BROWNIE MIX

Bliss

Also by Camilla V. Saulsbury

Cookie Dough Delights

BROWNIE MIX

More Than 175 Very Chocolate Recipes for Brownies, Bars,
Cookies, & Other Decadent Desserts
Made with Boxed Brownie Mix

Camilla V. Saulsbury

CUMBERLAND HOUSE
NASHVILLE, TN

To my parents, Daniel & Charlotte

Published by
Cumberland House Publishing, Inc.
431 Harding Industrial Drive
Nashville, TN 37211

Cover design: JulesRules Design
Text design: Lisa Taylor

Library of Congress Cataloging-in-Publication Data

Saulsbury, Camilla V.
   Brownie mix bliss : more than 175 very chocolate recipes for brownies, bars, cookies, & other decadent desserts made with boxed brownie mix / Camilla V. Saulsbury.
      p. cm.
   Includes index.
   ISBN 1-58182-444-0 (french-fold pbk.)
1. Brownies (Cookery) 2. Desserts. I. Title.
   TX771.S25 2005
   641.8'653—dc22
                                                                2005000753

Printed in Canada
1 2 3 4 5 6 7 — 11 10 09 08 07 06 05

Contents

Acknowledgments vii

Introduction 3

1/Brownies 15

2/Bar Cookies 85

3/Cookies and Bite-Sized Confections 133

4/Assorted Brownie Desserts 191

5/Frostings, Glazes, and Whipped Cream 243

Glossary 271

Index 273

Acknowledgments

Heaps of kudos and gratitude are owed to the entire team at Cumberland House Publishing, notably Lisa Taylor, Tracy Ford, Julia Pitkin, and Ron Pitkin. Endless thanks to my family, too: Daniel, Charlotte, Becca, Sean, Robin, Jean, and Ray. I could not have done this without your support and enthusiasm. Finally, three cheers for my husband Kevin, who never complained when all I made for dinner, for months on end, was batch after batch of brownies.

BROWNIE MIX
Bliss

Introduction

Brownies are quietly spectacular: moist, dense, and irresistibly intense, they are the pantheon of chocolate comfort. At once both reassuringly familiar and undeniably dazzling, brownies closely rival apple pie for top-rank, all-American status.

And as anyone who has ever had a still-warm-from-the-oven brownie can attest, brownie goodness increases exponentially when the sweet treats are made in the home kitchen. The evocative aroma of baking brownies wafting through the house makes everyone feel warm and fuzzy, and quite likely a bit weak in the knees.

That being said, why not make brownies more often, but easier and better than ever? The answer is as simple as a box of brownie mix.

As I wrote this book and developed an assortment of recipes, I kept in mind both novice and accomplished home cooks, and tried to create a wealth of brownie and chocolate options well-suited for home baking, all of which begin with a box of plain brownie mix. All of the recipes have been streamlined for easy, everyday baking—if you can wield a wooden spoon, you have all the skills necessary to start turning out any of the deep, dark, delicious chocolate treats herein. Beginning with a box of brownie mix is not only easier than pie, but also leads to sweet success; delicious proof is mere minutes away.

And oh, just try choosing which treat to make first. Consider, for example, Mocha Buttercream Brownies, Cinnamon-Buttermilk Brownies, Snickery Supreme Brownies, Almond Toffee-Topped Brownies, and Mint Julep Ganache Brownies. Yet that's but the tip of the chocolate iceberg. While brownie mix can be used to create all manner of mouthwatering brownie concoctions, it can also be transformed into countless other very easy, very chocolate desserts ranging from sophisticated biscotti, soufflé cakes, madeleines, and cheesecakes, to nostalgic drop cookies, ice cream novelties, gooey layered bar cookies, and so much more.

So whether it's a batch of Ultimate Fresh Raspberry Cheesecake Bars at a summertime cookout, Ginger-Jeweled Chocolate Biscotti with an afternoon cappuccino, Molten

Mocha Lava Cakes for two under the stars, or a Macadamia & White Chocolate Chunk Brownie tucked into a lunch bag, I'm confident you'll discover the perfect recipe for every chocolate occasion within these pages.

Once you taste these brownie mix treats, your fondness for brownies and chocolate desserts in general will undoubtedly reach a brand new level—bliss, perhaps?

Brownie Points: Suggestions for Sweet Success

To help make all of your brownie mix baking blissful, I offer here some tips, guidelines, and a smattering of personal opinions about getting started, selecting, prepping and measuring ingredients, and choosing equipment. But the best advice I can offer is to share your baking with the people you love and care about, by inviting them into the kitchen to assist, chat, keep you company, or anticipate the chocolate goodness soon to come, and, of course, then sharing the freshly baked fruits of your labor.

Ready-to-Bake Checklist

- ✓ Change into comfortable clothes and shoes and don an apron, if you like.
- ✓ Read the recipe thoroughly. Note the required ingredients and necessary equipment as well as the chilling, baking, and cooling times.
- ✓ Gather the necessary ingredients, checking for freshness (*see* the "Selecting Ingredients" section that follows for tips on how to do so).
- ✓ Gather the necessary equipment, including oven mitts and cooling racks.
- ✓ Prep the ingredients as needed, such as chopping nuts, zesting lemons, softening cream cheese, or melting butter.
- ✓ Prepare any baking pans or cookie sheets as specified in the recipe. If no advanced preparation is needed, set the pan or sheet aside so that it is ready to be used when needed.
- ✓ Reread the recipe.
- ✓ Preheat the oven. Turn the oven to the specified temperature for 10 to 15 minutes prior to baking to give the oven adequate time to heat up to the correct temperature.
- ✓ Use an oven thermometer. This can be a baker's best friend. Inexpensive ($3–$5) and available in the baking sections of most supermarkets or at any kitchen supply store, an oven thermometer allows you to check whether the temperature of your oven is accurate and consistent (since ovens and oven temperatures can vary). If your oven temperature is off (either too high or too low), adjust the temperature accordingly.

✓ Precisely measure all of the ingredients. Baking is a science, hence small variations can have a significant effect on the final product. *See* the "Measuring Ingredients" section for tips on measuring dry, liquid, and moist ingredients.

✓ Mix ingredients according to recipe specifications.

✓ Use a kitchen timer. This allows for precision and helps ensure the end product is not overcooked.

✓ Check the baked good at the earliest time specified. For example, if a recipe reads "Bake for 30–35 minutes, until toothpick inserted near the center comes clean," then check for doneness at 30 minutes. Continue baking if needed and continue checking every 1 minute.

✓ Tidy up as you go to make the final cleaning less toilsome (alternatively, bribe family members to clean in exchange for some of what you're baking).

Selecting Ingredients

Brownie Mix: All of the recipes in this book were tested using a 19.5- to 19.8-ounce box of brownie mix. These included, for example, name brand mixes such as Betty Crocker® Fudge Brownie mix and Pillsbury® Brownie Classics Traditional Fudge Brownie Mix, as well as store brand mixes such as the Kroger® label brownie mix. Check the weight, and then double-check that the mix does not include stir-ins such as chocolate syrup, nuts, caramel, or baking chips.

Several brands of brownie mix come in slightly larger sizes, such as Martha White® Chewy Fudge Brownie Mix (22.5 ounces), Krusteaz Fudge Brownie Mix® (22 ounces), Ghiradelli® Brownie Mix (20 ounces), Duncan Hines® Family Style Chewy Fudge Brownie Mix (21 ounces), and the Safeway® store-brand Fudge Brownie Mix (21.5 ounces). All of these are still suitable for any of the recipes in this book. However, for best success, use only 4 cups of the mix for the equivalent of a 19.5- to 19.8-ounce package.

Butter: Butter is used in many of the recipes throughout the book to bolster the flavor of the brownies, cookies, or bars. I recommend unsalted butter because salt is already included in the brownie mix, but lightly salted butter is a perfectly fine substitution.

Fresh butter should have a delicate cream flavor and pale yellow color. Butter quickly picks up off-flavors during storage and when exposed to oxygen; once the carton is opened place it in a resealable plastic bag or airtight container. Store it away from foods with strong odors, especially items such as onions or garlic.

Avoid using butter to coat baking pans and sheets. Because butter melts at a lower temperature than other "greasing" ingredients, such as vegetable shortening, it may leave ungreased gaps on sheets and pans, causing baked goods to stick. Second, butter can burn, particularly when baking above 350°. At best, what you're making will be overly brown, at worst, scorched.

Melted butter is used in many recipes throughout this book. For best results, cut the specified amount of butter into small pieces, place in a small saucepan, and allow to melt over the lowest heat setting of the burner. Once the butter has melted, remove pan from heat and cool. To speed the cooling, pour the melted butter into a small bowl or liquid measuring cup.

Browning butter is a simple way to enhance the already rich flavor of melted butter. To do it, melt the butter in a heavy saucepan over medium heat, stirring frequently as the butter bubbles and foams, until it just begins to turn a delicate golden brown. The browning happens quickly, so watch the pan closely. Immediately remove the pan from the heat and pour the melted browned butter into a bowl to cool (the butter will continue to brown if left in the hot pan).

Softened butter is also required in several recipes throughout the book. The easiest method for softening butter is to remove from the refrigerator the amount needed for the recipe. Let it stand 30–45 minutes at room temperature. Cutting the butter into small chunks will reduce the softening time to about 15 minutes. If time is really limited, try grating the cold butter on the large holes of a cheese grater. The small bits of butter will be soft in just a few minutes. Alternatively, place the cold butter between sheets of waxed paper and hit it several times with a rolling pin (this can also double as a means of stress relief!). Avoid softening butter in the microwave as it will typically melt at least part of the butter, even if you are watching it closely.

Chocolate: Two general types of chocolate are used throughout this book. First, chocolate chips, available in semisweet, milk, white, and miniature semisweet. Some premium brands offer bittersweet chocolate chips, which may be used interchangeably with semisweet. The second general type of chocolate is baking chocolate, which is typically available in 6- or 8-ounce packages with the chocolate most often individually wrapped in 1-ounce squares or occasionally in 2-ounce bars. It is available in unsweetened, bittersweet, semisweet, milk, and white chocolate varieties.

Store both chocolate chips and baking chocolate in a dry, cool place between 60° and 78°. Wrapping chocolate in moisture-proof wrap or in a ziplock plastic bag is a good idea if the temperature is higher or the humidity is above 50 percent. Chocolate can also be stored in the fridge, but let it stand at room temperature before using.

If the chocolate from your pantry has a white, crusty-looking film on it, don't toss it. This is commonly called "bloom" and develops when the chocolate is exposed to varying temperatures, from hot to cold. The change in heat allows the cocoa butter to melt and rise to the surface of the chocolate. Bloom does not affect the quality or flavor of the chocolate. The chocolate will look normal again once it is melted or used in baking.

Cream Cheese: All of the recipes in this book use "brick"-style cream cheese, which is typically packaged in 3-ounce and 8-ounce rectangular packages. Avoid using soft-spread, flavored, or whipped cream cheese to achieve the best results.

To soften cream cheese, unwrap it and cut it into chunks with a sharp knife. Let it stand at room temperature 30–45 minutes, until softened. For speed softening, place the chunks of cream cheese on a microwavable plate or in a microwavable bowl and microwave on high for 15 seconds. If necessary, microwave 5 or 10 seconds longer.

Eggs: Use large eggs in all of the recipes in this book. Select clean, fresh eggs that have been handled properly and refrigerated. Do not use dirty, cracked, or leaking eggs that have a bad odor or unnatural color when cracked open. They may have become contaminated with harmful bacteria such as salmonella. Cold eggs are easiest to separate; eggs at room temperature beat to high volume.

There's an easy way to check eggs for freshness. Simply fill a deep bowl with enough cold water to cover an egg. Place the egg in the water. If the egg lies on its side on the bottom of the bowl, it is fresh. If the egg stands up and bobs on the bottom, it isn't quite as fresh but is still acceptable for baking. If the egg floats on the surface, it should be discarded.

Margarine: Margarine may be substituted for butter, but it is not recommended because it lacks the rich flavor that butter offers. However, if using margarine in place of butter, it is essential that it is a 100 percent vegetable oil, solid stick. Margarine spreads—in tub or stick form—will alter the liquid and fat combination of the recipe, leading to either unsatisfactory or downright disastrous results. You can determine the fat percentage in one of two ways. In some cases, the percentage is printed on the box. If it reads anything less than 100 percent oil, it is a spread and should be avoided for baking purposes. If the percentage is not printed on the outside of the box, flip it over and check the calories. If it is 100 calories per tablespoon, it is 100 percent vegetable oil; any less, and it is less than 100 percent and should not be used.

Nonstick Cooking Spray: I prefer to use nonstick cooking spray, such as PAM, for "greasing" pans because of its convenience. However, solid vegetable shortening, such as Crisco, may also be used. Both are flavorless and coat pans and cookie sheets evenly.

When spraying or greasing baking pans for brownies, be sure to coat only the bottom of the pan. If the inside walls of the pan are coated, the brownies will not rise properly. When making bars, the entire inside of the pan may be coated in cooking spray. Cookie sheets should be given only a very light spraying or greasing for best results.

Shelled nuts: Use plain, unsalted nuts unless specified otherwise in the recipe. To determine whether shelled nuts are fresh, taste them: they should taste and smell fresh, not rancid with an off-flavor. Frozen nuts are prone to freezer burn if stored improperly and may taste old or stale (old, stale, or rancid nuts will ruin the baked product). Shelled nuts should also have a crisp texture, should be relatively uniform in color, and should not be shriveled or discolored in spots.

Toasting nuts before adding them to a recipe can greatly intensify their flavor and hence their contribution to a recipe. To toast without turning on the oven, place them in an ungreased skillet over medium heat (3–4 minutes), stirring frequently, until golden brown (note that this method works best with chopped, as opposed to whole, nuts). To oven-toast, spread the nuts in a single layer in a baking pan or on a cookie sheet. Bake at 350° for 10–15 minutes, stirring occasionally, or until golden brown. Cool the nuts before adding them to the recipe.

Spices: All of the recipes in this book use ground, as opposed to whole, spices. Freshness is everything with ground spices. The best way to determine if a ground spice is fresh is to open the container and smell it. If it still has a strong fragrance, it is acceptable for use. If not, toss it and make a new purchase.

Vanilla Extract: Vanilla extract adds a sweet, fragrant flavor to baked goods and is particularly good for enhancing the flavor of chocolate. It is produced by extracting the flavor of dried vanilla beans with an alcohol and water mixture. It is then aged for several months. The three most common types of beans used to make vanilla extract are Bourbon-Madagascar, Mexican, and Tahitian.

Store vanilla extract in a cool, dark place, with the bottle tightly closed, to prevent it from evaporating and losing flavor. It will stay fresh for about two years unopened and for one year after being opened.

Imitation vanilla flavoring can be substituted for vanilla extract, but it may have a slight or prominent artificial taste, depending on the brand. It is about half the cost of real vanilla extract; however, I believe the real thing is worth the extra expense.

Measuring Ingredients

Measuring Dry Ingredients: When measuring a dry ingredient such as sugar, flour, spices, or salt, spoon it into the appropriate-size dry measuring cup or measuring spoon, heaping it up over the top. Next, slide a straight-edged utensil, such as a knife, across the top to level off the extra. Be careful not to shake or tap the cup or spoon to settle the ingredient or you will have more than you need.

Measuring Liquid Ingredients: Use a clear plastic or glass measuring cup or container with lines up the sides to measure liquid ingredients. Set the container on the counter and pour the liquid to the appropriate mark. Lower your head to read the measurement at eye level.

Measuring Moist Ingredients: Some moist ingredients, such as brown sugar, coconut, and dried fruits, must be firmly packed into the measuring cup to be measured accurately. Use a dry measuring cup for these ingredients. Fill the measuring cup to slightly overflowing, then pack down the ingredient firmly with the back of a spoon. Add more of the ingredient and pack down again until the cup is full and even with the top of the measure.

Measuring Butter: Butter is typically packaged in stick form with markings on the wrapper indicating tablespoon and cup measurements. Use a sharp knife to cut off the amount needed for a recipe.

$\frac{1}{4}$ cup = $\frac{1}{2}$ stick = 4 tablespoons = 2 ounces
$\frac{1}{2}$ cup = 1 stick = $\frac{1}{4}$ pound = 4 ounces
1 cup = 2 sticks = $\frac{1}{2}$ pound = 8 ounces
2 cups = 4 sticks = 1 pound = 16 ounces

Measuring Cream Cheese: Like sticks of butter, bricks of cream cheese are typically packaged with markings on the wrapper indicating tablespoon and cup measurements. Use a sharp knife to cut off the amount needed for a recipe.

Measuring Spices, Salt, Baking Powder, & Baking Soda: Use the standard measuring spoon size specified in the recipe and be sure the spoon is dry when measuring. Fill a standard measuring spoon to the top and level with a spatula or knife. When a recipe calls for a dash of a spice or salt, use about $\frac{1}{16}$ of a teaspoon. A pinch is considered to be the amount of salt that can be held between the tips of the thumb and forefinger and is also approximately $\frac{1}{16}$ of a teaspoon.

Measuring Nuts: Spoon nuts into a dry measuring cup to the top. Four ounces of nuts is the equivalent of 1 cup chopped nuts.

Measuring Extracts & Flavorings: Fill the standard measuring spoon size specified in the recipe to the top, being careful not to let any spill over. It's a good idea to avoid measuring extracts or flavorings over the mixing bowl because the spillover will go into the bowl and you will not know the amount of extract or flavoring you have added.

Cooling & Serving

Cooling: Cool all baked goods on cooling racks immediately following baking unless specified otherwise in the recipe.

For best results, allow brownies and bars to cool in the pan before cutting. Cookies should be transferred to the cooling racks immediately following removal from the oven unless specified otherwise. A metal spatula or pancake turner is the best tool for transferring cookies to cooling racks. Some of the recipes in the cookies chapter note that the cookies should be left on the cookie sheets for several minutes after baking before being transferred to cooling racks. This allows the cookies to continue baking due to the heat of the hot pan (without overbaking and drying out in the oven).

Cutting Brownies & Bars: Cut cooled brownies with plastic or table knife to insure smooth-sided bars. For precision cutting, use a pastry scraper.

To cut particularly soft or gooey brownies or bars while they are still in the pan, move the knife across the pan in an up and down sawing motion from one end to the other until they are cut. Place the pan in the freezer for 30 minutes, if needed, to make the cutting job easier.

A hot knife will also make brownies and bars cut more easily: before starting, dip a sharp knife in hot water and wipe with a dry kitchen towel. When cutting gooey brownies or a similar type of bar, try not to press down with the knife or the cut edges will squish together. After each cut, clean and reheat the knife by dipping it in hot water and wiping with a paper towel before resuming.

Storage

General Storage: Store brownies, bars, and cookies at room temperature unless specified otherwise in the recipe. Store them in an airtight container for optimal freshness. Sturdier brownies, bars, and cookies can be place in a ziplock plastic bag; more delicate varieties are better off stacked between layers of waxed paper in a plastic container. Brownies and bar cookies can be stacked in a container between layers of waxed paper or stored in their baking pan. I prefer to cut them first and then place them back in the pan for easy removal. Cover the top tightly with aluminum foil, wrap, or a lid.

Freezing Already-Baked Cookies: Brownies and cookies may be frozen for future enjoyment. Bars (especially custard or gooey layered bars) and cream cheese–filled brownies do not fare as well when frozen. If the brownies or cookies have a frosting, do not add it until the baked good has been thawed at a future date. For best results, freeze brownies and cookies as soon as possible after they are completely cooled. Place them in freezer bags or airtight freezer containers for up to 6 months. Double wrap the brownies or cookies to prevent them from getting freezer burn or absorbing odors from the freezer and label the bag clearly with the name of the cookie and the date. Brownies and cookies can be frosted after thawing at room temperature for 15–30 minutes.

Equipment

Baking Pans: Using the size of pan specified in the recipe is critical to the success of all baking. Brownies, bars, and other baked goods that are made in a too-large pan, for example, will be overbaked, and those in a too-small pan will be underbaked.

If you only have a few pans, and none are the pan size specified, a solution still exists.

Use the pan size that you have. If it's larger than what is called for, use a shorter bake time. If it's smaller than what is called for, use a longer bake time and reduce the oven temperature 25°.

Only use glass or shiny metal pans. Dark pans will cause brownies to be soggy and low in volume. If a dark pan is all you have, reduce the oven temperature 25°.

Cookie Sheets: When baking cookies, choose light-colored, dull-finished, heavy-gauge cookie sheets. Shiny sheets work best for cookies that should not brown too much on the bottom. Avoid using cookie sheets with high sides; they can deflect heat as well as make it difficult to remove the cookies for cooling. As a general rule, cookie sheets should be two inches narrower and shorter than the oven to allow for even baking.

It is best to avoid dark aluminum cookie sheets. These sheets have a brown or almost black finish and may absorb heat, causing the bottoms of cookies to brown more quickly. If you do use dark aluminum sheets, decrease the baking time and lower the temperature 25°.

Nonstick cookie sheets are easier to clean and help ensure even baking; however, the dough may not spread as much and you may end up with a thicker cookie. On the other hand, rich cookies can spread if baked on a greased sheet. Follow the manufacturer's instructions if using a cookie sheet with a nonstick coating; the oven temperature may need to be reduced by 25°.

Also follow the manufacturer's instructions if using insulated cookie sheets, which are made from two sheets of metal with a layer of air between for insulation. Cookies will not brown as much on the bottom, so it may be hard to tell when the cookies are done. Also, cookies may take slightly longer to bake.

Aluminum Foil (Foil-Lining Pans): Lining baking pans with aluminum foil is great way to avoid messy clean-up whenever you bake brownies and bars. Doing so also makes it easy to remove the entire batch of brownies or bars from the pan at once, making the cutting of perfectly uniform squares and bars a snap. When the brownies or bars are cool or nearly cool, simply lift them out of the pan, peel back the foil and cut. Foil-lining is also a boon during holiday baking seasons, allowing for the production of multiple batches of bars and brownies in no time, with virtually no clean-up.

And foil-lining is easy. Begin by turning the pan upside down. Tear off a piece of aluminum foil longer than the pan, and shape the foil over the pan. Carefully remove the foil and set aside. Flip the pan over and gently fit the shaped foil into the pan, allowing the foil to hang over the sides (the overhang ends will work as "handles" when the brownies or bars are removed).

Essential Utensils Checklist

✓ Dry measuring cups in graduated sizes ¼, ⅓, ½, and 1 cup
✓ Liquid measuring cup (preferably clear glass or plastic)
✓ Measuring spoons in graduated sizes ¼, ½ and 1 teaspoon as well as 1 tablespoon
✓ Wooden spoon(s)
✓ Mixing bowls (at least one each of small, medium, and large sizes)
✓ Rubber or silicone spatula (for scraping the sides of a mixing bowl)
✓ Metal spatula or pancake turner for removing brownies and bars from pans and cookies from sheets (use a plastic spatula if you are using a nonstick-coated pan or sheet)
✓ Wire cooling racks
✓ Oven mitts or holders
✓ Kitchen timer
✓ Cutting board
✓ Pastry brush (a clean 1-inch paintbrush from the hardware store works fine)
✓ Rolling pin (only for Brownie Cut-outs, see page 162, and for crushing ingredients)
✓ Wire whisk
✓ Chef's knife
✓ Kitchen spoons (everyday place setting soup and teaspoons for drop cookies)
✓ Electric mixer (handheld or stand mixer)

Wish-List Utensils Checklist:

✓ Small off-set metal spatula (ideal for frosting brownies, bars, and cookies)
✓ Metal pastry scraper (the perfect tool for cutting brownies and bars into perfect squares and bars)
✓ Cookie scoops (look like small ice cream scoops—use for perfectly measured drop cookies)
✓ Food processor
✓ Cookie cutters
✓ Silicone cookie sheet liners (eliminates nonstick spray or greasing step)
✓ Zester

Baking Equipment Checklist:

- ✓ 8-inch square pan (plain aluminum or Pyrex)
- ✓ 9-inch square pan (plain aluminum or Pyrex)
- ✓ 13 x 9-inch rectangular pan (plain aluminum or Pyrex)
- ✓ Round cake pans (8- or 9-inch)
- ✓ Jelly roll pan (15 x 10-inch)
- ✓ Standard-size 12-cup muffin pan (2¾ x 1¼-inch cups)
- ✓ Miniature muffin pan
- ✓ Plain aluminum cookie sheets (at least 2)
- ✓ Madeleine pan (3 x 1¼-inch shell molds)
- ✓ Deep-dish pie pan (9-inch)
- ✓ Springform pan (9- or 10-inch)
- ✓ 12-cup Bundt pan

Chapter 1
Brownies

Classic Brownies

Few eating pleasures are greater than biting into a warm, chewy, chocolate brownie. There may be many brownie recipes around, but this classic version is a winner, on its own or doctored with any number of stir-ins. You can also up the flavor ante by making them with buttermilk and melted butter in place of water and vegetable oil. To create your own original brownie, consider stirring in one or two of the stir-in options listed on the next page or adding a special frosting or glaze from chapter five.

1	19.5- to 19.8-ounce package brownie mix
½	cup vegetable oil or 1 stick (½ cup) unsalted butter, melted
¼	cup water or buttermilk
2	large eggs
1–2	of the stir-ins listed on the next page (optional)
	Any of the frostings or glazes listed in chapter five (optional)

Preheat oven to 350° (325° for dark-coated metal pan). Position a rack in the lower third of the oven. Spray the bottom only of an 8-inch square baking pan with nonstick cooking spray (or foil-line pan; see page 11).

In a medium mixing bowl mix the brownie mix, oil, water, and eggs with a wooden spoon until just blended and all dry ingredients are moistened. Spread batter into prepared pan.

Bake 40–44 minutes or until toothpick inserted 2 inches from side of pan comes out clean or almost clean (do not overbake). Transfer to a wire rack and cool completely. Cut into squares. Makes 9 large or 16 small brownies.

(variations on next page)

Classic Brownie Variations

Cake-style Brownies
Increase number of eggs to three. Prepare, bake, cool, and cut as directed above.

Pan Size Options
(1) 9-inch square pan: Prepare as directed above but bake 38–42 minutes.
(2) 13 x 9-inch pan: Prepare as directed above but bake 28–30 minutes.
(3) 9-inch springform pan: Prepare as directed above but bake 38–42 minutes.

Stir-in Options
Stir in 1 cup of any one of the following options into prepared brownie batter and bake as directed. If adding two stir-ins (e.g., chocolate chips and nuts), decrease the quantity to ½ cup for each stir-in.

(1) *Baking chips and bits:* chocolate chips (e.g., semisweet, milk, or white chocolate chips) or other baking chips (e.g., butterscotch, peanut butter, or cinnamon baking chips or English toffee baking bits).
(2) *Nuts:* chopped nuts (e.g., pecans, walnuts, almonds, hazelnuts, roasted peanuts, roasted cashews, lightly salted mixed nuts, roasted Brazil nuts, macadamia nuts, or pistachios).
(3) *Fruit and coconut:* coconut or dried fruit (e.g., shredded coconut (sweetened or unsweetened), cranberries, raisins (regular or golden), currants, dried cherries, dried cranberries, chopped dried apricots, dried tropical fruit bits, or chopped banana chips).

Chocolate Cream Cheese Chocolate-Chip Brownies

Old-fashioned brownies get a triple dose of chocolate in this very easy but very delicious recipe. In case you have any doubts, these are a huge hit with kids.

1	19.5- to 19.8-ounce package brownie mix
½	cup vegetable oil
¼	cup water
2	large eggs
1½	cups miniature semisweet chocolate chips, divided
1	recipe Chocolate Cream Cheese Frosting (see page 252)

Preheat oven to 350° (325° for dark-coated metal pan). Position a rack in the lower third of the oven. Spray the bottom only of an 8-inch square baking pan with nonstick cooking spray (or foil-line pan; see page 11).

In a medium mixing bowl mix the brownie mix, oil, water, and eggs with a wooden spoon until just blended and all dry ingredients are moistened; stir in 1 cup of the miniature chocolate chips. Spread batter into prepared pan.

Bake 40–44 minutes or until toothpick inserted 2 inches from side of pan comes out clean or almost clean (do not overbake). Transfer to a wire rack and cool completely.

Prepare the chocolate cream cheese frosting. Frost brownies with frosting and sprinkle with remaining ½ cup chocolate chips. Cut into squares. Store in refrigerator. Makes 9 large or 16 small brownies.

Big-Batch Brownies

2   19.5- to 19.8-ounce packages brownie mix
4   large eggs
½   cup water or buttermilk
1   cup vegetable oil or 2 sticks (1 cup) unsalted
     butter, melted

Preheat oven to 350°. Position a rack in the lower third of the oven. Foil-line the pan (see page 11), letting the foil overlap just two of the pan's sides.

In a large mixing bowl mix the brownie mixes, eggs, water and oil with a wooden spoon until well blended. Spread batter into prepared pan.

Bake 50–55 minutes or until toothpick inserted 2 inches from side of pan comes out clean or almost clean (do not over-bake). Transfer to a wire rack and cool completely.

When cool, slide a knife between the pan and the brownies on the unlined sides. Lift the ends of the foil liner and transfer to a cutting board. Cut brownies into squares. Makes 36 large or 48 small brownies.

Brownies are a perennial hit for great big gatherings. This doubled recipe lets you satisfy the whole gang while keeping your kitchen time minimal. To gild the lily in a matter of minutes, smooth a layer of prepared chocolate frosting over the cooled brownies, or take a few minutes more to prepare and spread with any of the frostings or glazes listed in chapter five. You can also incorporate any one, or several, of the stir-in options suggested for Classic Brownies (page 16) but increase the total amount of your ingredient(s) choice to 2 cups (e.g., 2 cups chocolate chips or 1 cup dried cranberries plus 1 cup chopped pecans).

Vanilla and Butter-Rich Glazed Buttermilk Brownies

Vanilla and chocolate are the yin and yang of the dessert world. Here I match vanilla with butter in the batter and glaze, which brings out the best in the chocolate and leads to a newfangled brownie few can turn down. The glaze seeps into the top half of the brownie, adding to the fudgy-ness of every bite.

1	19.5- to 19.8-ounce package brownie mix
1	stick (½ cup) unsalted butter, melted
¼	cup buttermilk
1	tablespoon vanilla extract
2	large eggs
1	recipe Vanilla-Butter Glaze (see page 264)

Preheat oven to 350° (325° for dark-coated metal pan). Position a rack in the lower third of the oven. Spray the bottom only of an 8-inch square baking pan with nonstick cooking spray (or foil-line pan; see page 11).

In a medium mixing bowl mix the brownie mix, melted butter, buttermilk, vanilla, and eggs with a wooden spoon until just blended and all dry ingredients are moistened. Spread batter into prepared pan.

Bake 40–44 minutes or until toothpick inserted 2 inches from side of pan comes out clean or almost clean (do not overbake). Transfer to a wire rack. Prepare Vanilla-Butter Glaze; spread over warm brownies and cool completely. Cut into squares. Makes 9 large or 16 small brownies.

Caramelicious Turtle Brownies

1	19.5- to 19.8-ounce package brownie mix
½	cup vegetable oil
¼	cup water
2	large eggs
1½	cups semisweet or milk chocolate chips, divided
1	cup coarsely chopped pecans
16	caramels, unwrapped
1½	tablespoons milk

Preheat oven to 350° (325° for dark-coated metal pan). Position a rack in the lower third of the oven. Spray the bottom only of an 8-inch square baking pan with nonstick cooking spray (or foil-line pan; see page 11).

In a medium mixing bowl mix the brownie mix, oil, water, and eggs with a wooden spoon until just blended and all dry ingredients are moistened; stir in ¾ cup of the chocolate chips. Spread batter into prepared pan.

Bake 40–44 minutes or until toothpick inserted 2 inches from side of pan comes out clean or almost clean (do not overbake). During last 10 minutes of baking, sprinkle the top with the pecans (so that they will toast). Remove from oven and immediately sprinkle with remaining chocolate chips. Transfer to a wire rack.

In a medium saucepan set over low heat, melt the caramels with the milk until melted and smooth. Drizzle caramel over brownies and cool completely. Cut into squares. Makes 9 large or 16 small brownies.

Because I am crazy for caramel, this recipe is my brownie nirvana. Decked out with gooey caramel, chocolate chips, and pecans, it's hard to find something better—I can't!

Almond Toffee-Topped Brownies

If you like brown sugar (and would anyone who doesn't please step forward?), these are your brownies. With tempting toffee and crunchy bits of brown-sugary almonds, each square tastes like an English toffee chocolate bar transformed into a brownie.

1	19.5- to 19.8-ounce package brownie mix
½	cup vegetable oil
¼	cup water
2	large eggs
1	cup English toffee baking bits
⅓	cup unsalted butter
½	cup packed dark brown sugar
1	tablespoon all-purpose flour
2	tablespoons milk
1	cup sliced almonds

Preheat oven to 350° (325° for dark-coated metal pan). Position a rack in the lower third of the oven. Spray the bottom only of a 13 x 9-inch baking pan with nonstick cooking spray (or foil-line pan; see page 11).

In a medium mixing bowl mix the brownie mix, oil, water, and eggs with a wooden spoon until just blended and all dry ingredients are moistened; stir in toffee bits. Spread batter into prepared pan.

Bake 28–30 minutes or until toothpick inserted 2 inches from side of pan comes out clean or almost clean (do not overbake).

While brownies bake, in a medium saucepan combine the butter, brown sugar, flour, milk, and almonds. Cook and stir over medium heat until sugar is dissolved, about 4–5 minutes.

Remove brownies from oven and turn oven to broiler setting; position oven rack 4–6 inches from the heat. Pour almond topping over brownies, spreading evenly. Broil 1–2½ minutes, until bubbly and light golden. Transfer to wire rack and cool completely. Cut into squares. Makes 24 large or 36 small brownies.

Black & Tan Layered Brownies

1	19.5- to 19.8-ounce package brownie mix
½	cup vegetable oil
¼	cup water
2	large eggs
1	cup chopped pecans, divided
1	cup semisweet chocolate chips
2	cups butterscotch chips, divided
2	cups sifted powdered sugar
¼	cup unsweetened cocoa powder
3	tablespoons hot water
¼	cup (½ stick) unsalted butter, melted
1	teaspoon vanilla extract

Old-fashioned brownies get a new treatment with a middle layer of butterscotch and a generous spread of cocoa icing as the crowning touch. For "Black & White" brownies, substitute white chocolate chips for the butterscotch chips.

Preheat oven to 350° (325° for dark-coated metal pan). Position a rack in the lower third of the oven. Spray the bottom only of a 13 x 9-inch baking pan with nonstick cooking spray (or foil-line pan; see page 11).

In a medium mixing bowl mix the brownie mix, oil, water, and eggs with a wooden spoon until just blended and all dry ingredients are moistened; stir in ½ cup of the chopped pecans, all of the chocolate chips, and ½ cup of the butterscotch chips. Spread batter into prepared pan.

Bake 28–30 minutes or until toothpick inserted 2 inches from side of pan comes out clean or almost clean (do not overbake). Remove from oven and immediately sprinkle with remaining 1 cup butterscotch chips. Return to oven for 1 minute to soften chips; spread the melted chips evenly over brownies with the back of a spoon. Transfer to a wire rack and cool completely.

In small mixing bowl whisk the powdered sugar, cocoa powder, hot water, melted butter, and vanilla until blended and smooth (mixture will be thin). Carefully spoon over butterscotch layer, spreading to cover; sprinkle with remaining pecans. Cool completely to set the glaze. Cut into squares. Makes 24 large or 36 small brownies.

Best "Boosted" Brownies

What's the secret to this incredibly delicious, intensely chocolate batch of brownies? Butter in place of oil for added flavor and richness, buttermilk in place of water for an extra tender-chewy crumb, and a splash of vanilla and a dash of espresso powder, both of which deepen the dark chocolate flavor. And, of course, more chocolate, in the form of bittersweet chocolate chunks.

1	tablespoon instant espresso or coffee powder
2	teaspoons vanilla extract
1	19.5- to 19.8-ounce package brownie mix
½	cup (1 stick) unsalted butter, melted
¼	cup buttermilk
2	large eggs
4	1-ounce squares bittersweet chocolate, coarsely chopped into chunks

Preheat oven to 350° (325° for dark-coated metal pan). Position a rack in the lower third of the oven. Spray the bottom only of an 8-inch square baking pan with nonstick cooking spray (or foil-line pan; see page 11).

In a small cup combine espresso powder and vanilla until dissolved.

In a medium mixing bowl mix the brownie mix, melted butter, buttermilk, eggs, and vanilla-espresso mixture with a wooden spoon until just blended and all dry ingredients are moistened. Stir in the chopped chocolate. Spread batter into prepared pan.

Bake 40–44 minutes or until toothpick inserted 2 inches from side of pan comes out clean or almost clean (do not overbake). Transfer to a wire rack and cool completely. Cut into squares. Makes 9 large or 16 small brownies.

Sour Cream Brownies with Chocolate Velvet Frosting

1	19.5- to 19.8-ounce package brownie mix
⅓	cup butter, melted
½	cup sour cream (not reduced fat)
2	large eggs
1	recipe Chocolate Velvet Frosting (see page 249)

Preheat oven to 350° (325° for dark-coated metal pan). Position a rack in the lower third of the oven. Spray the bottom only of an 8-inch square baking pan with nonstick cooking spray (or foil-line pan; see page 11).

In a medium mixing bowl mix the brownie mix, melted butter, sour cream, and eggs with a wooden spoon until just blended and all dry ingredients are moistened. Spread batter into prepared pan.

Bake 40–44 minutes or until toothpick inserted 2 inches from side of pan comes out clean or almost clean (do not overbake). Transfer to a wire rack and cool completely.

Prepare Chocolate Velvet Frosting. Spread over cooled brownies. Cut into squares. Store in refrigerator. Makes 9 large or 16 small brownies.

I tested and retested this recipe until I came up with this moist, incredibly flavorful rendition. The velvety sour cream frosting pushes them over the top. One 8-ounce container of sour cream provides enough to make both the brownies and the Chocolate Velvet Frosting.

Triple-Shot
Espresso Layered Brownies

The bold flavor of espresso is a perfect partner to the chocolate in these sophisticated, triple-layered (brownie-brown sugar espresso-chocolate glaze) brownies.

1	19.5- to 19.8-ounce package brownie mix
½	cup vegetable oil
¼	cup water
3	large eggs
2	tablespoons plus 1 teaspoon instant espresso or coffee powder, divided
2	teaspoons vanilla extract, divided
6	tablespoons unsalted butter, softened, divided
½	cup firmly packed brown sugar
1	cup coarsely chopped walnuts
3	cups semisweet chocolate chips
1–2	teaspoons milk

Preheat oven to 350° (325° for dark-coated metal pan). Position a rack in the lower third of the oven. Spray the bottom only of a 13 x 9-inch baking pan with nonstick cooking spray (or foil-line pan; see page 11).

In a medium mixing bowl mix the brownie mix, oil, water, 2 of the eggs, 1 tablespoon espresso powder, and 1 teaspoon vanilla with a wooden spoon until just blended and all dry ingredients are moistened. Spread batter into prepared pan.

Bake 26–28 minutes or until just barely set at center (do not overbake). Transfer to a wire rack momentarily (leave oven on).

Meanwhile, in a medium mixing bowl beat 4 tablespoons (½ stick) butter and brown sugar with an electric mixer set on medium until light and fluffy. Add remaining 1 egg, 1 tablespoon espresso powder, and remaining 1 teaspoon vanilla; beat with electric mixer set on low until just blended. Mix in walnuts and 2 cups of the chocolate chips.

Spoon and carefully spread brown sugar filling over baked brownies. Return to oven; bake 17–20 minutes or until light brown. Transfer to a wire rack and cool.

In small saucepan, melt remaining 1 cup chocolate chips and remaining 2 tablespoons butter over low heat, stirring constantly until smooth. Remove from heat. With wire whisk, whisk in remaining teaspoon espresso powder and enough milk for desired drizzling consistency. Spread or drizzle over warm brownies. Cool completely. Cut into squares. Makes 24 large or 36 small brownies.

Monkey Business Banana Brownies

These easy, banana-enhanced brownies are just right for a week's worth of lunch bag goodies or after-school snacks. For a delicious dress-up, consider frosting these with either the Caramel or Milk Chocolate Frosting in chapter five, then sprinkle with chopped banana chips.

1	19.5- to 19.8-ounce package brownie mix
¾	cup mashed very ripe bananas (about 2 medium)
3	tablespoons vegetable oil
2	large eggs
1	cup milk chocolate chips
1	cup chopped walnuts or pecans

Preheat oven to 350° (325° for dark-coated metal pan). Position a rack in the lower third of the oven. Spray the bottom only of a 13 x 9-inch baking pan with nonstick cooking spray (or foil-line pan; see page 11).

In a medium mixing bowl mix the brownie mix, mashed bananas, oil, and eggs with a wooden spoon until just blended and all dry ingredients are moistened. Spread batter into prepared pan; sprinkle with chocolate chips and nuts.

Bake 28–30 minutes or until toothpick inserted 2 inches from side of pan comes out clean or almost clean (do not overbake). Transfer to a wire rack and cool completely. Cut into squares. Makes 24 large or 36 small brownies.

Cookies 'n' Cream Brownies

1	19.5- to 19.8-ounce package brownie mix
½	cup vegetable oil
¼	cup water
2	large eggs
3	cups coarsely crushed creme-filled chocolate sandwich cookies, divided
1	recipe Cream Cheese Frosting (see page 261)

This is one of my favorite brownies, at once familiar and new-fangled. And if I don't make a batch of them at least once a month, one of my colleagues won't speak to me.

Preheat oven to 350° (325° for dark-coated metal pan). Position a rack in the lower third of the oven. Spray the bottom only of a 13 x 9-inch baking pan with nonstick cooking spray (or foil-line pan; see page 11).

In a medium mixing bowl mix the brownie mix, oil, water, and eggs with a wooden spoon until just blended and all dry ingredients are moistened; stir in 1½ cups cookie crumbs. Spread batter into prepared pan.

Bake 28–30 minutes or until toothpick inserted 2 inches from side of pan comes out clean or almost clean (do not overbake). Transfer to a wire rack and cool completely.

Prepare Cream Cheese Frosting. Spread brownies with frosting and sprinkle with remaining cookie crumbs. Cut into squares. Store in refrigerator. Makes 24 large or 36 small brownies.

Easy Mississippi Mud Brownies

Some families believe that blood is thicker than water; others believe chocolate is, and that their shared bond is an intrinsic love of the dark, delicious stuff. This recipe is just the thing for strengthening such familial bonds. Positively sumptuous, these brownies are also a breeze to put together, making them great for last-minute chocolate cravings.

1	19.5- to 19.8-ounce package brownie mix
½	cup vegetable oil
¼	cup water
2	large eggs
1	7-ounce jar marshmallow creme
1¼	cups ready-to-spread milk chocolate frosting (from a 16-ounce tub)

Preheat oven to 350° (325° for dark-coated metal pan). Position a rack in the lower third of the oven. Spray the bottom only of a 13 x 9-inch baking pan with nonstick cooking spray (or foil-line pan; see page 11).

In a medium mixing bowl mix the brownie mix, oil, water, and eggs with a wooden spoon until just blended and all dry ingredients are moistened. Spread batter into prepared pan.

Bake 28–30 minutes or until toothpick inserted 2 inches from side of pan comes out clean or almost clean (do not overbake).

Transfer to a wire rack. Dollop marshmallow creme evenly over hot brownies; gently spread with knife.

Place frosting in small saucepan set over low heat; heat until melted, about 2 minutes, stirring until smooth. Pour frosting over marshmallow creme. Swirl with knife to marbleize. Cool completely. Cut into squares. Makes 24 large or 36 small brownies.

Julie's Cinnamon Buttermilk Brownies

1	19.5- to 19.8-ounce package brownie mix
½	cup (1 stick) unsalted butter, melted
¼	cup buttermilk
2	large eggs
1	teaspoon ground cinnamon
1	cup cinnamon baking chips

Preheat oven to 350° (325° for dark-coated metal pan). Position a rack in the lower third of the oven. Spray the bottom only of an 8-inch square baking pan with nonstick cooking spray (or foil-line pan; see page 11).

In a medium mixing bowl mix the brownie mix, melted butter, buttermilk, eggs, and cinnamon with a wooden spoon until just blended and all dry ingredients are moistened; stir in cinnamon chips. Spread batter into prepared pan.

Bake 40–44 minutes or until toothpick inserted 2 inches from side of pan comes out clean or almost clean (do not overbake). Transfer to a wire rack and cool completely. Cut into squares. Makes 9 large or 16 small brownies.

I had my friend Julie Artis—a terrific cook, great scholar, and diehard cinnamon lover—in mind when I developed these cinnamon-scented treats. The cinnamon chips are an easy way to intensify the cinnamon flavor—look for them in the baking aisle alongside chocolate chips. If you cannot find them, leave them out or substitute semisweet chocolate chips in their place for double the chocolate goodness. And if you don't have buttermilk, plain yogurt may be substituted. Be sure to serve these brownies alongside your favorite hot drink for the epitome of cozy.

Mint Julep Ganache Brownies

Some people (like me) want too much of a good thing. This recipe suits such types by combining just enough of several extremely good things to produce an elegant but still easy-to-assemble brownie inspired by the Kentucky Derby drink of choice. You can use this recipe as a template for other liqueur ganache brownies: simply leave out the peppermint extract and substitute the liqueur or spirit of your choice in place of the bourbon.

1	19.5- to 19.8-ounce package brownie mix
2	large eggs
5	tablespoons bourbon or whiskey, divided
½	cup (1 stick) unsalted butter, melted
1	teaspoon peppermint extract

Topping:

1	cup semisweet chocolate chips
¼	cup heavy cream

Preheat oven to 350° (325° for dark-coated metal pan). Position a rack in the lower third of the oven. Spray the bottom only of an 8-inch square baking pan with nonstick cooking spray (or foil-line pan; see page 11).

In a medium mixing bowl mix the brownie mix, eggs, 4 tablespoons bourbon, melted butter, and peppermint extract with a wooden spoon until well blended. Spread batter into prepared pan.

Bake 40–44 minutes or until toothpick inserted 2 inches from side of pan comes out clean or almost clean (do not overbake). Transfer to a wire rack and cool completely. Using a toothpick, poke holes all over the top of the brownies.

To make ganache topping, whisk the chocolate chips and heavy cream in a small saucepan set over medium-low heat until melted and smooth. Remove from heat and whisk in remaining tablespoon bourbon. Pour and spread evenly over brownies in pan.

Refrigerate brownies until topping is set, about 2 hours (or as long as overnight). Cut brownies into squares. Store in refrigerator. Makes 9 large or 16 small brownies.

Raspberry Cream Cheese Brownies

1	19.5- to 19.8-ounce package brownie mix
½	cup vegetable oil
¼	cup water
2	large eggs
1	8-ounce package cream cheese, softened
½	cup sifted powdered sugar
½	cup seedless raspberry preserves
1	1-ounce square unsweetened baking chocolate, chopped
1	tablespoon unsalted butter

Preheat oven to 350° (325° for dark-coated metal pan). Position a rack in the lower third of the oven. Spray the bottom only of a 13 x 9-inch baking pan with nonstick cooking spray (or foil-line pan; see page 11).

In a medium mixing bowl mix the brownie mix, oil, water, and eggs with a wooden spoon until just blended and all dry ingredients are moistened. Spread batter into prepared pan.

Bake 28–30 minutes or until toothpick inserted 2 inches from side of pan comes out clean or almost clean (do not over-bake). Transfer to a wire rack and cool completely.

In a small mixing bowl beat cream cheese, powdered sugar, and preserves with an electric mixer set on medium until smooth; spread over cooled brownies.

Place chopped chocolate and butter in a small saucepan set over low heat; stir until melted and smooth. Drizzle off the edge of a spoon in decorative swirls or lines over brownies. Refrigerate at least 1 hour or until chocolate is firm. Cut into squares. Store in refrigerator. Makes 24 large or 36 small brownies.

With a swath of pretty-in-pink frosting and dark chocolate drizzle, small squares of these brownies are perfect for bridal and baby showers or as part of a spring luncheon dessert buffet. The creamy berry frosting is a great foil to the dark chocolate drizzle.

Amaretto Café Cream Brownies

Here the archetypal brownie is taken to new coffeehouse-inspired heights with the enhancement of almonds, coffee, and cream.

1	19.5- to 19.8-ounce package brownie mix
1	stick (½ cup) unsalted butter, softened
⅓	cup milk
2	large eggs
12	ounces (1½ 8-ounce packages) cream cheese, softened
1	7-ounce jar marshmallow creme
1½	tablespoons instant espresso or coffee powder
1	teaspoon almond extract
1	cup chopped walnuts

Preheat oven to 350° (325° for dark-coated metal pan). Position a rack in the lower third of the oven. Spray the bottom only of a 13 x 9-inch baking pan with nonstick cooking spray (or foil-line pan; see page 11).

In a large mixing bowl mix the brownie mix and softened butter with an electric mixer set on low for 1 minute or until crumbly. Reserve 1 cup of the mixture in small mixing bowl for topping. Add milk and eggs to remaining brownie mixture; mix with a wooden spoon until blended and smooth. Spread batter evenly into prepared pan.

In a medium mixing bowl beat cream cheese, marshmallow creme, espresso powder, and almond extract with electric mixer set on medium until smooth. Spread evenly over brownie mixture.

Add walnuts to reserved 1 cup brownie mixture; mix well. Sprinkle evenly over cream cheese mixture.

Bake 28–30 minutes or until toothpick inserted 2 inches from side of pan comes out clean or almost clean (do not over-bake). Transfer to a wire rack and cool completely. Cut into squares. Store in refrigerator. Makes 24 large or 36 small brownies.

Almond Joyful Coconut Brownies

Inspired by a favorite candy bar of similar name, these moist, almond-, coconut-, and milk chocolate–packed brownies are more confection than brownie. To enhance the almond flavor, lightly toast the almonds before sprinkling onto the brownies.

1	19.5- to 19.8-ounce package brownie mix
½	cup vegetable oil
¼	cup water
2	large eggs
1	teaspoon almond extract
2	cups sweetened shredded coconut, divided
1½	cups milk chocolate chips
½	cup sliced almonds, preferably lightly toasted

Preheat oven to 350° (325° for dark-coated metal pan). Position a rack in the lower third of the oven. Spray the bottom only of a 13 x 9-inch baking pan with nonstick cooking spray (or foil-line pan; see page 11).

In a medium mixing bowl mix the brownie mix, oil, water, eggs, and almond extract with a wooden spoon until just blended and all dry ingredients are moistened; stir in 1 cup coconut. Spread batter into prepared pan.

Bake 28–30 minutes or until toothpick inserted 2 inches from side of pan comes out clean or almost clean (do not overbake). Remove from oven and immediately sprinkle with chocolate chips. Return to oven for 1 minute to soften chips; spread the melted chips evenly over brownies with the back of a metal spoon.

Transfer to a wire rack and sprinkle with almonds and remaining 1 cup coconut. Gently press into melted chocolate. Cool completely. Refrigerate 1 hour to set the chocolate. Cut into squares. Makes 24 large or 36 small brownies.

Milk Chocolate Malt Brownies

1	19.5- to 19.8-ounce package brownie mix
½	cup vegetable oil
¼	cup water
3	large eggs
2	cups malted milk balls, coarsely chopped
1	cup milk chocolate chips
1	tablespoon vegetable shortening

Preheat oven to 350° (325° for dark-coated metal pan). Position a rack in the lower third of the oven. Spray the bottom only of a 13 x 9-inch baking pan with nonstick cooking spray (or foil-line pan; see page 11).

In a medium mixing bowl mix the brownie mix, oil, water, and eggs with a wooden spoon until just blended and all dry ingredients are moistened. Spread batter into prepared pan; sprinkle with malted milk balls.

Bake 28–30 minutes or until toothpick inserted 2 inches from side of pan comes out clean or almost clean (do not over-bake). Transfer to a wire rack.

In a small saucepan set over low heat, melt chocolate chips and shortening until smooth, stirring. Drizzle over topping; cool completely. Refrigerate about 10 minutes or until chocolate is firm. Cut into squares. Makes 24 large or 36 small brownies.

If any brownie can make you feel like a kid again, this is it. It's bound to become a favorite. When baked in the brownies, the malt balls add both old-fashioned flavor and richness.

Spicy Aztec Brownies

Melted butter, a handful of dark chocolate, a kick of cayenne, and a sheen of cinnamon glaze makes for one intensely delicious Aztec-inspired brownie.

1½	tablespoons instant espresso or coffee powder
1	tablespoon vanilla extract
1	19.5- to 19.8-ounce package brownie mix
1	stick (½ cup) unsalted butter, melted
¼	cup water
2	large eggs
¼	teaspoon cayenne pepper
3	1-ounce squares bittersweet chocolate, finely chopped
1	recipe Cinnamon Glaze (see page 248)

Preheat oven to 350° (325° for dark-coated metal pan). Position a rack in the lower third of the oven. Spray the bottom only of an 8-inch square baking pan with nonstick cooking spray (or foil-line pan; see page 11).

In a small cup dissolve the espresso powder in the vanilla. In a medium mixing bowl mix the brownie mix, melted butter, water, vanilla-espresso mixture, eggs, and cayenne pepper with a wooden spoon until just blended and all dry ingredients are moistened; stir in chopped chocolate. Spread batter into prepared pan.

Bake 40–44 minutes or until toothpick inserted 2 inches from side of pan comes out clean or almost clean (do not overbake). Transfer to a wire rack.

Prepare Cinnamon Glaze; spread over warm brownies. Cool completely. Cut into squares. Makes 9 large or 16 small brownies.

Turtle Cheesecake Brownies

1	19.5- to 19.8-ounce package brownie mix
½	cup vegetable oil
¼	cup water
3	large eggs
1	8-ounce package cream cheese, softened
½	teaspoon vanilla extract
⅔	cup caramel ice cream topping
1	cup chopped pecans

Preheat oven to 350° (325° for dark-coated metal pan). Position a rack in the lower third of the oven. Spray the bottom only of a 13 x 9-inch baking pan with nonstick cooking spray (or foil-line pan; see page 11).

In a medium mixing bowl mix the brownie mix, oil, water, and 2 eggs with a wooden spoon until just blended and all dry ingredients are moistened. Spread batter into prepared pan.

In a medium mixing bowl beat the cream cheese with an electric mixer set on medium until smooth. Beat in vanilla and remaining egg until thoroughly blended.

Spoon cream cheese mixture over brownie batter in pan (need not cover completely); dollop with spoonfuls of caramel topping. Cut through mixture with knife several times for marbled design. Sprinkle with pecans.

Bake 32–35 minutes or until toothpick inserted 2 inches from side of pan comes out clean or almost clean (do not overbake). Transfer to a wire rack and cool completely. Cut into squares. Store in refrigerator. Makes 24 large or 36 small brownies.

A rich brownie base, a silken layer of cheesecake, crunchy pecans, and buttery caramel? I call it perfection. These outstanding brownies make a delicious present for a very lucky friend.

Pecan Pie Brownies

My love of pecan pie was the inspiration for this new-fashioned brownie. The combination of chewy chocolate brownie and familiar brown sugar pecan goodness is out of this world. I prefer a cakey brownie to contrast with the pecan filling (hence the three eggs in the brownie batter) but you can certainly reduce the number of eggs in the brownie batter to two for a fudgy effect. I am confident these will become a fast favorite for you, too.

¼	cup (½ stick) unsalted butter
2	tablespoons all-purpose flour
¼	cup packed brown sugar
¼	cup corn syrup
5	large eggs
1	teaspoon vanilla extract
1½	cups very coarsely chopped pecans
1	19.5- to 19.8-ounce package brownie mix
½	cup vegetable oil
¼	cup water

Preheat oven to 350° (325° for dark-coated metal pan). Position a rack in the lower third of the oven. Spray the bottom only of a 13 x 9-inch baking pan with nonstick cooking spray (or foil-line pan; see page 11).

In a medium saucepan set over medium heat, melt the butter; stir in flour until blended. Stir in brown sugar, corn syrup, and 2 of the eggs until well blended. Cook over medium heat about 4–5 minutes, stirring constantly, until bubbly. Remove from heat. Stir in vanilla and pecans. Set aside.

In a medium mixing bowl mix the brownie mix, oil, water, and remaining 3 eggs with a wooden spoon until just blended and all dry ingredients are moistened. Spread batter into prepared pan; spoon pecan mixture evenly over top.

Bake 32–35 minutes or until toothpick inserted 2 inches from side of pan comes out clean or almost clean (do not overbake).

Transfer to a wire rack and cool completely. Cut into squares. Makes 24 large or 36 small brownies.

Whiskey-Glazed
Double Chocolate Brownies

1   19.5- to 19.8-ounce package brownie mix
1   stick (½ cup) unsalted butter, melted
¼   cup whiskey
2   large eggs
1   cup semisweet chocolate chunks or chips

1   recipe Whiskey Glaze (see page 264)

Preheat oven to 350° (325° for dark-coated metal pan). Position a rack in the lower third of the oven. Spray the bottom only of an 8-inch square baking pan with nonstick cooking spray (or foil-line pan; see page 11).

In a medium mixing bowl combine the brownie mix, melted butter, whiskey, and eggs with a wooden spoon until well blended; stir in chocolate chunks or chips. Spread batter into the prepared pan.

Bake 40–44 minutes or until toothpick inserted 2 inches from side of pan comes out clean or almost clean (do not over-bake). Transfer to a wire rack.

Prepare Whiskey Glaze. Spread glaze evenly over warm brownies. Cool completely. Cut into squares. Makes 9 large or 16 small brownies.

This variation on traditional brownies features a generous dose of whiskey. Not for the faint of heart, they are simple yet wickedly rich. You can use this recipe as a template—substitute the liqueur or spirit of your choice in place of the whiskey.

Cream Cheese Swirled Brownies

Take note: the aroma

of these luscious

brownies baking will

quickly lure family and

friends to the kitchen.

The marbled effect

looks elaborate but is

in fact simple to

accomplish with a few

swirls of a kitchen

knife. Don't worry

about making perfect

swirls—"mistakes"

look every bit as beau-

tiful. Warm cocoa is

the beverage of choice

here.

1	19.5- to 19.8-ounce package brownie mix
½	cup vegetable oil
¼	cup water
3	large eggs
1	8-ounce package cream cheese, softened
3	tablespoons sugar
2	teaspoons all-purpose flour
1	teaspoon vanilla extract

Preheat oven to 350° (325° for dark-coated metal pan). Position a rack in the lower third of the oven. Spray the bottom only of a 13 x 9-inch baking pan with nonstick cooking spray (or foil-line pan; see page 11).

In a medium mixing bowl mix the brownie mix, oil, water, and 2 eggs with a wooden spoon until just blended and all dry ingredients are moistened. Spread all but about ½ cup of the batter into prepared pan.

In a medium mixing bowl beat the cream cheese with an electric mixer set on medium until smooth. Beat in the sugar, flour, vanilla, and remaining egg until well blended and smooth.

Spoon cream cheese mixture over brownie batter in pan; dollop remaining brownie batter over the spoonfuls of cream cheese batter. Swirl the batters with the tip of a knife to create a marbled design.

Bake 28–30 minutes or until toothpick inserted in brownie 2 inches from side of pan comes out clean or almost clean (do not overbake).

Transfer to a wire rack and cool completely. Cut into squares. Store in refrigerator. Makes 24 large or 36 small brownies.

Chocolate-Chip Cookie Bull's-Eye Brownies

1	19.5- to 19.8-ounce package brownie mix
1/2	cup vegetable oil
1/4	cup water
3	large eggs
1	cup semisweet chocolate chips
1	18-ounce package refrigerated chocolate-chip cookie dough
28	chocolate "kiss" or white chocolate striped "hugs" candies, unwrapped

Preheat oven to 350° (325° for dark-coated metal pan). Position a rack in the lower third of the oven. Spray the bottom only of a 13 x 9-inch baking pan with nonstick cooking spray (or foil-line pan; see page 11).

In a medium mixing bowl mix the brownie mix, oil, water, and eggs with a wooden spoon until just blended and all dry ingredients are moistened; stir in chocolate chips. Spread batter into prepared pan.

Cut cookie dough in half, then in half again (for 4 equal pieces). Cut each quarter of dough into 7 pieces. Roll each piece into a ball, then flatten slightly. Evenly space pieces atop brownie layer in rows (4 across, 7 down).

Bake 28–30 minutes or until just set. Remove from oven and immediately press a chocolate kiss into each cookie mound. Transfer to a wire rack and cool completely. Cut into squares with one "bull's-eye" in the center of each brownie. Makes 28 large brownies.

If you're one of those home cooks who is always looking for the "next new thing," place your bookmark here. What's more, these brownies are simple to make since the chocolate-chip "bull's-eyes" are made with refrigerated cookie dough. Whether for a picnic, pitch-in, or your own enjoyment, these chocolate-chipcookie-bolstered brownies are both excitingly modern and reassuringly conventional.

Brandy-Laced "Fruitcake" Brownies

You have to try these brownies to believe how yummy they are. If you love fruitcake, this may supplant your favorite recipe, and if you're not a fan, you will become a fast convert with one or two bites of these rich, delicious holiday treats, which boast four kinds of dried fruit (no glacé cherries!), toasted walnuts, and a generous pour of brandy.

1	19.5- to 19.8-ounce package brownie mix
1	stick (½ cup) unsalted butter, melted
¼	cup brandy or dark rum
3	large eggs
½	cup chopped walnuts, preferably lightly toasted
⅓	cup chopped dried apricots
⅓	cup chopped dried figs
⅓	cup chopped pitted dates
⅓	cup dried tart cherries or cranberries
1	recipe Cream Cheese Frosting (see page 261)

Preheat oven to 350° (325° for dark-coated metal pan). Position a rack in the lower third of the oven. Spray the bottom only of a 13 x 9-inch baking pan with nonstick cooking spray (or foil-line pan; see page 11).

In a medium mixing bowl mix the brownie mix, melted butter, brandy, and eggs with a wooden spoon until just blended and all dry ingredients are moistened. Stir in the walnuts and dried fruits. Spread batter into prepared pan.

Bake 28–30 minutes or until toothpick inserted 2 inches from side of pan comes out clean or almost clean (do not overbake). Transfer to a wire rack and cool completely.

Prepare Cream Cheese Frosting. Spread frosting over cooled brownies. Cut into squares. Store in refrigerator. Makes 24 large or 36 small brownies.

Jim & Anna's Dark Rum Brownies

1	19.5- to 19.8-ounce package brownie mix
½	cup (1 stick) unsalted butter, melted
¼	cup dark rum
2	large eggs
¼	teaspoon ground nutmeg
4	1-ounce squares bittersweet chocolate, coarsely chopped
1	recipe Chocolate Rum Glaze (see page 256)

Preheat oven to 350° (325° for dark-coated metal pan). Position a rack in the lower third of the oven. Spray the bottom only of an 8-inch square baking pan with nonstick cooking spray (or foil-line pan; see page 11).

In a medium mixing bowl mix the brownie mix, melted butter, dark rum, eggs, and nutmeg with a wooden spoon until just blended and all dry ingredients are moistened; stir in chopped chocolate. Spread batter into prepared pan.

Bake 40–44 minutes or until toothpick inserted 2 inches from side of pan comes out clean or almost clean (do not overbake). Transfer to a wire rack and cool for 15 minutes.

Prepare Chocolate Rum Glaze. Spread glaze over warm brownies; cool completely. Cut into squares. Makes 9 large or 16 small brownies.

My friends Jim and Anna Lynch are two of the most generous people I have ever known. Lucky for me, they are always happy to be thanked with chocolate. They both came close to swooning when they tasted these brownies which, fittingly, are extremely generous in both chocolate and rum.

Oatmeal Cookie–Bottomed Brownies

If there is a way to build on the brownie's old-fashioned, homey goodness, it's by fortifying its foundation with a brown sugar oatmeal base. Pour a glass of cold milk to complement the renovation.

$2\frac{1}{2}$	cups quick-cooking or old-fashioned oats
$\frac{3}{4}$	cup all-purpose flour
$\frac{3}{4}$	cup packed dark brown sugar
$\frac{1}{2}$	teaspoon baking soda
$\frac{3}{4}$	cup ($1\frac{1}{2}$ sticks) butter, softened
1	19.5- to 19.8-ounce package brownie mix
$\frac{1}{2}$	cup vegetable oil
$\frac{1}{4}$	cup water
2	large eggs
1	cup semisweet chocolate chips

Preheat oven to 350° (325° for dark-coated metal pan). Position a rack in the lower third of the oven. Spray the bottom only of a 13 x 9-inch baking pan with nonstick cooking spray (or foil-line pan; see page 11).

In a large mixing bowl mix oats, flour, brown sugar, and baking soda; mix in softened butter with wooden spoon or electric mixer set on low until well blended. Reserve 1 cup of the oat mixture; press remaining oat mixture into prepared pan. Bake 10 minutes; transfer to wire rack and cool 5 minutes (leave oven on).

In a medium mixing bowl mix the brownie mix, oil, water and eggs with a wooden spoon until just blended and all dry ingredients are moistened; stir in chocolate chips. Spread batter over partially baked crust; sprinkle with reserved oat mixture.

Bake 30–35 minutes or until toothpick inserted 2 inches from side of pan comes out clean or almost clean (do not overbake). Transfer brownies to a wire rack and cool completely. Cut into squares. Makes 24 large or 36 small brownies.

Chocolate-Glazed Mint-Frosted Brownies

1	19.5- to 19.8-ounce package brownie mix
½	cup vegetable oil
¼	cup water
2	large eggs
½	teaspoon peppermint extract
1	cup semisweet chocolate chips
1	recipe Mint Frosting (see page 265)
1	recipe Shiny Chocolate Glaze (see page 258)

Preheat oven to 350° (325° for dark-coated metal pan). Position a rack in the lower third of the oven. Spray the bottom only of a 13 x 9-inch baking pan with nonstick cooking spray (or foil-line pan; see page 11).

In a medium mixing bowl mix the brownie mix, oil, water, eggs, and peppermint extract with a wooden spoon until just blended and all dry ingredients are moistened. Stir in the chocolate chips. Spread batter into prepared pan.

Bake 28–30 minutes or until toothpick inserted 2 inches from side of pan comes out clean or almost clean (do not overbake). Transfer to a wire rack and cool completely.

Prepare Mint Frosting. Spread frosting over cooled brownies.

Prepare Shiny Chocolate Glaze; drizzle over frosting. Refrigerate 1 hour to set the glaze. Cut into squares. Store in refrigerator. Makes 24 large or 36 small brownies.

Much to my joy, my mother made a version of these layered brownies every Christmas of my childhood. Using brownie mix streamlines her recipe for these festive cookies that are lovely for the winter holidays but also welcome year-round.

Orange Cream–Frosted Brownies

Accented with a creamy orange frosting, these brownies are a heavenly marriage of flavors. One 6-ounce container of frozen orange juice concentrate is enough to make both the brownies and the frosting.

1	19.5- to 19.8-ounce package brownie mix
½	cup vegetable oil
¼	cup frozen (thawed) orange juice concentrate
2	large eggs
1	recipe Orange Cream Cheese Frosting (see page 266)
½	cup semisweet chocolate chips
1	tablespoon shortening

Preheat oven to 350° (325° for dark-coated metal pan). Position a rack in the lower third of the oven. Spray the bottom only of a 13 x 9-inch baking pan with nonstick cooking spray (or foil-line pan; see page 11).

In a medium mixing bowl mix the brownie mix, oil, orange juice concentrate, and eggs with a wooden spoon until just blended and all dry ingredients are moistened. Spread batter into prepared pan.

Bake 28–30 minutes or until toothpick inserted 2 inches from side of pan comes out clean or almost clean (do not overbake). Transfer to a wire rack and cool completely.

Prepare Orange Cream Cheese Frosting; spread over cooled brownies.

Place chocolate chips and shortening in small saucepan set over low heat; stir until melted and smooth. Drizzle over brownies. Refrigerate at least 1 hour, until chocolate is set. Cut into squares. Store in refrigerator. Makes 24 large or 36 small brownies.

Peppermint Patty–Frosted Brownies

1	19.5- to 19.8-ounce package brownie mix
½	cup vegetable oil
¼	cup water
2	large eggs
28	chocolate-covered miniature peppermint patties, unwrapped

Preheat oven to 350° (325° for dark-coated metal pan). Position a rack in the lower third of the oven. Spray the bottom only of a 13 x 9-inch baking pan with nonstick cooking spray (or foil-line pan; see page 11).

In a medium mixing bowl mix the brownie mix, oil, water, and eggs with a wooden spoon until just blended and all dry ingredients are moistened. Spread batter into prepared pan.

Bake 28–30 minutes or until toothpick inserted 2 inches from side of pan comes out clean or almost clean (do not overbake).

Remove pan from oven and immediately place peppermint patties to cover top of brownies. Return to oven 3–4 minutes or until patties are softened. Remove from oven and immediately spread evenly with a small offset metal spatula or butter knife, swirling the melted chocolate and mint of the candies for a marbled design.

Transfer to a wire rack and cool completely. Cut into squares. Makes 24 large or 36 small brownies.

The impressive mint and dark-chocolate swirled frosting on these brownies is almost embarrassingly easy to make. The marbled result looks professional and the taste is fantastic. Good luck making them last!

Peanut Butter Cup Brownies

If chocolate–peanut butter cravings are part of your genetic blueprint, you'll want to whip up these easy-to-assemble brownies ASAP.

1	19.5- to 19.8-ounce package brownie mix
½	cup vegetable oil
¼	cup water
2	large eggs
28	1-inch chocolate-covered peanut butter cup candies, unwrapped

Preheat oven to 350° (325° for dark-coated metal pan). Position a rack in the lower third of the oven. Spray the bottom only of a 13 x 9-inch baking pan with nonstick cooking spray (or foil-line pan; see page 11).

In a medium mixing bowl mix the brownie mix, oil, water, and eggs with a wooden spoon until just blended and all dry ingredients are moistened. Spread batter into prepared pan. Arrange candies in rows (7 across, 4 down) on batter. Press candies into batter slightly.

Bake 28–30 minutes or until toothpick inserted 2 inches from side of pan comes out clean or almost clean (do not overbake). Transfer to a wire rack and cool completely.

Cut into 28 squares (with peanut butter cup at center of each brownie). Makes 28 large brownies.

Rocky Road Brownies

1   19.5- to 19.8-ounce package brownie mix
½   cup vegetable oil
¼   cup water
3   large eggs
2   cups semisweet chocolate chips, divided
2   cups miniature marshmallows
1   cup coarsely chopped roasted, lightly salted peanuts

Preheat oven to 350° (325° for dark–coated metal pan). Position a rack in the lower third of the oven. Spray the bottom only of a 13 x 9-inch baking pan with nonstick cooking spray (or foil-line pan; see page 11).

In a medium mixing bowl mix the brownie mix, oil, water, and eggs with a wooden spoon until just blended and all dry ingredients are moistened; stir in 1 cup of the chocolate chips. Spread batter into prepared pan.

Bake 28–30 minutes or until toothpick inserted 2 inches from side of pan comes out clean or almost clean (do not overbake).

Remove pan from oven and immediately sprinkle with marshmallows, remaining 1 cup chocolate chips, and the peanuts. Cover pan with cookie sheet for about 5 minutes to soften (slightly) the chocolate chips and marshmallows. Remove cookie sheet. Transfer to a wire rack and cool completely. Makes 24 large or 36 small brownies.

Make this marshmallow, chocolate chip, and nut-topped rendering of the all-American brownie on a Saturday afternoon when everyone seems too busy to slow down and enjoy the day. The wafting smells of baking chocolate will silently summon everyone around the kitchen table in no time for some good old-fashioned conversation and commensality.

Dad's Double Peanut Butter Frosted Brownies

Oh, that peanut butter/chocolate combination—who can resist? Not me, and certainly not my peanut-butter-loving Dad. To push the envelope, consider sprinkling the frosted brownies with some coarsely chopped peanut butter cups.

1	19.5- to 19.8-ounce package brownie mix
½	cup vegetable oil
¼	cup water
4	large eggs
⅓	cup packed brown sugar
⅓	cup creamy peanut butter
1	recipe Peanut Butter Frosting (see page 268)

Preheat oven to 350° (325° for dark-coated metal pan). Position a rack in the lower third of the oven. Spray the bottom only of a 13 x 9-inch baking pan with nonstick cooking spray (or foil-line pan; see page 11).

In a medium mixing bowl mix the brownie mix, oil, water, and 3 of the eggs with a wooden spoon until just blended and all dry ingredients are moistened. Spread batter into prepared pan.

In a small mixing bowl mix brown sugar, peanut butter, and remaining egg until blended. Drop by tablespoonfuls onto batter. Cut through batter several times with the tip of a knife to create a marble effect.

Bake 32–35 minutes or until toothpick inserted 2 inches from side of pan comes out clean or almost clean (do not overbake). Transfer to a wire rack and cool completely.

Prepare Peanut Butter Frosting. Spread frosting over cooled brownies. Cut into squares. Makes 24 large or 36 small brownies.

Caramel-Butterscotch-Loaded Brownies

1	19.5- to 19.8-ounce package brownie mix
½	cup vegetable oil
¼	cup water
2	large eggs
2	cups butterscotch-flavored baking chips, divided
24	caramels, unwrapped
2	tablespoons milk

Wow! If you're a butterscotch and caramel lover (as I am), you'll move these brownies to the top of your must-make-immediately list.

Preheat oven to 350° (325° for dark-coated metal pan). Position a rack in the lower third of the oven. Spray the bottom only of a 13 x 9-inch baking pan with nonstick cooking spray (or foil-line pan; see page 11).

In a medium mixing bowl mix the brownie mix, oil, water, and eggs with a wooden spoon until just blended and all dry ingredients are moistened. Stir in 1 cup butterscotch chips. Spread batter into prepared pan.

Bake 28–30 minutes or until toothpick inserted 2 inches from side of pan comes out clean or almost clean (do not overbake). Remove from oven and immediately sprinkle with remaining butterscotch chips. Return to oven for 1 minute to soften chips. Transfer to a wire rack and cool (do not spread melted chips).

In a medium saucepan set over low heat combine caramels and milk, stirring until melted and smooth; drizzle over brownies. Transfer to a wire rack and cool completely. Cut into squares. Makes 24 large or 36 small brownies.

Rum Raisin Brownies

Here you have brownies with a grown-up taste and the sophisticated balance of sweetness and rum. Try them warm with vanilla ice cream or, if you can find it, rum raisin ice cream.

1	cup raisins, packed
½	cup dark rum
1	19.5- to 19.8-ounce package brownie mix
½	cup (1 stick) butter, melted
2	large eggs
1	cup semisweet chocolate chips

In a small mixing bowl combine the raisins and rum; soak until raisins are plump, about 30 minutes (do not drain).

Preheat oven to 350° (325° for dark-coated metal pan). Position a rack in the lower third of the oven. Spray the bottom only of an 8-inch square baking pan with nonstick cooking spray (or foil-line pan; see page 11).

In a medium mixing bowl mix the brownie mix, melted butter, eggs, and raisins and their liquid with a wooden spoon until just blended and all dry ingredients are moistened; stir in chocolate chips. Spread batter into prepared pan.

Bake 40–44 minutes or until toothpick inserted 2 inches from side of pan comes out clean or almost clean (do not overbake). Transfer to a wire rack and cool completely. Cut into squares. Makes 9 large or 16 small brownies.

Browned Butter Cashew Brownies

1   19.5- to 19.8-ounce package brownie mix
½   cup (1 stick) unsalted butter, melted
¼   cup water
2   large eggs
2   cups coarsely chopped roasted, lightly salted
      cashews, divided

1   recipe Browned Butter Icing (see page 263)

Punctuated with velvety bits of roasted cashews and finished with a sleek spread of browned-butter frosting, this is a winning new twist on classic brownies. Prepare for this page to become dog-eared and batter-splattered from repeated use.

Preheat oven to 350° (325° for dark-coated metal pan). Position a rack in the lower third of the oven. Spray the bottom only of an 8-inch square baking pan with nonstick cooking spray (or foil-line pan; see page 11).

In a medium mixing bowl mix the brownie mix, melted butter, water, and eggs with a wooden spoon until just blended and all dry ingredients are moistened; stir in 1 cup chopped cashews. Spread batter into prepared pan.

Bake 40–44 minutes or until toothpick inserted 2 inches from side of pan comes out clean or almost clean (do not overbake). Transfer to a wire rack and cool completely.

Prepare Browned Butter Icing. Spread over cooled brownies; sprinkle with remaining cashews. Cut into squares. Makes 9 large or 16 small brownies.

Mocha Buttercream Brownies

Making brownies for a coffee-loving friend? Give them the special treatment by adding embellishments that show you care, namely a swath of smooth Mocha Buttercream. A few extra ingredients from the pantry and several strokes of the spoon are all it takes.

1	19.5- to 19.8-ounce package brownie mix
1/2	cup vegetable oil
1/4	cup water
2	large eggs
1	tablespoon instant espresso or coffee powder
1/2	teaspoon ground cinnamon
1/4	teaspoon ground cardamom (optional)
1	recipe Mocha Buttercream Frosting (see page 267)

Preheat oven to 350° (325° for dark-coated metal pan). Position a rack in the lower third of the oven. Spray the bottom only of an 8-inch square baking pan with nonstick cooking spray (or foil-line pan; see page 11).

In a medium mixing bowl mix the brownie mix, oil, water, eggs, espresso powder, cinnamon, and cardamom with a wooden spoon until just blended and all dry ingredients are moistened. Spread batter into prepared pan.

Bake 40–44 minutes or until toothpick inserted 2 inches from side of pan comes out clean or almost clean (do not overbake). Transfer to a wire rack and cool completely.

Prepare Mocha Buttercream Frosting. Spread frosting over cooled brownies. Refrigerate at least 1 hour or until frosting is set. Cut into squares. Store in refrigerator. Makes 9 large or 16 small brownies.

Tennessee Jam Cake Brownies

1	19.5- to 19.8-ounce package brownie mix
½	cup vegetable oil
¼	cup buttermilk or water
2	large eggs
½	teaspoon ground cinnamon
¼	teaspoon ground cloves
1	cup chopped pecans or walnuts
¾	cup blackberry jam, stirred to loosen
1	recipe Caramel Penuche Frosting (see page 259)

This recipe takes its inspiration from traditional Tennessee jam cake, a rich spice cake made with blackberry jam and a brown sugar "penuche" frosting. The chocolate rendition here is wonderful.

Preheat oven to 350° (325° for dark-coated metal pan). Position a rack in the lower third of the oven. Spray the bottom only of a 13 x 9-inch baking pan with nonstick cooking spray (or foil-line pan; see page 11).

In a medium mixing bowl mix the brownie mix, oil, buttermilk, eggs, cinnamon, and cloves with a wooden spoon until just blended and all dry ingredients are moistened; stir in nuts. Spread batter into prepared pan. Dollop jam randomly over top of batter; swirl into batter with the tip of a knife.

Bake 28–30 minutes or until toothpick inserted 2 inches from side of pan comes out clean or almost clean (do not overbake). Transfer to a wire rack and cool completely.

Prepare Caramel Penuche Frosting. Spread frosting evenly over cooled brownies. Cut into squares. Makes 24 large or 36 small brownies.

Fudge-Frosted Walnut Brownies

Just about every cof-
feehouse has a version
of these classic brown-
ies. Elegant in their
simplicity of flavors,
they are dressy
enough to close out a
posh supper party or
give as a special gift.
To intensify the flavor
of the walnuts, lightly
toast and cool them
before adding to the
brownie batter—it's
well worth the extra
step.

1	19.5- to 19.8-ounce package brownie mix
½	cup (1 stick) unsalted butter, melted
¼	cup buttermilk
2	large eggs
1	teaspoon vanilla extract
¼	teaspoon almond extract
1	cup coarsely chopped walnuts, preferably lightly toasted
1	recipe Chocolate Fudge Frosting (see page 250)

Preheat oven to 350° (325° for dark-coated metal pan). Position a rack in the lower third of the oven. Spray the bottom only of an 8-inch square baking pan with nonstick cooking spray (or foil-line pan; see page 11).

In a medium mixing bowl mix the brownie mix, melted butter, buttermilk, eggs, vanilla extract, and almond extract with a wooden spoon until just blended and all dry ingredients are moistened; stir in the walnuts. Spread batter into prepared pan.

Bake 40–44 minutes or until toothpick inserted 2 inches from side of pan comes out clean or almost clean (do not overbake). Transfer to a wire rack and cool completely.

Prepare Chocolate Fudge Frosting. Spread frosting over cooled brownies. Cut into squares. Makes 9 large or 16 small brownies.

Macadamia & White Chocolate Chunk Brownies

1	19.5- to 19.8-ounce package brownie mix
½	cup vegetable oil
¼	cup water
2	large eggs
1	cup coarsely chopped macadamia nuts
1	6-ounce white chocolate baking bar, coarsely chopped into chunks, divided
2	teaspoons vegetable shortening

Preheat oven to 350° (325° for dark-coated metal pan). Position a rack in the lower third of the oven. Spray the bottom only of an 8-inch square baking pan with nonstick cooking spray (or foil-line pan; see page 11).

In a medium mixing bowl mix the brownie mix, oil, water, and eggs with a wooden spoon until just blended and all dry ingredients are moistened; stir in the macadamia nuts and two-thirds of the white chocolate chunks. Spread batter into prepared pan.

Bake 40–44 minutes or until toothpick inserted 2 inches from side of pan comes out clean or almost clean (do not overbake). Transfer to a wire rack and cool completely.

Place remaining white chocolate and shortening in small saucepan set over low heat; stir until melted and smooth. Drizzle melted chocolate over brownies. Refrigerate at least 1 hour until chocolate is set. Cut into squares. Makes 9 large or 16 small brownies.

Few can resist these brownies, not that anyone I know has ever tried. Studded with chunks of white chocolate and macadamia nuts, they were inspired by a nearly identical brownie at one of my favorite local coffeehouses.

S'mores Brownies

No tents or sleeping bags are required for this brownie rendition of a classic campfire treat. Gooey marshmallows and melted chocolate chips piled atop a graham cracker and brownie base? It doesn't get much better than this.

10	whole graham crackers, broken crosswise in half (20 squares), divided
1	19.5- to 19.8-ounce package brownie mix
½	cup vegetable oil
¼	cup water
2	large eggs
2	cups semisweet chocolate chips, divided
2½	cups miniature marshmallows

Preheat oven to 350° (325° for dark-coated metal pan). Position a rack in the lower third of the oven. Line a 13 x 9-inch baking pan with foil, with ends of foil extending beyond sides of pan; spray bottom of foil-lined pan with nonstick cooking spray.

Place 15 of the graham squares in bottom of pan, overlapping slightly. Break remaining 5 graham squares into large pieces; set aside.

In a medium mixing bowl mix the brownie mix, oil, water, and eggs with a wooden spoon until just blended and all dry ingredients are moistened; stir in 1 cup of the chocolate chips. Carefully spread batter into graham cracker–lined pan.

Bake 28–30 minutes or until toothpick inserted 2 inches from side of pan comes out clean or almost clean (do not overbake). Sprinkle evenly with marshmallows and remaining chocolate chips. Bake an additional 3–5 minutes or until marshmallows begin to puff. Poke reserved graham pieces gently through marshmallows into the brownie (let them stick out).

Transfer to a wire rack and cool completely. Lift brownies out of pan onto cutting board using foil handles. Cut into bars. Makes 24 large or 36 small brownies.

Raspberry Brownies

1	19.5- to 19.8-ounce package brownie mix
½	cup vegetable oil
¼	cup water
2	large eggs
½	cup seedless raspberry jam
1	cup white chocolate chips
2	teaspoons vegetable shortening

Preheat oven to 350° (325° for dark-coated metal pan). Position a rack in the lower third of the oven. Spray the bottom only of an 8-inch square baking pan with nonstick cooking spray (or foil-line pan; see page 11).

In a medium mixing bowl mix the brownie mix, oil, water, and eggs with a wooden spoon until just blended and all dry ingredients are moistened. Spread batter into prepared pan.

Bake 40–44 minutes or until toothpick inserted 2 inches from side of pan comes out clean or almost clean (do not overbake). Immediately spread jam over brownies. Transfer to a wire rack and cool completely.

In a small saucepan set over low heat melt the white chocolate with the shortening until smooth; drizzle over brownies. Refrigerate 1 hour to set chocolate. Cut into squares. Makes 9 large or 16 small brownies.

The combination of raspberry and chocolate has timeless appeal. No one will guess that these beautiful, scrumptious brownies are so easy to prepare.

Toasted Coconut White Chocolate Fudge Brownies

Tropical coconut, white chocolate, and rum flavoring pump up the volume of these part brownie, part fudge treats. Semisweet chocolate may be substituted for the white chocolate, if desired.

1	19.5- to 19.8-ounce package brownie mix
½	cup oil
¼	cup water
2	large eggs
3	teaspoons rum extract, divided
1	5-ounce can evaporated milk
3	cups miniature marshmallows
1½	cups white chocolate chips
2	cups sweetened shredded coconut, toasted

Preheat oven to 350° (325° for dark-coated metal pan). Position a rack in the lower third of the oven. Spray the bottom only of a 13 x 9-inch baking pan with nonstick cooking spray (or foil-line pan; see page 11).

In a medium mixing bowl mix the brownie mix, oil, water, eggs, and 1½ teaspoons of the rum extract with a wooden spoon until just blended and all dry ingredients are moistened. Spread batter into prepared pan.

Bake 28–30 minutes or until toothpick inserted 2 inches from side of pan comes out clean or almost clean (do not overbake). Transfer to a wire rack to cool.

Meanwhile, place evaporated milk and marshmallows in a large saucepan; cook on medium-low heat until mixture is melted and smooth, stirring constantly (to avoid scorching). Remove pan from heat and add white chocolate; stir until completely melted. Remove from heat and stir in remaining 1½ teaspoons rum extract. Immediately pour over brownies, spreading to cover evenly.

Immediately sprinkle with toasted coconut; press lightly into white chocolate fudge layer. Cool completely. Refrigerate 2 hours or until firm. Cut into bars. Store in airtight container in refrigerator. Makes 24 large or 36 small bars.

Milk Chocolate Buttermilk Brownies

Rich, moist, and sweet with chocolate, these buttermilk-enhanced, milk chocolate–frosted brownies are a quick and easy path to chocolate heaven.

1	19.5- to 19.8-ounce package brownie mix
½	cup (1 stick) unsalted butter, melted
¼	cup buttermilk
3	large eggs
1½	teaspoons vanilla extract
1½	cups milk chocolate chips, divided
2	teaspoons vegetable shortening

Preheat oven to 350° (325° for dark-coated metal pan). Position a rack in the lower third of the oven. Spray the bottom only of an 8-inch square baking pan with nonstick cooking spray (or foil-line pan; see page 11).

In a medium mixing bowl mix the brownie mix, melted butter, buttermilk, eggs, and vanilla with a wooden spoon until just blended and all dry ingredients are moistened; stir in 1 cup of the chocolate chips. Spread batter into prepared pan.

Bake 40–44 minutes or until toothpick inserted 2 inches from side of pan comes out clean or almost clean (do not overbake). Transfer to a wire rack and cool completely.

In a small saucepan set over low heat melt the remaining ½ cup chocolate chips with the shortening until smooth; drizzle over brownies. Refrigerate 1 hour to set the chocolate. Cut into squares. Makes 9 large or 16 small brownies.

Maple-Frosted Brownies

1	19.5- to 19.8-ounce package brownie mix
½	cup vegetable oil
¼	cup water
2	large eggs
2	teaspoons maple-flavored extract
1	cup coarsely chopped walnuts, preferably lightly toasted
1	recipe Maple Frosting (see page 267)

Preheat oven to 350° (325° for dark-coated metal pan). Position a rack in the lower third of the oven. Spray the bottom only of an 8-inch square baking pan with nonstick cooking spray (or foil-line pan; see page 11).

In a medium mixing bowl mix the brownie mix, oil, water, eggs, and maple extract with a wooden spoon until just blended and all dry ingredients are moistened; stir in chopped walnuts. Spread batter into prepared pan.

Bake 40–44 minutes or until toothpick inserted 2 inches from side of pan comes out clean or almost clean (do not overbake). Transfer to a wire rack and cool completely.

Prepare Maple Frosting. Spread frosting over cooled brownies. Cut into squares. Store in refrigerator. Makes 9 large or 16 small brownies.

You may not have known before now that chocolate and maple make a perfect match. These brownies are indisputable proof. Look for maple flavoring where vanilla extract is sold in the baking section of your supermarket.

Apricot Macaroon Brownies

Te quiero. Je t'aime. S'ayapo. There are many ways to say I love you, but a batch of these toasty coconut and apricot brownies will do it in any language. They come together in a flash, allowing plenty of time to sit back and savor.

1	19.5- to 19.8-ounce package brownie mix
½	cup vegetable oil
¼	cup water
2	large eggs
⅔	cup apricot preserves
⅓	cup butter
1	10-ounce package marshmallows
1	7-ounce package shredded coconut, toasted

Preheat oven to 350° (325° for dark-coated metal pan). Position a rack in the lower third of the oven. Spray the bottom only of a 13 x 9-inch baking pan with nonstick cooking spray (or foil-line pan; see page 11).

In a medium mixing bowl mix the brownie mix, oil, water, and eggs with a wooden spoon until just blended and all dry ingredients are moistened. Spread batter into prepared pan.

Bake 28–30 minutes or until toothpick inserted 2 inches from side of pan comes out clean or almost clean (do not overbake). Transfer to a wire rack and cool completely. Spread evenly with apricot preserves.

Meanwhile, melt butter in a large saucepan set over low heat. Add marshmallows; cook until marshmallows are completely melted and mixture is well blended, stirring frequently. Remove from heat; stir in toasted coconut. Spread evenly over apricot layer using back of large spoon or spatula. Cool completely. Cut into squares. Makes 24 large or 36 small bars.

Cranberry Brownies with Cranberry Ganache Topping

1	19.5- to 19.8-ounce package brownie mix
½	cup vegetable oil
¼	cup freshly squeezed orange juice
2	teaspoons grated orange zest
2	large eggs
1¼	cups dried cranberries
1	cup semisweet chocolate chips
¼	cup heavy whipping cream
¼	cup canned jelly cranberry sauce

Preheat oven to 350° (325° for dark-coated metal pan). Position a rack in the lower third of the oven. Spray the bottom only of an 8-inch square baking pan with nonstick cooking spray (or foil-line pan; see page 11).

In a medium mixing bowl mix the brownie mix, oil, orange juice, orange zest, and eggs with a wooden spoon until just blended and all dry ingredients are moistened; stir in the cranberries. Spread batter into prepared pan.

Bake 40–44 minutes or until toothpick inserted 2 inches from side of pan comes out clean or almost clean (do not overbake). Transfer to a wire rack and cool completely.

In a medium saucepan melt the chocolate chips, heavy cream, and cranberry sauce over low heat, stirring until melted and smooth. Remove from heat and let cool 5 minutes. Spread over cooled brownies. Let stand in refrigerator 1 hour to set chocolate. Cut into squares. Makes 9 large or 16 small brownies.

Cloaked with a layer of chocolate-cranberry ganache, these moist, cranberry-packed brownies are a harmonious marriage of sweet and tart flavors. Although I wouldn't pass on the ganache layer myself, I will readily admit that these are every bit as good without it.

Almond Fudge Brownies

If you can't resist the urge to overindulge, serve the brownies warm with premium ice cream, whipped cream, more almonds, and a cherry.

1	19.5- to 19.8-ounce package brownie mix
½	cup vegetable oil
¼	cup water
2	large eggs
2	cups semisweet chocolate chips
1	14-ounce can sweetened condensed milk
1	teaspoon almond extract
1½	cups sliced almonds, toasted

Preheat oven to 350° (325° for dark-coated metal pan). Position a rack in the lower third of the oven. Spray the bottom only of a 13 x 9-inch baking pan with nonstick cooking spray (or foil-line pan; see page 11).

In a medium mixing bowl mix the brownie mix, oil, water, and eggs with a wooden spoon until just blended and all dry ingredients are moistened. Spread batter into prepared pan.

Bake 28–30 minutes or until toothpick inserted 2 inches from side of pan comes out clean or almost clean (do not overbake). Transfer to a wire rack and cool.

Meanwhile, in heavy saucepan set over low heat, melt chips with condensed milk, stirring constantly. Remove from heat; stir in almond extract. Spread evenly over brownies. Sprinkle with toasted almonds; press down firmly. Chill 3 hours or until firm. Cut into squares. Store in the refrigerator. Makes 24 large or 36 small brownies.

Craggy-Topped Toffee Fudge Brownies

1	19.5- to 19.8-ounce package brownie mix
½	cup vegetable oil
¼	cup water
2	large eggs
2	cups semisweet chocolate chips, divided
2	cups coarsely chopped almonds
4	1.4-ounce milk chocolate–covered toffee candy bars, very coarsely chopped

Preheat oven to 350° (325° for dark-coated metal pan). Position a rack in the lower third of the oven. Spray the bottom only of a 13 x 9-inch baking pan with nonstick cooking spray (or foil-line pan; see page 11).

In a medium mixing bowl mix the brownie mix, oil, water, and eggs with a wooden spoon until just blended and all dry ingredients are moistened; stir in 1 cup chocolate chips. Spread batter into prepared pan; evenly sprinkle with the almonds.

Bake 28–30 minutes or until toothpick inserted 2 inches from side of pan comes out clean or almost clean (do not overbake).

Transfer to a wire rack and immediately sprinkle with remaining chocolate chips and chopped candy bars while brownies are still hot. Cover with a cookie sheet for 5 minutes. Remove cookie sheet and cool completely. Refrigerate 1 hour to set the chocolate. Cut into squares. Makes 24 large or 36 small brownies.

Anything goes with these over-the-(craggy) top brownies. You can, with terrific success, use any variety of chips (e.g., white chocolate, milk chocolate, cinnamon, butterscotch) in place of the semisweet chocolate chips and change out the almonds for your favorite nut—you'll still get a craggy-topped brownie!

Gooey Baby Ruthy Brownies

Few sentences are more welcoming when crossing the threshold of home than "there's a batch of brownies just out of the oven." Why not intensify the pleasure and excitement by adding ". . . and they're loaded with chunks of gooey Baby Ruthy bars!"

1	19.5- to 19.8-ounce package brownie mix
½	cup vegetable oil
¼	cup water
3	large eggs
3	2.1-ounce chocolate covered peanut-nougat candy bars (e.g., Baby Ruth® or Snickers®), coarsely chopped
1	8-ounce package cream cheese, softened
3	tablespoons packed brown sugar
2	teaspoons milk

Preheat oven to 350° (325° for dark-coated metal pan). Position a rack in the lower third of the oven. Spray the bottom only of a 13 x 9-inch baking pan with nonstick cooking spray (or foil-line pan; see page 11).

In a medium mixing bowl mix the brownie mix, oil, water, and 2 of the eggs with a wooden spoon until just blended and all dry ingredients are moistened. Stir in chopped candy bars. Reserve 1 cup of the batter. Spread remaining batter into prepared pan.

In a medium mixing bowl beat the cream cheese and brown sugar with an electric mixer set on medium until blended and smooth. Beat in milk and remaining egg. Spoon and spread over brownie batter in pan (need not cover completely). Dollop reserved brownie batter over cream cheese layer. Use the tip of a knife to swirl the batters for a marbled effect.

Bake 30–35 minutes or until toothpick inserted 2 inches from side of pan comes out clean or almost clean (do not overbake). Transfer to a wire rack and cool completely. Cut into squares. Store in refrigerator. Makes 24 large or 36 small brownies.

Chocolate Covered Cherry Brownies

2	6-ounce jars maraschino cherries without stems, drained, liquid reserved
1	19.5- to 19.8-ounce package brownie mix
10	tablespoons (1¼ sticks) unsalted butter, melted, divided
2	large eggs
½	teaspoon almond extract
1½	cups semisweet chocolate chips
1½	cups sifted powdered sugar

Preheat oven to 350° (325° for dark-coated metal pan). Position a rack in the lower third of the oven. Spray the bottom only of a 13 x 9-inch baking pan with nonstick cooking spray (or foil-line pan; see page 11).

Coarsely chop maraschino cherries; set aside.

In a medium mixing bowl mix the brownie mix, 8 tablespoons (1 stick) melted butter, ¼ cup reserved cherry liquid, eggs, and almond extract with a wooden spoon until just blended and all dry ingredients are moistened; stir in cherries and chocolate chips. Spread batter into prepared pan.

Bake 28–30 minutes or until toothpick inserted 2 inches from side of pan comes out clean or almost clean (do not over-bake). Transfer to a wire rack and cool completely.

In a small mixing bowl combine powdered sugar, remaining 2 tablespoons melted butter and 2 teaspoons reserved cherry liquid in small mixing bowl; stir. Add enough additional reserved cherry liquid, if needed, to make glazing consistency. Spread over brownies. Cut into squares. Makes 24 large or 36 small brownies.

These brownies remind me of a hard-to-find candy bar from my childhood known as a "mountain bar." It came in several flavors but my favorite was the cherry version, which had a crispy chocolate exterior and a cherry and almond-flavored cream filling. But as good as these candy shop–inspired brownies are, I guarantee they're even better warm, topped with vanilla ice cream.

Black Forest Brownies

I cannot speak for everyone, but by the time Valentine's Day rolls around, I'm either stumped for ideas or strapped for time. Enter in these Black Forest Brownies, an easy yet extravagant treat that solves any such Valentine's crises. They look gorgeous (and very festive with the contrasts of dark brownie, snowy whipped cream, and bright red cherries) and they taste spectacular. You're sure to earn kudos and win hearts.

1	19.5- to 19.8-ounce package brownie mix
½	cup vegetable oil
¼	cup water
2	large eggs
1	21-ounce can cherry pie filling
1	2-cup recipe for Sweetened Whipped Cream (see page 269)
2	1-ounce semisweet chocolate baking bars, grated with vegetable peeler

Preheat oven to 350° (325° for dark-coated metal pan). Position a rack in the lower third of the oven. Spray the bottom only of an 8-inch square baking pan with nonstick cooking spray (or foil-line pan; see page 11).

In a medium mixing bowl mix the brownie mix, oil, water, and eggs with a wooden spoon until just blended and all dry ingredients are moistened. Spread batter into prepared pan.

Bake 40–44 minutes or until toothpick inserted 2 inches from side of pan comes out clean or almost clean (do not over-bake). Transfer to a wire rack and cool. Cut into 9 squares. Top each brownie (warm or completely cooled) with pie filling, Sweetened Whipped Cream, and grated chocolate. Makes 9 servings.

Truffle-Topped Brownies

1	19.5- to 19.8-ounce package brownie mix
½	cup (1 stick) unsalted butter, melted
¼	cup water
2	large eggs
2	cups semisweet chocolate chips
1	14-ounce can sweetened condensed milk
2	teaspoons vanilla extract
1–2	tablespoons unsweetened cocoa powder (optional)

Chocolate euphoria? It's right here. These deep chocolate brownies are super rich—a small square goes a long way. Sifting the squares with unsweetened cocoa powder adds to the truffle resemblance.

Preheat oven to 350° (325° for dark-coated metal pan). Position a rack in the lower third of the oven. Spray the bottom only of a 13 x 9-inch baking pan with nonstick cooking spray (or foil-line pan; see page 11).

In a medium mixing bowl mix the brownie mix, melted butter, water, and eggs with a wooden spoon until just blended and all dry ingredients are moistened. Spread batter into prepared pan.

Bake 28–30 minutes or until toothpick inserted 2 inches from side of pan comes out clean or almost clean (do not overbake).

During last 10 minutes of brownies baking, prepare topping. In a heavy saucepan set over low heat, melt chocolate chips with condensed milk, stirring until smooth. Remove from heat and stir in vanilla.

Remove brownies from oven and immediately spread with chocolate mixture. Transfer to a wire rack and cool completely. Chill 1 hour in refrigerator to set topping. Cut into bars. If desired, sift squares with cocoa powder. Store in refrigerator. Makes 24 large or 36 small brownies.

Dark Chocolate Gingerbread Brownies

Rich with redolent spices, these brownies are a perfect autumn day detour or departure from the daily grind.

1	19.5- to 19.8-ounce package brownie mix
2	teaspoons ground ginger
¾	teaspoon ground cinnamon
½	teaspoon ground nutmeg
¼	teaspoon ground cloves
½	cup (1 stick) unsalted butter, melted
¼	cup dark molasses
3	large eggs
2	teaspoons vanilla extract
4	1-ounce squares bittersweet chocolate, coursely chopped
1	recipe Vanilla-Butter Glaze (see page 264)

Preheat oven to 350° (325° for dark-coated metal pan). Position a rack in the lower third of the oven. Spray the bottom only of an 8-inch square baking pan with nonstick cooking spray (or foil-line pan; see page 11).

In a medium mixing bowl toss brownie mix with the ginger, cinnamon, nutmeg, and cloves. Add the melted butter, molasses, eggs, and vanilla and mix with a wooden spoon until just blended and all dry ingredients are moistened; stir in chopped chocolate. Spread batter into prepared pan.

Bake 40–44 minutes or until toothpick inserted 2 inches from side of pan comes out clean or almost clean (do not overbake). Transfer to a wire rack.

Prepare Vanilla-Butter Glaze. Spread glaze over warm brownies; cool completely. Cut into squares. Makes 9 large or 16 small brownies.

Strawberries & Cream Brownies

1   19.5- to 19.8-ounce package brownie mix
½   cup vegetable oil
¼   cup water
2   large eggs
¾   cup strawberry jam, stirred to loosen
1   cup white chocolate chips
¾   cup (1½ sticks) butter, softened
¼   cup sifted powdered sugar

Preheat oven to 350° for metal or glass pan (325° for dark-coated metal pan). Position a rack in the lower third of the oven. Spray the bottom only of a 13 x 9-inch baking pan with nonstick cooking spray (or foil-line pan; see page 11).

In a medium mixing bowl mix the brownie mix, oil, water, and eggs with a wooden spoon until just blended and all dry ingredients are moistened. Spread batter into prepared pan.

Bake 28–30 minutes or until toothpick inserted 2 inches from side of pan comes out clean or almost clean (do not over-bake). Transfer to wire rack and cool 10 minutes; spread with jam. Cool completely.

Melt the white chocolate chips according to package directions; cool 30 minutes. In a medium bowl beat the butter and powdered sugar with electric mixer set on medium-high until light and fluffy. Gradually beat in cooled white chocolate until smooth, light, and fluffy. Carefully spread mixture over preserves. Store in refrigerator. Cut into squares. Let stand at room temperature 5–10 minutes before serving. Makes 24 large or 36 small brownies.

Everyone loves traditions because they are familiar and comforting, especially when it comes to food. But to keep things exciting, sometimes you need to inject an element of surprise in even your most steadfast of rituals. Case in point these brownies, which transform the perennial favorite of strawberries & cream into a berry-layered, buttercream-rich chocolate treat.

Swirled Tuxedo-Top Brownies

The beautifully marbleized pattern on these brownies is surprisingly simple to do, but the result is stunning. Consider making them in a 9-inch round cake pan (reducing the baking time to 38–42 minutes), then cut into wedges and serve with raspberry sauce for an elegant plated dessert.

1	19.5- to 19.8-ounce package brownie mix
½	cup vegetable oil
¼	cup water
2	large eggs
1	cup chopped walnuts, lightly toasted
1¼	cups semisweet chocolate chips, divided
1¼	cups white chocolate chips, divided

Preheat oven to 350° (325° for dark-coated metal pan). Position a rack in the lower third of the oven. Spray the bottom only of an 8-inch square baking pan with nonstick cooking spray (or foil-line pan; see page 11).

In a medium mixing bowl mix the brownie mix, oil, water, and eggs with a wooden spoon until just blended and all dry ingredients are moistened; stir in the toasted walnuts, ½ cup of the semisweet chocolate chips, and ½ cup of the white chocolate chips. Spread batter into prepared pan.

Bake 40–44 minutes or until toothpick inserted 2 inches from side of pan comes out clean or almost clean (do not overbake).

Remove pan from oven and immediately sprinkle with remaining ¾ cup semisweet and ¾ cup white chocolate chips; cover with cookie sheet. Let stand 5 minutes or until chocolates are melted. Remove sheet and swirl with the tip of a knife for a marbled effect. Transfer pan to a wire rack and cool completely. Refrigerate 1 hour to set the chocolate. Cut into squares. Makes 9 large or 16 small brownies.

Snickery Supreme Brownies

1	19.5- to 19.8-ounce package brownie mix
½	cup vegetable oil
¼	cup water
2	large eggs
1	cup semisweet chocolate chips
¼	cup (½ stick) unsalted butter
3	2.1-ounce chocolate covered peanut-caramel nougat candy bars (e.g., Snickers®), coarsely chopped

Supreme indeed! Take these to any gathering and I guarantee you will come home with an empty plate. Best of all, they are a snap to make.

Preheat oven to 350° (325° for dark-coated metal pan). Position a rack in the lower third of the oven. Spray the bottom only of an 8-inch square baking pan with nonstick cooking spray (or foil-line pan; see page 11).

In a medium mixing bowl mix the brownie mix, oil, water, and eggs with a wooden spoon until just blended and all dry ingredients are moistened. Spread batter into the prepared pan.

Bake 40–44 minutes or until toothpick inserted 2 inches from side of pan comes out clean or almost clean (do not overbake). Transfer to a wire rack to cool.

In a medium saucepan combine chocolate chips and butter; cook and stir over low heat until chocolate is melted and mixture is smooth. Pour and spread over brownies and immediately sprinkle with chopped candy bars. Gently press chopped candy into chocolate layer. Cool. Cut into squares. Makes 9 large or 16 small brownies.

Oh-So-Orange Brownies

A refreshing change of pace from traditional brownies, this recipe features the full flavor of orange throughout. Make sure to choose a relatively thin-skinned navel orange for best flavor.

1	large navel orange
1	19.5- to 19.8-ounce package brownie mix
½	cup oil
2	large eggs

Preheat oven to 350° (325° for dark-coated metal pan). Position a rack in the lower third of the oven. Spray the bottom only of an 8-inch square baking pan with nonstick cooking spray (or foil-line pan; see page 11).

Gently scrub the orange under warm water with a vegetable brush; pat dry. Cut the orange into quarters, trimming off ends (do not remove peel); remove any stray seeds. Place quarters into blender or food processor; purée until smooth.

In a medium mixing bowl mix orange purée, brownie mix, oil, and eggs with a wooden spoon until just blended. Spread batter into prepared pan.

Bake 40–44 minutes or until toothpick inserted 2 inches from side of pan comes out clean or almost clean (do not overbake). Transfer to a wire rack and cool completely. Cut into squares. Makes 9 large or 16 small brownies.

Sour Cream Brownies with Broiled Brown Sugar Topping

1	19.5- to 19.8-ounce package brownie mix
3	large eggs
1	cup sour cream, divided
½	cup (1 stick) unsalted butter, melted, divided
1½	cups sweetened shredded coconut
½	cup chopped pecans
1	cup packed brown sugar

Preheat oven to 350° (325° for dark-coated metal pan). Position a rack in the lower third of the oven. Spray the bottom only of an 8-inch square baking pan with nonstick cooking spray (or foil-line pan; see page 11).

In a medium mixing bowl mix the brownie mix, eggs, ¾ cup of the sour cream, and ¼ cup melted butter with a wooden spoon until just blended and all dry ingredients are moistened. Spread batter into prepared pan.

Bake 40–44 minutes or until toothpick inserted 2 inches from side of pan comes out clean or almost clean (do not overbake).

While brownies bake, in a medium mixing bowl combine the coconut, chopped pecans, brown sugar, remaining ¼ cup sour cream and remaining ¼ cup melted butter and blend with a wooden spoon. Remove brownies from oven and turn oven to broiler setting. Spread brownies evenly with the prepared topping.

Broil 4 inches from heat for 2–3 minutes or until golden brown (watch carefully to avoid burning). Transfer to a wire rack and cool completely. Cut into squares. Makes 9 large or 16 small brownies.

These irresistible brownies are the stuff from which the concept "comfort food" is derived. Frankly, I could eat the topping on its own straight from a spoon (it's a brown sugar thing), but it is truly delectable atop the sour cream brownie base.

Gianduia Brownies (Italian Chocolate Hazelnut Brownies)

The Italian combination of chocolate and hazelnuts, called *gianduia*, is used here to create a dense, sumptuous brownie. You can typically find chocolate hazelnut spread (Nutella® is the most common brand) in one of two places in the supermarket: in the peanut butter section or in the international foods section.

1	19.5- to 19.8-ounce package brownie mix
½	cup (1 stick) unsalted butter, melted
¼	cup water
2	large eggs
1	13-ounce jar chocolate-hazelnut spread (e.g., Nutella®), divided
2	tablespoons all-purpose flour
1	large egg yolk
1	cup coarsely chopped, lightly toasted hazelnuts (optional)

Preheat oven to 350° (325° for dark-coated metal pan). Position a rack in the lower third of the oven. Spray the bottom only of an 8-inch square baking pan with nonstick cooking spray (or foil-line pan; see page 11).

In a medium mixing bowl mix the brownie mix, melted butter, water, and eggs with a wooden spoon until just blended and all dry ingredients are moistened. Spread batter into prepared pan.

In a small mixing bowl mix ⅓ cup chocolate-hazelnut spread, flour, and the egg yolk until blended. Drop by spoonfuls onto batter. Cut through batter several times with tip of a knife for a marbled effect.

Bake 40–44 minutes or until toothpick inserted 2 inches from side of pan comes out clean or almost clean (do not overbake). Transfer to a wire rack and cool completely.

Spread cooled brownies with remaining hazelnut spread and, if desired, sprinkle with chopped hazelnuts. Cut into squares. Makes 9 large or 16 small brownies.

Baker's Note: To skin hazelnuts, boil 3 cups of water; add ¼ cup baking soda and then the hazelnuts. Boil 3 minutes; drain and rinse. Under running water pinch off the hazelnut skins. Dry completely. Toast at 350° for 10–15 minutes.

Cappuccino Brownies

Think of the layers of a perfect cappuccino and you will understand the construction of these brownies: an espresso/brownie base, a layer of cinnamon-flecked creaminess, and a smooth chocolate finish. Coffee lovers will be transported.

1	tablespoon instant espresso or coffee powder
¼	cup water
1	19.5- to 19.8-ounce package brownie mix
½	cup vegetable oil
2	large eggs

Topping:

1	8-ounce package cream cheese, softened
¾	cup sifted powdered sugar
1	teaspoon vanilla extract
½	teaspoon cinnamon
1	recipe Shiny Chocolate Glaze (See page 258; prepare full recipe, not the 8-inch square pan size option.)

Preheat oven to 350° (325° for dark-coated metal pan). Position a rack in the lower third of the oven. Spray an 8-inch square baking pan with nonstick cooking spray (or foil-line pan; see page 11).

In a medium mixing bowl dissolve the espresso powder in the water. Add the brownie mix, oil, and eggs and mix with a wooden spoon until just blended and all dry ingredients are moistened. Spread batter into prepared pan.

Bake 40–44 minutes or until toothpick inserted 2 inches from side of pan comes out clean or almost clean (do not overbake). Transfer to a wire rack and cool completely.

In a medium mixing bowl the beat cream cheese with an electric mixer until light and fluffy. Add powdered sugar, vanilla, and cinnamon; beat until well blended and smooth.

Spread mixture evenly over brownie layer. Chill brownies 1 hour in the refrigerator.

Prepare Shiny Chocolate Glaze. Spread glaze carefully over frosting. Chill brownies, covered, until cold, at least 3 hours. Cut into squares. Store in refrigerator. Makes 9 large or 16 small brownies.

Peanut Butter Cheesecake
Swirl Brownies

These thick, chewy brownies are loaded. With a chocolaty base, a rich swirl of peanut butter–infused cheesecake batter, and a handful of peanut butter baking chips, they're decadence to the max.

1	19.5- to 19.8-ounce package brownie mix
½	cup vegetable oil
¼	cup water
3	large eggs
1	cup peanut butter baking chips
1	8-ounce package cream cheese, softened
¼	cup creamy peanut butter
3	tablespoons packed brown sugar
1½	tablespoons all-purpose flour

Preheat oven to 350° (325° for dark-coated metal pan). Position a rack in the lower third of the oven. Spray the bottom only of a 13 x 9-inch baking pan with nonstick cooking spray (or foil-line pan; see page 11).

In a medium mixing bowl mix the brownie mix, oil, water, and 2 eggs with a wooden spoon until just blended and all dry ingredients are moistened; stir in peanut butter chips. Spread two-thirds of the batter in prepared pan.

In a medium mixing bowl beat the cream cheese, peanut butter, brown sugar, flour, and remaining egg with an electric mixer set on medium until smooth.

Spoon and spread peanut butter mixture over batter in pan. Drop remaining brownie batter by spoonfuls onto peanut butter mixture; swirl with tip of knife for marbled effect.

Bake 28–30 minutes or until toothpick inserted 2 inches from side of pan comes out clean or almost clean (do not overbake). Transfer to a wire rack and cool completely. Cut into squares. Store in refrigerator. Makes 24 large or 36 small brownies.

Chapter 2
Bar Cookies

Toasted Coconut Cheesecake Bars

Oh, to be basking on a Bahamas beach enjoying the island breezes and tropical treats. Consider these bars your passport.

1	19.5- to 19.8-ounce package brownie mix
½	cup (1 stick) unsalted butter, melted
5	large eggs
1	7-ounce package shredded coconut (about 2⅔ cups), divided
2	8-ounce packages cream cheese, softened
⅓	cup sugar
¾	cup canned sweetened cream of coconut
2	tablespoons dark rum or 2 teaspoons rum extract

Preheat oven to 350° (325° for dark-coated metal pan). Position a rack in the lower third of the oven. Spray the bottom only of a 13 x 9-inch baking pan with nonstick cooking spray (or foil-line pan; see page 11).

In a medium mixing bowl mix the brownie mix, melted butter, 2 of the eggs, and ⅔ cup coconut with a wooden spoon until just blended and all dry ingredients are moistened. Press mixture into prepared pan.

Bake 15 minutes. Remove from oven (leave oven on).

Meanwhile, in a medium mixing bowl beat the cream cheese, sugar, cream of coconut, and rum with an electric mixer set on medium until well blended. Beat in remaining 3 eggs, one at a time, until just blended. Pour cream cheese mixture over partially baked crust. Sprinkle with remaining coconut; gently press coconut into cheesecake batter.

Bake an additional 15 minutes. Loosely cover pan with foil (to prevent coconut from overbrowning) and bake 10–12 minutes longer, until just barely set when pan is jiggled. Transfer to a wire rack and cool completely. Refrigerate at least 3 hours or up to overnight before serving. Cut into bars. Makes 24 large or 36 small bars.

New York Cheesecake Brownie Bars

1	19.5- to 19.8-ounce package brownie mix
½	cup (1 stick) unsalted butter, melted
4	8-ounce packages cream cheese, softened
1	cup plus 2 tablespoons sugar, divided
4	teaspoons vanilla extract, divided
4	large eggs
1	16-ounce container (2 cups) sour cream

Preheat oven to 350° (325° for dark-coated metal pan). Position a rack in the lower third of the oven. Spray the bottom only of a 13 x 9-inch baking pan with nonstick cooking spray (or foil-line pan; see page 11).

In a medium mixing bowl mix the brownie mix and melted butter with a wooden spoon until just blended and all dry ingredients are moistened. Press mixture into prepared pan.

Bake 15 minutes. Remove from oven (leave oven on).

While crust bakes, beat cream cheese, 1 cup of the sugar, and 3 teaspoons of the vanilla with an electric mixer set on medium until well blended. Add eggs, one at a time, mixing on low after each addition just until blended. Pour over hot crust.

Bake 23–26 minutes or until center is just barely set when pan is jiggled (do not overbake); remove from oven (leave oven on).

In a medium mixing bowl whisk the sour cream with the remaining 2 tablespoons sugar and 1 teaspoon vanilla; spread evenly over bars. Return bars to oven for 5 minutes. Transfer to a wire rack and cool completely. Refrigerate at least 4 hours or overnight. Cut into bars. Makes 36 medium or 48 small bars.

Take the silken simplicity of New York–style cheesecake, layer it atop a rich, dark chocolate base and what have you got? An irresistible bar cookie. But not for long— they will disappear fast. These bars are very rich, very high, and very creamy, as New York cheesecake should be. One batch easily makes forty-eight servings when cut small, enough for a good-sized crowd.

Cashew Crunch Brownie Bars

Looking for a show-stopper bar cookie? You've turned to the right page, and it couldn't be easier than with this tiered treat. With but a few steps, you can take brownie mix to the ooh-aah level by covering it in layers of marshmallows, nuts, and chow mein noodles. The contrast of crispy and chewy is guaranteed to make this a "Wow!"-inducing dessert.

1	19.5- to 19.8-ounce package brownie mix
½	cup (1 stick) unsalted butter, melted
1	large egg
3	cups miniature marshmallows
1	14-ounce can sweetened condensed milk
½	cup creamy peanut butter
2	teaspoons vanilla extract
1	3-ounce can chow mein noodles
1	cup coarsely chopped roasted, lightly salted cashews or peanuts

Preheat oven to 350° (325° for dark-coated metal pan). Position a rack in the lower third of the oven. Spray the bottom only of a 13 x 9-inch baking pan with nonstick cooking spray (or foil-line pan; see page 11).

In a medium mixing bowl mix the brownie mix, melted butter, and egg with a wooden spoon until just blended and all dry ingredients are moistened. Press mixture into prepared pan. Bake 22–24 minutes, until just set at center (do not overbake).

Transfer to a wire rack and immediately sprinkle with marshmallows. Return to oven and bake 2 minutes longer or until marshmallows begin to puff. Remove from oven; transfer to a wire rack to cool.

Meanwhile, in heavy saucepan over medium heat, combine condensed milk and peanut butter; cook and stir until slightly thickened, 5–6 minutes. Remove from heat; stir in vanilla, noodles, and nuts. Spread evenly over marshmallows. Transfer to wire rack and cool completely. Chill 1 hour in refrigerator. Cut into bars. Store loosely covered at room temperature. Makes 24 large or 36 small bars.

Cheesecake-Filled Chocolate Streusel Bars

1	19.5- to 19.8-ounce package brownie mix
2¼	cups quick-cooking oats
1	cup (2 sticks) unsalted butter, melted
2	8-ounce packages cream cheese, softened
½	cup sugar
2	large eggs
1½	teaspoons vanilla extract

Preheat oven to 350° (325° for dark-coated metal pan). Position a rack in the lower third of the oven. Spray the bottom only of a 13 x 9-inch baking pan with nonstick cooking spray (or foil-line pan; see page 11).

In a large mixing bowl mix the brownie mix, oats, and melted butter with a wooden spoon until just blended and all dry ingredients are moistened. Press half of mixture evenly into prepared pan.

In a medium mixing bowl beat the cream cheese and sugar with electric mixer set on high until smooth. Add eggs and vanilla; beat until just blended. Spoon and spread cheesecake mixture over base layer; top with reserved crumb mixture and press down gently.

Bake 30–34 minutes or until topping is firm to the touch. Transfer to a wire rack and cool completely. Cut into bars. Makes 24 large or 36 small bars.

Take heart as you take up spoon and bowl to make these soon-to-be-classic bar cookies. A chocolate crumble cookie bottom and topping with a smooth layer of cheesecake sandwiched in between? Pure comfort.

Ultimate Fresh Raspberry Cheesecake Bars

I cannot say enough good things about these brownie bars. One bite and you'll agree that they live up to their "ultimate" name. As indicated in the recipe, frozen unsweetened raspberries (individually frozen in bags, not in sweetened syrup) may be substituted for fresh if you're making these when berries are out of season. It is essential, however, that the frozen raspberries are not thawed or the

1	19.5- to 19.8-ounce package brownie mix
½	cup (1 stick) unsalted butter, melted
4	large eggs
2	8-ounce packages cream cheese, softened
⅓	cup sugar
1	teaspoon vanilla extract
2	tablespoons all-purpose flour
2	cups (1 pint) fresh raspberries or frozen (not thawed) unsweetened raspberries
1–2	tablespoons powdered sugar (optional)

Preheat oven to 350° (325° for dark-coated metal pan). Position a rack in the lower third of the oven. Spray the bottom only of a 13 x 9-inch baking pan with nonstick cooking spray (or foil-line pan; see page 11).

In a medium mixing bowl mix the brownie mix, melted butter, and 2 of the eggs with a wooden spoon until just blended and all dry ingredients are moistened. Spread batter into prepared pan.

Bake 18 minutes. Remove from oven (leave oven on).

While the brownie base bakes, in a medium mixing bowl beat the cream cheese and sugar with an electric mixer set on medium until light and fluffy. Add the remaining 2 eggs, vanilla, and flour and beat until smooth, scraping down sides with rubber spatula. Spread cream cheese mixture evenly over batter. Distribute the raspberries evenly over the cream cheese layer.

Bake bars on a middle oven rack for 22–25 minutes, or until topping is just barely set when the pan is jiggled (do not overbake). Transfer to a wire rack and cool completely. Chill in refrigerator at least 3 hours or until firm. Cut into bars or squares and sprinkle with powdered sugar, if desired. Makes 24 large or 36 small bars.

brownie base will become goopy (from extra liquid seeping into the batter) and the topping will not set properly.

Apricot Coconut Bars

Whenever I return home to the San Francisco Bay Area to visit family, I try to stop by Yanni's produce store on College Avenue in Oakland to pick up a bag of apricot candies from their large bin selection of natural foods. They are so good because they are so very apricot: finely chopped dried apricots pressed together and rolled in shredded coconut. These bars capture the same ambrosial combination of apricot and coconut with the added, unbeatable base layer of chocolate.

1	19.5- to 19.8-ounce package brownie mix
½	cup (1 stick) unsalted butter, melted
1	14-ounce can sweetened condensed milk
2	large eggs
1½	cups sweetened shredded coconut
1½	cups finely chopped dried apricots

Preheat oven to 350° (325° for dark-coated metal pan). Position a rack in the lower third of the oven. Spray the bottom only of a 13 x 9-inch baking pan with nonstick cooking spray (or foil-line pan; see page 11).

In a medium mixing bowl mix the brownie mix and melted butter with a wooden spoon until just blended and all dry ingredients are moistened. Press mixture into prepared pan.

Bake 15 minutes. Remove from oven (leave oven on).

Meanwhile, in a medium mixing bowl whisk condensed milk and eggs until blended. Stir in coconut and apricots. Spread mixture evenly over hot crust.

Return to oven and bake 22–25 minutes longer or until golden around edges. Transfer to a wire rack and cool completely. Cut into bars. Makes 24 large or 36 small bars.

Chocolate Raisin Pecan Bars

1	19.5- to 19.8-ounce package brownie mix
½	cup (1 stick) unsalted butter, melted
1	14-ounce can sweetened condensed milk
¾	teaspoon ground cinnamon
1½	cups raisins
2	cups semisweet chocolate chips
1	cup coarsely chopped pecans

Preheat oven to 350° (325° for dark-coated metal pan). Position a rack in the lower third of the oven. Spray the bottom only of a 13 x 9-inch baking pan with nonstick cooking spray (or foil-line pan; see page 11).

In a medium mixing bowl mix the brownie mix and butter with a wooden spoon until just blended and all dry ingredients are moistened. Press mixture into prepared pan.

Bake 15 minutes. Remove from oven (leave oven on).

In a medium mixing bowl combine condensed milk, cinnamon, and raisins and stir until blended. Spoon and spread mixture over hot crust. Sprinkle with chocolate chips and pecans; gently press into condensed milk layer.

Bake 16–18 minutes longer or until lightly browned at edges. Transfer to a wire rack and cool completely. Cut into bars. Store loosely covered at room temperature. Makes 24 large or 36 small bars.

No reason is needed for stirring up a batch of these rich bar cookies—the arrival of the weekend or the end of the workday is grounds enough. Raisins are my favorite for this recipe, but feel free to substitute an equal amount of dried cranberries or chopped dried apricots.

Funky, Chunky Chocolate Banana Chip Bars

Banana chips definitely add the "funky" to these chunky bars. Look for them in the health food or dried fruit sections of the supermarket. To break them up for this recipe, place in a large ziplock plastic bag and hit several times with a can or rolling pin.

1	19.5- to 19.8-ounce package brownie mix
½	cup (1 stick) unsalted butter, melted
1	large egg
2	cups broken banana chips
2	cups miniature marshmallows
1	cup milk or semisweet chocolate chips
1	cup chopped walnuts or pecans

Preheat oven to 350° (325° for dark-coated metal pan). Position a rack in the lower third of the oven. Spray the bottom only of a 13 x 9-inch baking pan with nonstick cooking spray (or foil-line pan; see page 11).

In a medium mixing bowl mix the brownie mix, melted butter, and egg with a wooden spoon until just blended and all dry ingredients are moistened. Press mixture into prepared pan.

Bake 20 minutes.

Remove pan from oven and layer with the banana chips, marshmallows, chocolate chips, and nuts; press down gently. Bake 7–8 minutes more, until marshmallows are puffed and golden. Transfer to a wire rack and cool completely. Cut into bars. Store loosely covered at room temperature. Makes 24 large or 36 small bars.

Berry-Berry Chocolate Streusel Bars

1	19.5- to 19.8-ounce package brownie mix
2¼	cups quick-cooking oats
2	teaspoons ground cinnamon
1	cup (2 sticks) unsalted butter, melted
1	12-ounce package frozen blueberries, thawed
¾	cup seedless raspberry jam
2	tablespoons all-purpose flour
1	tablespoon grated lemon peel

When the next pitch-in party comes along, make a batch of these bars and prepare for accolades. I guarantee you won't be bringing any home.

Preheat oven to 350° (325° for dark-coated metal pan). Position a rack in the lower third of the oven. Spray the bottom only of a 13 x 9-inch baking pan with nonstick cooking spray (or foil-line pan; see page 11).

In a large mixing bowl mix the brownie mix, oats, cinnamon, and melted butter with a wooden spoon until just blended and all dry ingredients are moistened. Press half of mixture evenly into prepared pan.

In a medium mixing bowl stir together the blueberries, jam, flour, and lemon peel. Spoon and spread berry mixture over prepared crust; top with reserved crumb mixture and press down gently.

Bake 30–34 minutes or until topping is set and firm to the touch. Transfer to wire rack and cool completely. Makes 24 large or 36 small bars.

Peanut-Butterscotch Fudge-Filled Bars

Ultra rich with chocolate, butterscotch, and a double dose of peanut butter, these are bars everyone will give in to, kids to grown-ups. If it's more peanut buttery-ness you're after, substitute peanut butter baking chips for the butterscotch chips. Or if it's more chocolate you crave, use semisweet or milk chocolate chips.

1	19.5- to 19.8 ounce package brownie mix
1¾	cups peanut butter, divided
½	cup (1 stick) unsalted butter, melted, plus 2 tablespoons (¼ stick) butter (not melted)
2	large eggs
1	14-ounce can sweetened condensed milk
1½	cups butterscotch baking chips
2	teaspoons vanilla extract

Preheat oven to 350° (325° for dark-coated metal pan). Position a rack in the lower third of the oven. Spray the bottom only of a 13 x 9-inch baking pan with nonstick cooking spray (or foil-line pan; see page 11).

In a large mixing bowl, mix the brownie mix, 1 cup peanut butter, ½ cup melted butter, and eggs with electric mixer set on medium until blended and thick. Reserve 1½ cups for topping; press remaining batter into bottom of prepared pan.

In a medium saucepan set over low heat combine the sweetened condensed milk, remaining ¾ cup peanut butter, remaining 2 tablespoons butter, and 1 cup butterscotch chips, stirring until melted and smooth, about 3–4 minutes. Remove from heat and stir in vanilla. Pour and spread mixture over prepared crust. Crumble reserved crumb mixture over the top; sprinkle with remaining ½ cup butterscotch chips.

Bake 25–30 minutes or until topping is firm to the touch. Transfer to a wire rack and cool completely. Cut into bars. Store loosely covered at room temperature. Makes 24 large or 36 small bars.

Candy Bar Bars

1	19.5- to 19.8-ounce package brownie mix
2¼	cups quick-cooking oats
1	cup (2 sticks) unsalted butter, melted
4	cups chopped candy bars (such as Snickers® or chocolate-covered toffee bars)
1	14-ounce can sweetened condensed milk

These over-the-top bars are intense, rich, and chocolate to the max.

Preheat oven to 350° (325° for dark-coated metal pan). Position a rack in the lower third of the oven. Spray the bottom only of a 13 x 9-inch baking pan with nonstick cooking spray (or foil-line pan; see page 11).

In a medium mixing bowl mix the brownie mix, oats, and melted butter with a wooden spoon until just blended and all dry ingredients are moistened. Press half of mixture evenly into prepared pan; sprinkle with candy bar pieces.

Evenly spoon condensed milk over candy bar layer. Top with reserved crumb mixture; press down firmly.

Bake 30–34 minutes or until topping is firm. Transfer to wire rack and cool. Cut into bars while still slightly warm. Makes 24 large or 36 small bars.

Caramel Apple
Chocolate Crumble Bars

We all know what a ho-hum cookie is; we've had many too many of them in our times. These cookie bars are the exact opposite. Like a chocolate-dipped caramel apple, they are pure panache.

1	19.5- to 19.8-ounce package brownie mix
2¼	cups quick-cooking oats
1	cup (2 sticks) unsalted butter, melted
1	cup semisweet or milk chocolate chips
4½	cups coarsely chopped peeled tart apples (about 3 medium apples)
3	tablespoons all-purpose flour
1	14-ounce bag caramels, unwrapped
2	tablespoons cream or milk

Preheat oven to 350° (325° for dark-coated metal pan). Position a rack in the lower third of the oven. Spray the bottom only of a 13 x 9-inch baking pan with nonstick cooking spray (or foil-line pan; see page 11).

In a large mixing bowl mix the brownie mix, oats, and melted butter with a wooden spoon until just blended and all dry ingredients are moistened. Press half of mixture evenly into prepared pan. Add chocolate chips to remaining crumbs.

In another large mixing bowl toss together the chopped apples and flour. Spread over prepared crust; set aside.

In a medium saucepan set over low heat, melt caramels with cream, stirring occasionally, until melted. Pour caramel mixture evenly over apples. Top with reserved crumb mixture and press down gently.

Bake 30–34 minutes or until topping is set and firm to the touch. Transfer to wire rack and cool completely. Makes 24 large or 36 small bars.

Cinnamon-Chip Cranberry Walnut Bars

1	19.5- to 19.8-ounce package brownie mix
½	cup (1 stick) unsalted butter, melted
1	14-ounce can sweetened condensed milk
1½	cups cinnamon flavored baking chips
1⅓	cups sweetened dried cranberries
1	cup chopped walnuts

Preheat oven to 350° (325° for dark-coated metal pan). Position a rack in the lower third of the oven. Spray the bottom only of a 13 x 9-inch baking pan with nonstick cooking spray (or foil-line pan; see page 11).

In a medium mixing bowl mix the brownie mix and melted butter with a wooden spoon until just blended and all dry ingredients are moistened. Press mixture into prepared pan.

Bake 15 minutes. Remove from oven (leave oven on).

Spoon and spread condensed milk over partially baked crust. Sprinkle cinnamon chips, dried cranberries, and nuts over condensed milk layer; press down firmly. Bake 16–18 minutes longer or until lightly browned at edges.

Transfer to a wire rack and cool. Cut into bars while still slightly warm. Store loosely covered at room temperature. Makes 24 large or 36 small bars.

Here's a bar cookie that is as versatile as it is delicious. You can vary it in several ways: change the cranberries to another dried fruit (such as dried cherries, raisins, or snipped apricots), vary the choice of chips, or pick your favorite chopped nuts. Any way is a good way here.

White Chocolate Fudge Fantasy Bars

A thick layer of white chocolate fudge nestled between two more layers of chocolate brownie cookie make these quick-to-assemble bars a chocoholic's dream come true. The flavor of the fudge can be tailored to suit your tastes. Consider using maple, rum, brandy, mint, or orange extract in place of the vanilla. Alternatively, milk or semisweet chocolate chips may be substituted for the white chocolate chips. And if you really want to change things up, try butterscotch, peanut butter or cinnamon chips in place of the white chocolate chips.

1	19.5- to 21.5-ounce package brownie mix
$\frac{1}{3}$	cup vegetable oil
1	large egg
1	cup chopped pecans or walnuts
2	cups white chocolate chips
1	14-ounce can sweetened condensed milk
2	teaspoons vanilla extract

Preheat oven to 350° (325° for dark-coated metal pan). Position a rack in the lower third of the oven. Spray the bottom only of a 13 x 9-inch baking pan with nonstick cooking spray (or foil-line pan; see page 11).

In a large mixing bowl mix the brownie mix, oil, and egg with an electric mixer set on medium until blended. Stir in the nuts. Set aside $1\frac{1}{2}$ cups of the crumb mixture. Firmly press remaining crumb mixture into bottom of prepared pan.

In a small saucepan set over low heat, melt the chips with condensed milk, stirring until smooth. Remove from heat and stir in the vanilla. Pour and spread evenly over prepared crust. Sprinkle reserved crumb mixture evenly over top.

Bake 25–30 minutes or until topping is set and firm to the touch. Transfer to wire rack and cool completely. Cut into bars. Store loosely covered at room temperature. Makes 24 large or 36 small bars.

Very Apricot Chocolate Streusel Bars

1	19.5- to 19.8-ounce package brownie mix
2¼	cups quick-cooking oats
2½	teaspoons ground ginger
1	cup (2 sticks) unsalted butter, melted
2	cups chopped dried apricots
1	12-ounce jar apricot preserves
1	tablespoon grated lemon peel

Preheat oven to 350° (325° for dark-coated metal pan). Position a rack in the lower third of the oven. Spray the bottom only of a 13 x 9-inch baking pan with nonstick cooking spray (or foil-line pan; see page 11).

In a large mixing bowl mix the brownie mix, oats, ginger, and melted butter with a wooden spoon until just blended and all dry ingredients are moistened. Press half of mixture evenly into prepared pan.

In a medium mixing bowl stir together the chopped dried apricots, apricot preserves, and lemon peel. Spoon and spread apricot mixture over prepared crust. Top with reserved crumb mixture and press down gently.

Bake 30–34 minutes or until topping is set and firm to the touch. Transfer to wire rack and cool completely. Makes 24 large or 36 small bars.

These delicious bars would be right at home in the pastry case of your favorite coffeehouse (for about $2.50 per square). Yet despite having the look and taste of a pedigree bar cookie, these apricot-filled chocolate bars are deceptively easy to make, proving that elegant does not have to equal time-consuming.

Cardamom, Almond & Orange Bars

Fragrant and flavorful are the catchwords for these elegant bars. Cardamom is often used in Scandinavian baking and is particularly delicious here in combination with chocolate and citrus. If you cannot find it, ground coriander or nutmeg may be substituted. Perfect for spring dining and celebrating, these delicious mouthfuls are sure to awaken your taste buds.

1	19.5- to 19.8-ounce package brownie mix
½	cup (1 stick) unsalted butter, melted
3	large eggs
3½	tablespoons all-purpose flour
2	teaspoons vanilla extract
¾	teaspoon ground cardamom
¼	teaspoon salt
1½	cups sliced almonds
1½	cups powdered sugar
2	tablespoons freshly squeezed orange juice
2	teaspoons grated orange zest

Preheat oven to 350° (325° for dark-coated metal pan). Position a rack in the lower third of the oven. Spray the bottom only of a 13 x 9-inch baking pan with nonstick cooking spray (or foil-line pan; see page 11).

In a medium mixing bowl mix the brownie mix and melted butter with a wooden spoon until just blended and all dry ingredients are moistened. Press mixture into prepared pan.

Bake 15 minutes. Remove from oven (leave oven on).

Meanwhile, in a medium mixing bowl mix the eggs, flour, vanilla, cardamom, and salt with an electric mixer set on medium about 2 minutes or until blended and smooth; stir in the almonds. Spread the mixture over hot crust.

Bake 18–21 minutes or until top is golden brown and set around edges. Transfer to wire rack to cool. In a small mixing bowl whisk the powdered sugar, orange juice, and zest until smooth; spread evenly over bars. Makes 24 large or 36 small bars.

Mint-Chip Cheesecake Brownie Bars

1	19.5- to 19.8-ounce package brownie mix
½	cup (1 stick) unsalted butter, melted
3	large eggs
2	8-ounce packages cream cheese, softened
½	cup sugar
1	teaspoon peppermint extract
2	cups miniature semisweet chocolate chips, divided
2	teaspoons vegetable shortening
16	red and white striped round peppermint hard candies, coarsely crushed

Preheat oven to 350° (325° for dark-coated metal pan). Position a rack in the lower third of the oven. Spray the bottom only of a 13 x 9-inch baking pan with nonstick cooking spray (or foil-line pan; see page 11).

In a medium mixing bowl mix the brownie mix, butter, and 1 egg with a wooden spoon until just blended and all dry ingredients are moistened. Press mixture into prepared pan.

Bake 18 minutes or until center is partially set (do not overbake). Remove from oven (leave oven on).

While crust bakes, beat cream cheese and sugar in a medium mixing bowl with electric mixer set on high until smooth. Gradually beat in remaining 2 eggs and peppermint extract until smooth. Stir in 1 cup of the miniature chocolate chips. Pour over partially baked crust.

Bake 20–22 minutes, until just barely set at center (do not overbake). Transfer to a wire rack and cool completely.

In heavy saucepan melt remaining 1 cup chocolate chips with shortening, stirring until smooth; drizzle over cooled bars and sprinkle with crushed mint candies. Chill at least 3 hours in refrigerator. Cut into bars. Store in refrigerator. Makes 24 large or 36 small bars.

'Tis the season for delectable cookie making with these festive, peppermint-y bar cookies. Feel free to experiment with other extracts such as rum, almond, orange, or maple—just be sure to leave off the peppermint candies if you do.

Coconut, Rum, & White Chocolate Macadamia Bars

Consider this an island escape bar. For a fruitier bar, consider using dried tropical fruit bits—found in the dried fruit section of the supermarket—in place of all or part of the shredded coconut.

1	19.5- to 19.8-ounce package brownie mix
½	cup (1 stick) unsalted butter, melted
1	14-ounce can sweetened condensed milk
2	large eggs
2	tablespoons dark rum or 2 teaspoons rum-flavored extract
1½	cups sweetened shredded coconut
1	cup chopped macadamia nuts
1	cup white chocolate chips
1	tablespoon vegetable shortening

Preheat oven to 350° (325° for dark-coated metal pan). Position a rack in the lower third of the oven. Spray the bottom only of a 13 x 9-inch baking pan with nonstick cooking spray (or foil-line pan; see page 11).

In a medium mixing bowl mix the brownie mix and melted butter with a wooden spoon until just blended and all dry ingredients are moistened. Press mixture into prepared pan.

Bake 15 minutes. Remove from oven (leave oven on).

In a medium bowl combine condensed milk, eggs, rum, coconut, and nuts. Pour over partially baked crust.

Bake 18–20 minutes longer or until golden at edges and just set at the center. Transfer to a wire rack.

In small saucepan set over low heat melt the chocolate chips with the shortening until melted and smooth. Drizzle over bars; cool completely. Makes 24 large or 36 small bars.

Almond Brickle Brownie Bars

1	19.5- to 19.8-ounce package brownie mix
2⅓	cups quick-cooking oats
1	cup (2 sticks) unsalted butter, melted
1	14-ounce can sweetened condensed milk
¾	cup creamy peanut butter
1	teaspoon almond extract
⅔	cup English toffee baking bits
½	cup slivered almonds

Preheat oven to 350° (325° for dark-coated metal pan). Position a rack in the lower third of the oven. Spray the bottom only of a 13 x 9-inch baking pan with nonstick cooking spray (or foil-line pan; see page 11).

In a medium mixing bowl mix the brownie mix, oats, and melted butter with a wooden spoon until just blended and all dry ingredients are moistened. Press ⅔ of mixture evenly into prepared pan.

In a large mixing bowl beat condensed milk, peanut butter, and almond extract with electric mixer set on medium until smooth. Spread evenly over base layer.

In a medium mixing bowl combine reserved crumb mixture with toffee bits and almonds. Sprinkle mixture evenly over filling; press down firmly.

Bake 30–34 minutes or until topping is firm. Transfer to a wire rack and cool completely. Cut into bars. Makes 24 large or 36 small bars.

These bars showcase two favorite flavors—chocolate and toffee—in all their delicious glory. The peanut butter in the filling adds a creamy nuttiness, but the almond extract makes the filling distinctively almond, a delicious complement to the toffee.

Backpacker Bars

Just one of these bars is enough to help you hit the trail running—with a big smile, to boot. Carob chips are my preference for these energy-boosting bars. You can find them at your local health food store and at some supermarkets in the baking, health food, or bulk foods section. Of course, chocolate chips are always a very fine substitute.

1	19.5- to 19.8-ounce package brownie mix
½	cup vegetable oil or ½ cup (1 stick) unsalted butter, melted
⅓	cup milk
3	large eggs
1⅓	cups quick-cooking or old-fashioned oats, divided
1½	cups carob chips or semisweet chocolate chips, divided
1½	cups lightly salted mixed nuts, coarsely chopped, divided
1	cup dried cranberries

Preheat oven to 350° (325° for dark-coated metal pan). Position a rack in the lower third of the oven. Spray the bottom only of a 13 x 9-inch baking pan with nonstick cooking spray (or foil-line pan; see page 11).

In a large mixing bowl mix the brownie mix, oil, milk, and eggs with a wooden spoon until just blended and all dry ingredients are moistened. Stir in 1 cup of the oats, 1 cup of the chips, 1 cup of the nuts, and the dried cranberries. Spread batter into prepared pan. Sprinkle with remaining ⅓ cup oats, remaining ½ cup chips, and remaining ½ cup nuts; gently press into batter.

Bake 28–30 minutes or until toothpick inserted 2 inches from side of pan comes out clean or almost clean (do not overbake). Transfer to a wire rack and cool completely. Cut into squares. Makes 24 large or 36 small bars.

Maple Pecan Bars

1	19.5- to 19.8-ounce package brownie mix
½	cup (1 stick) unsalted butter, melted
1	14-ounce can sweetened condensed milk
1	large egg
2½	teaspoons maple extract
2	cups chopped pecans
1¼	cups milk chocolate chips

Impressive and unexpected, but still easy to prepare, these maple-accented bars can be made at the last minute when necessary.

Preheat oven to 350° (325° for dark-coated metal pan). Position a rack in the lower third of the oven. Spray the bottom only of a 13 x 9-inch baking pan with nonstick cooking spray (or foil-line pan; see page 11).

In a medium mixing bowl mix the brownie mix and melted butter with a wooden spoon until just blended and all dry ingredients are moistened. Press mixture into prepared pan.

Bake 15 minutes. Remove from oven (leave oven on).

Meanwhile, in a medium mixing bowl whisk together the condensed milk, egg, and maple extract; stir in pecans. Spoon and spread pecan mixture over hot crust; sprinkle with milk chocolate chips.

Return to oven and bake 20–22 minutes longer, until golden at edges and just set at the center. Transfer to a wire rack and cool completely. Cut into bars. Makes 24 large or 36 small bars.

Chocolate, Chocolate, Chocolate-Chip Cheesecake Bars

These bars describe themselves: a crunchy chocolate cookie-like base layer, a luscious chocolate cheesecake layer, and chocolate chips scattered throughout. Yes, they are heavenly, so help yourself—go ahead, you deserve it!

1	19.5- to 19.8-ounce package brownie mix
½	cup (1 stick) unsalted butter, melted
3	large eggs
½	cup heavy whipping cream
2½	cups semisweet chocolate chips
2	8-ounce packages cream cheese, room temperature
⅓	cup sugar
1	tablespoon cornstarch
2	teaspoons vanilla extract

Preheat oven to 350° (325° for dark-coated metal pan). Position a rack in the lower third of the oven. Spray the bottom only of a 13 x 9-inch baking pan with nonstick cooking spray (or foil-line pan; see page 11).

In a medium mixing bowl mix the brownie mix, melted butter, and 1 egg with a wooden spoon until just blended and all dry ingredients are moistened. Press mixture into prepared pan.

Bake 18 minutes or until center is partially set (do not overbake). Remove from oven (leave oven on).

While crust bakes, heat the cream in a medium saucepan set over medium heat until hot but not boiling. Reduce heat to low. Add 1½ cups of the chocolate chips; whisk until chocolate melts and mixture is smooth. Remove from heat and cool 10 minutes.

Meanwhile, beat cream cheese and sugar in a large mixing bowl with electric mixer set on high until well blended. Beat in cornstarch and vanilla. Add remaining 2 eggs, 1 at a time, beating just until blended after each addition.

Whisk 1 cup of the cream cheese mixture into chocolate mixture. Return chocolate mixture to remaining cheese mixture; whisk until smooth. Pour batter over hot crust and sprinkle with remaining 1 cup chocolate chips.

Bake 20–25 minutes, until just barely set at center (do not overbake). Transfer to a wire rack and cool completely. Chill at least 3 hours in refrigerator. Cut into bars. Store in refrigerator. Makes 24 large or 36 small bars.

Pumpkin Swirl Cheesecake Bars

Looking for a tempting alternative to traditional Thanksgiving pumpkin pie? It's right here. The chocolate brownie base is a fine foil for the creamy layer of pumpkin-swirled cheesecake. If you want a formal presentation, cut them into large squares and serve, plated, with whipped cream; if informal is more your style, cut them into small squares to serve as part of a casual dessert buffet.

1	19.5- to 19.8-ounce package brownie mix
½	cup (1 stick) unsalted butter, melted
2	teaspoons pumpkin pie spice, divided
4	large eggs
½	cup canned pumpkin purée
1½	tablespoons all-purpose flour
3	8-ounce packages cream cheese, softened
¾	cup sugar
2	teaspoons vanilla extract

Preheat oven to 350° (325° for dark-coated metal pan). Position a rack in the lower third of the oven. Spray the bottom only of a 13 x 9-inch baking pan with nonstick cooking spray (or foil-line pan; see page 11).

In a medium mixing bowl combine brownie mix, melted butter, 1 teaspoon of the pumpkin pie spice, and 1 egg until just blended and all dry ingredients are moistened. Press into bottom of prepared pan.

Bake 18 minutes. Remove from oven (leave oven on).

Meanwhile, in a medium mixing bowl mix the pumpkin purée, flour, and remaining 1 teaspoon pumpkin pie spice; set aside.

In a large mixing bowl, beat cream cheese with electric mixer set on high until smooth. Add the sugar, beating until blended. Beat in vanilla and remaining 3 eggs, one at a time, until just blended.

Stir ½ cup of the cream cheese mixture into the pumpkin mixture. Pour remaining cream cheese mixture over prepared crust, spreading evenly to cover. Distribute large spoonfuls of the pumpkin batter randomly over cream cheese layer. Carefully swirl the batters with the tip of a knife.

Bake 25–30 minutes or until just barely set at the center. Transfer to a wire rack and cool completely. Chill 2 hours or overnight in refrigerator; cut into bars. Store covered in refrigerator. Makes 24 large or 36 small bars.

Chocolate Carmelitas

When life becomes particularly frantic and stressful, bake a batch of these bars. They have the flavor and richness of your favorite candy bar all wrapped up into a streusel-layered cookie. Once you're done, pour yourself a glass of cold milk, grab the latest issue of your favorite magazine, turn off the telephone ringer, sit in a comfy chair and prop up your feet—and enjoy!

1	19.5- to 19.8-ounce package brownie mix
2¼	cups quick-cooking oats
1	cup (2 sticks) unsalted butter, melted
1	cup miniature semisweet chocolate chips
1	14-ounce bag caramels, unwrapped
1	14-ounce can sweetened condensed milk

Preheat oven to 350° (325° for dark-coated metal pan). Position a rack in the lower third of the oven. Spray the bottom only of a 13 x 9-inch baking pan with nonstick cooking spray (or foil-line pan; see page 11).

In a medium mixing bowl mix the brownie mix, oats, and melted butter with a wooden spoon until just blended and all dry ingredients are moistened. Press half of mixture evenly into prepared pan. Stir miniature chocolate chips into remaining mixture; set aside.

In a medium saucepan set over low heat combine the caramels and the sweetened condensed milk, stirring until melted and smooth. Pour caramel mixture over prepared crust and sprinkle with reserved crumb mixture.

Bake 28–30 minutes or until topping is firm to the touch. Transfer to a wire rack and cool completely. Cut into bars. Makes 24 large or 36 small bars.

Chocolate Date Bars

2½	cups water
½	cup fresh lemon juice
3	cups chopped pitted dates
2	teaspoons vanilla extract
1	19.5- to 19.8-ounce package brownie mix
2¼	cups quick-cooking oats
2½	teaspoons ground cinnamon
1	cup (2 sticks) unsalted butter, melted

In a medium saucepan combine water and lemon juice. Bring to a boil over medium heat. Add dates; simmer until very soft and thick, stirring occasionally, about 10 minutes. Cool to room temperature. Stir in vanilla.

Preheat oven to 350° (325° for dark-coated metal pan). Position a rack in the lower third of the oven. Spray the bottom only of a 13 x 9-inch baking pan with nonstick cooking spray (or foil-line pan; see page 11).

In a medium mixing bowl mix the brownie mix, oats, cinnamon, and melted butter with a wooden spoon until just blended and all dry ingredients are moistened. Press half of mixture evenly into prepared pan.

Spoon and spread date mixture over prepared crust; top with reserved crumb mixture and press down gently.

Bake 30–34 minutes or until topping is firm to the touch. Transfer to wire rack and cool completely. Makes 24 large or 36 small bars.

Traditional date bars just got better than ever thanks to a chocolate-cinnamon streusel in place of the traditional crumb component. For some additional chocolate revving, stir 1 cup miniature semisweet chocolate chips into the chocolate streusel topping before popping them in the oven.

Brown Sugar & Toffee Cheesecake Bars

This cookie is dedicated to all of my fellow brown sugar lovers. Restraint is futile here, so be sure to invite a gaggle of good friends over to share the joy.

1	19.5- to 19.8-ounce package brownie mix
½	cup (1 stick) unsalted butter, melted
4	large eggs
3	8-ounce packages cream cheese, softened
¾	cup packed dark brown sugar
2	teaspoons vanilla extract
1	10-ounce package English toffee baking bits, divided

Preheat oven to 350° (325° for dark-coated metal pan). Position a rack in the lower third of the oven. Spray the bottom only of a 13 x 9-inch baking pan with nonstick cooking spray (or foil-line pan; see page 11).

In a medium mixing bowl mix the brownie mix, melted butter, and 1 egg with a wooden spoon until just blended and all dry ingredients are moistened. Press mixture into prepared pan.

Bake 18 minutes. Remove from oven (leave oven on).

While crust bakes, beat cream cheese and brown sugar with electric mixer set on high until smooth. Add the remaining 3 eggs and vanilla; beat until just blended. Stir in 1 cup of the toffee bits; pour mixture over hot crust and sprinkle with remaining toffee bits.

Return to oven and bake 25–28 minutes, until center is just barely set. Transfer to a wire rack and cool completely. Refrigerate at least 3 hours until chilled. Makes 24 large or 36 small bars.

Milk Chocolate Macaroon Bars

1	19.5- to 19.8-ounce package brownie mix
½	cup (1 stick) unsalted butter, melted
2	cups shredded coconut
1	14-ounce can sweetened condensed milk
1	cup milk chocolate chips
1	teaspoon almond extract

Preheat oven to 350° (325° for dark-coated metal pan). Position a rack in the lower third of the oven. Spray a 13 x 9-inch baking pan with nonstick cooking spray (or foil-line pan; see page 11).

In a medium mixing bowl mix the brownie mix and melted butter with a wooden spoon until all dry ingredients are moistened (mixture will be stiff). Press into prepared pan.

Bake 15 minutes. Remove from oven (leave oven on).

While crust bakes, in a medium mixing bowl combine coconut, condensed milk, chocolate chips, and almond extract; carefully spread over warm brownie base.

Bake an additional 16–18 minutes or until topping is set and golden brown. Transfer to a wire rack and cool completely. Cut into bars. Makes 24 large or 36 small bars.

Don't fuss the next time you need to make dessert for a party crowd. Rather, whip up a batch of these jazzed-up, milk chocolate and coconut-adorned bar cookies. With such a fast and versatile recipe, you'll have plenty of time to celebrate yourself.

Dulce de Leche Cream Bars

Inspired by Latin and South America's beloved dessert, these creamy, caramel-filled bars are inarguably awesome.

1	19.5- to 19.8-ounce package brownie mix
½	cup (1 stick) unsalted butter, melted
4	large eggs
2	8-ounce packages cream cheese, softened
½	cup firmly packed brown sugar
3	tablespoons flour
1	tablespoon vanilla extract
1	cup sour cream
1	17-ounce jar premium caramel ice cream topping

Preheat oven to 350° (325° for dark-coated metal pan). Position a rack in the lower third of the oven. Spray a 13 x 9-inch baking pan with nonstick cooking spray (or foil-line pan; see page 11).

In a medium mixing bowl mix the brownie mix, melted butter, and 1 egg with a wooden spoon until just blended and all dry ingredients are moistened. Spread mixture into prepared pan.

Bake 18 minutes. Remove from oven (leave oven on).

Meanwhile, in a large bowl beat the cream cheese, brown sugar, flour, and vanilla with electric mixer set on high until well blended. Add sour cream; mix until blended. Add remaining 3 eggs, one at a time, mixing on low after each addition until just blended. Add half of the caramel topping; mix on low until blended. Pour over hot crust.

Bake 32–35 minutes or until center is just barely set. Transfer to a wire rack and cool completely. Refrigerate at least 4 hours or overnight.

Drizzle remaining caramel topping over bars; refrigerate until set. Cut into bars. Makes 24 large or 36 small bars.

Coffee Toffee Cream Bars

1	19.5- to 19.8-ounce package brownie mix
½	cup (1 stick) butter, melted
2	tablespoons water
2	large eggs
4	teaspoons instant espresso or coffee powder, divided
6	1.4-ounce chocolate covered toffee bars, chopped
1	cup slivered lightly toasted almonds, divided
2	teaspoons vanilla extract
4	ounces (half of an 8-ounce package) cream cheese, softened
⅓	cup packed dark brown sugar
1½	cups heavy whipping cream

Preheat oven to 350° (325° for dark-coated metal pan). Position a rack in the lower third of the oven. Spray the bottom only of a 13 x 9-inch baking pan with nonstick cooking spray (or foil-line pan; see page 11).

In a medium mixing bowl mix the brownie mix, melted butter, water, eggs, and 2 teaspoons espresso powder with a wooden spoon until just blended and all dry ingredients are moistened; stir in one-third of the chopped toffee bars and ½ cup of the toasted almonds. Spread batter into prepared pan. Bake 24–27 minutes or until just set (do not overbake).

Transfer to wire rack and cool completely.

In a medium bowl dissolve the remaining 2 teaspoons espresso powder in the vanilla. Add cream cheese and brown sugar; beat with electric mixer set on medium until smooth. Increase speed to high; beat in the heavy whipping cream until soft peaks form.

Spread cream mixture over cooled brownie base. Sprinkle remaining chopped toffee bars and toasted almonds over top. Refrigerate at least 1 hour before serving. Cut into bars. Makes 24 large or 36 small bars. Store, loosely covered, in refrigerator.

These charming black and tan bars are infused with the bold flavor of coffee and the double crunch of toffee and toasted almonds—who can (or would want to) resist? A pleasure to eat out of hand, they can also be cut into larger squares and plated for dessert.

"Caramel Delightful" Bars

These bars were inspired by a scrumptious Girl Scout cookie of similar name, though made even better with the addition of a chocolate cookie crust. Perhaps "delirium" would be more apropos than "delightful."

1	19.5- to 19.8-ounce package brownie mix
½	cup (1 stick) unsalted butter, melted
1	7-ounce package (about 2⅔ cups) sweetened shredded coconut
1	14-ounce can sweetened condensed milk
2	teaspoons vanilla extract
1	cup semisweet chocolate chunks or chips
1	cup chopped pecans
30	caramels, unwrapped
2	tablespoons milk

Preheat oven to 350° (325° for dark-coated metal pan). Position a rack in the lower third of the oven. Spray a 13 x 9-inch baking pan with nonstick cooking spray (or foil-line pan; see page 11).

In a medium mixing bowl mix the brownie mix and melted butter with a wooden spoon until just blended and all dry ingredients are moistened. Press mixture into prepared pan.

Bake 15 minutes. Remove from oven (leave oven on).

Meanwhile, in a medium mixing bowl mix the coconut, condensed milk, and vanilla until blended; spread over hot crust and sprinkle with chocolate chunks and pecans.

Bake an additional 18–20 minutes or until coconut is lightly browned. Transfer to wire rack.

In a medium saucepan set over low heat melt caramels and milk, stirring until melted and smooth. Drizzle over bars. Transfer to a wire rack and cool completely. Cut into bars. Makes 24 large or 36 small bars.

Pineapple–White Chocolate Aloha Bars

1	19.5- to 19.8-ounce package brownie mix
2½	teaspoons ground ginger
1⅔	cups quick-cooking oats
1	cup sweetened shredded coconut
1	cup (2 sticks) unsalted butter, melted
1	16-ounce can crushed pineapple, well drained
⅔	cup pineapple preserves
2	tablespoons lime juice
1	cup white chocolate chips

Preheat oven to 350° (325° for dark-coated metal pan). Position a rack in the lower third of the oven. Spray a 13 x 9-inch baking pan with nonstick cooking spray (or foil-line pan; see page 11).

In a large mixing bowl mix the brownie mix, ginger, oats, coconut, and melted butter with a wooden spoon until just blended and all dry ingredients are moistened. Press half of mixture evenly into prepared pan.

In a medium mixing bowl combine the drained pineapple, preserves, and lime juice. Spoon mixture over prepared crust. Sprinkle reserved topping and white chocolate chips evenly over filling; press down gently.

Bake 30–34 minutes or until topping is firm. Transfer to a wire rack and cool completely. Cut into bars. Makes 24 large or 36 small bars.

The dark chocolate brownie base of these island-inspired bars takes beautifully to the contrasting flavors of white chocolate and pineapple in the filling. I highly recommend them for summertime picnics and barbecues.

Five-Layer Chocolate Marshmallow Brownie Bars

Versions of this bar—typically with a graham cracker crust—abound. This version surpasses the rest. The bars are big and gooey, and everybody who has one is going to demand seconds.

1	19.5- to 19.8-ounce package brownie mix
½	cup (1 stick) unsalted butter, melted
1	large egg
3	cups miniature marshmallows
1	cup semisweet chocolate chunks or chips
1	cup sweetened shredded coconut
1	cup chopped pecans or walnuts

Preheat oven to 350° (325° for dark-coated metal pan). Position a rack in the lower third of the oven. Spray the bottom only of a 13 x 9-inch baking pan with nonstick cooking spray (or foil-line pan; see page 11).

In a medium mixing bowl mix the brownie mix, melted butter, and egg with a wooden spoon until just blended and all dry ingredients are moistened. Spread mixture into prepared pan.

Bake 22–25 minutes or until center is just set (do not overbake; leave oven on).

Layer marshmallows, chocolate chunks, coconut, and nuts over crust; press down gently. Bake an additional 3–5 minutes or until marshmallows begin to puff. Transfer to a wire rack and cool completely. Cut into bars. Makes 24 large or 36 small bars.

Caramel Mallow Brownie Bars

1	19.5- to 19.8-ounce package brownie mix
½	cup (1 stick) unsalted butter, melted
1	large egg
1	17-ounce jar premium caramel ice cream topping
3	cups miniature marshmallows

Preheat oven to 350° (325° for dark–coated metal pan). Position a rack in the lower third of the oven. Spray the bottom only of a 13 x 9–inch baking pan with nonstick cooking spray (or foil-line pan; see page 11).

In a medium mixing bowl mix the brownie mix, melted butter, and egg with a wooden spoon until just blended and all dry ingredients are moistened. Reserve ⅔ cup of mixture; press remaining mixture into prepared pan.

Bake 21–24 minutes or until center is set (do not overbake). Pour caramel topping over hot crust.

Sprinkle with marshmallows. Spoon remaining brownie mixture randomly over bars.

Bake an additional 6–8 minutes or until marshmallows are puffed and lightly browned (do not overbake). Transfer to a wire rack and cool completely. Cut into bars. Makes 24 large or 36 small bars.

Bauer's Candies, Inc., located in Lawrenceburg, Kentucky, makes a special candy that ranks at the very top of my all-time favorites. Known as a "modjeska," it is a caramel-covered marshmallow that tastes like a piece of heaven. These bars were inspired by modjeskas, with an additional tweak of chocolate. You won't be disappointed!

Tri-Level Peanut Butter Marshmallow Crispy Bars

Layers of chocolate, marshmallows, peanut butter chips, and crisp rice cereal? Sounds like kid stuff, but think again. The reality is a chewy-gooey, candy bar–like confection that everyone, of every age, will love.

1	19.5- to 19.8-ounce package brownie mix
10	tablespoons (1¼ sticks) unsalted butter, softened, divided
2	large egg yolks
3	cups miniature marshmallows

Topping:

⅔	cup light corn syrup
1	10-ounce package peanut butter chips
2	teaspoons vanilla extract
2	cups crisp rice cereal
2	cups lightly salted peanuts

Preheat oven to 350° (325° for dark-coated metal pan). Position a rack in the lower third of the oven. Spray the bottom only of a 13 x 9-inch baking pan with nonstick cooking spray (or foil-line pan; see page 11).

In a large mixing bowl mix the brownie mix, 6 tablespoons softened butter, and egg yolks with an electric mixer set on low until mixture is combined and crumbly. Press mixture firmly into the bottom of the prepared pan.

Bake 18 minutes or until set at edges. Remove crust from oven (leave oven on). Immediately sprinkle with marshmallows. Return to oven; bake an additional 3–5 minutes or until marshmallows just begin to puff. Transfer to a wire rack and cool while preparing topping.

In a large saucepan, combine the corn syrup, remaining 4 tablespoons butter and peanut butter chips. Cook and stir constantly over low heat until the chips are melted and smooth.

Remove from heat; stir in vanilla, cereal, and peanuts. Immediately spoon warm topping over marshmallows; spread to cover. Place pan of bars in refrigerator for 1 hour or until firm. Cut into bars or squares. Makes 36 medium bars or 48 small squares.

Chocolate Linzer Bars

These bars are loosely based on Linzer Torte, an Austrian pastry concoction made with almonds and raspberry jam. For a more pronounced almond accent, mix the preserves with 1 teaspoon almond extract before spreading over bars.

1	19.5- to 19.8-ounce package brownie mix
1½	teaspoons ground cinnamon
1½	cups quick-cooking oats
1	cup finely chopped almonds
1	cup (2 sticks) unsalted butter, melted
1	12-ounce jar seedless raspberry preserves
1	cup miniature semisweet chocolate chips

Preheat oven to 350° (325° for dark-coated metal pan). Position a rack in the lower third of the oven. Spray the bottom only of a 13 x 9-inch baking pan with nonstick cooking spray (or foil-line pan; see page 11).

In a medium mixing bowl mix the brownie mix, cinnamon, oats, almonds, and melted butter with a wooden spoon until just blended and all dry ingredients are moistened. Press half of mixture evenly into prepared pan.

Spread base layer with preserves. Add chocolate chips to remaining crumb mixture. Sprinkle over preserves, and press down firmly.

Bake 28–30 minutes or until topping is firm to the touch. Transfer to a wire rack and cool completely. Cut into bars. Makes 24 large or 36 small bars.

Extra-Easy Chocolate-Frosted Rocky Road Bars

1   19.5- to 19.8-ounce package brownie mix
½   cup (1 stick) unsalted butter, melted
1   large egg
1   16-ounce tub ready-to-spread chocolate frosting
2   cups miniature marshmallows
1   cup chopped peanuts

Yes, comfort can arrive in bar cookie form—here it is.

Preheat oven to 350° (325° for dark-coated metal pan). Position a rack in the lower third of the oven. Spray the bottom only of a 13 x 9-inch baking pan with nonstick cooking spray (or foil-line pan; see page 11).

In a medium mixing bowl mix the brownie mix, melted butter, and egg with a wooden spoon until all dry ingredients are moistened. Press mixture into prepared pan.

Bake 22–25 minutes or until center is set (do not overbake). Transfer to a wire rack and cool completely.

In a medium mixing bowl stir frosting until smooth; stir in marshmallows. Spoon and spread frosting mixture over brownie base. Sprinkle with peanuts. Refrigerate 1 hour. Cut into bars. Makes 24 large or 36 small bars.

Sour Cream Cranberry Bars

These stellar bars are a delicious contrast of flavors and textures, from the chocolate streusel top and bottom to the slightly tart middle layer, smooth with sour cream and loaded with dried cranberries.

1	19.5- to 19.8-ounce package brownie mix
2¼	cups quick-cooking oats
1	cup (2 sticks) unsalted butter, melted
1¼	cups sour cream
⅓	cup sugar
2½	tablespoons all-purpose flour
1	tablespoon grated lemon zest
1	teaspoon vanilla extract
1	large egg
2	cups dried cranberries

Preheat oven to 350° (325° for dark–coated metal pan). Position a rack in the lower third of the oven. Spray the bottom only of a 13 x 9-inch baking pan with nonstick cooking spray (or foil-line pan; see page 11).

In a large mixing bowl mix the brownie mix, oats, and melted butter with a wooden spoon until just blended and all dry ingredients are moistened. Press half of the mixture evenly into prepared pan.

In a separate medium mixing bowl whisk the sour cream, sugar, flour, lemon zest, vanilla, and egg until smooth; stir in the cranberries and spread over base layer. Sprinkle with remaining crumb mixture; press gently into filling.

Bake 30–34 minutes or until topping is firm. Transfer to a wire rack and cool completely. Cut into bars. Makes 24 large or 36 small bars.

One Bowl
Triple-Chocolate Cherry Bars

1	19.5- to 19.8-ounce package brownie mix
1	21-ounce can cherry pie filling
3	tablespoons vegetable oil
2	large eggs, lightly beaten
1	cup miniature semisweet chocolate chips
1	recipe Chocolate Fudge Frosting (see page 250; prepare 13 x 9-inch pan size option) or 1 16-ounce tub ready-to-spread chocolate frosting (optional)

Preheat oven to 350° (325° for dark-coated metal pan). Position a rack in the lower third of the oven. Spray a 15 x 10-inch jelly roll baking pan with nonstick cooking spray (or foil-line pan; see page 11).

In a medium mixing bowl mix the brownie mix, pie filling, oil, eggs, and chocolate chips with a wooden spoon until just blended and all dry ingredients are moistened. Spread mixture evenly into prepared pan.

Bake 28–32 minutes or until just set and firm to the touch (do not overbake). Transfer to a wire rack and cool completely.

If desired, prepare Chocolate Fudge Frosting; spread over cooled bars. Cut into bars. Makes 24 large or 36 small bars.

Cherry filling makes these bars moist, cake-like, and cherry all over. I personally refer to these as "procrastination bars" because they are the ideal solution for last-minute baking. Just one bowl, five ingredients, and a bit of stirring are all that's needed to get them in the oven. A gilding of chocolate frosting ensures that these will be surefire hits for any and every occasion.

Pretty-in-Pink Strawberry Streusel Bars

Anyone who has had a chocolate-dipped strawberry knows how well this combination of flavors works. The strawberry jam gets used twice here: first to flavor and turn the creamy filling pink, then again dolloped on top before adding the second layer of chocolate streusel. This recipe also works very well with apricot or seedless raspberry preserves.

1	19.5- to 19.8-ounce package brownie mix
2¼	cups quick-cooking oats
1	cup (2 sticks) unsalted butter, melted
2	8-ounce packages cream cheese, softened
1¼	cups strawberry jam, divided
2	large eggs

Preheat oven to 350° (325° for dark-coated metal pan). Position a rack in the lower third of the oven. Spray the bottom only of a 13 x 9-inch baking pan with nonstick cooking spray (or foil-line pan; see page 11).

In a large mixing bowl mix the brownie mix, oats, and melted butter with a wooden spoon until just blended and all dry ingredients are moistened. Press half of mixture evenly into prepared pan.

In a medium mixing bowl beat the cream cheese and ½ cup jam with electric mixer set on medium until smooth. Beat in eggs until just blended; spread over base layer. Dollop remaining ¾ cup jam, in teaspoons, on top of the filling. Sprinkle with remaining crumb mixture; press gently into filling.

Bake 32–34 minutes or until topping is firm and center is just set. Transfer to a wire rack and cool completely. Refrigerate at least 2 hours before serving. Cut into bars. Makes 24 large or 36 small bars.

White Chocolate Brown Sugar Meringue Bars

1	19.5- to 19.8-ounce package brownie mix
½	cup (1 stick) unsalted butter, melted
1	large egg
1	12-ounce package white chocolate chips
4	large egg whites
1	cup packed dark brown sugar
1	cup slivered almonds

Preheat oven to 375° (350° for dark-coated metal pan). Position a rack in the lower third of the oven. Spray the bottom only of a 13 x 9-inch baking pan with nonstick cooking spray (or foil-line pan; see page 11).

In a medium mixing bowl mix the brownie mix, melted butter, and egg with a wooden spoon until just blended and all dry ingredients are moistened. Press mixture into prepared pan.

Bake about 12 minutes, until partially set at center. Remove pan from oven (leave oven on). Sprinkle with white chocolate chips. Transfer to wire rack while preparing meringue.

In a medium mixing bowl beat the egg whites with an electric mixer set on high until frothy. Gradually add brown sugar; beat until stiff peaks form. Carefully spread meringue over chips and nuts. Sprinkle with almonds.

Bake an additional 13–15 minutes or until meringue is golden brown. Transfer to a wire rack and cool completely. Cut into bars. Makes 24 large or 36 small bars.

These elegant bars have a touch of drama. It's dark chocolate versus white chocolate, dense chewy brownie against light, airy meringue. The contrasts add up to a lot of excitement.

Chocolate-Chip Pecan Pie Bars

This inventive take on pecan pie gets a double dose of chocolate. It's a no-fail pleaser you can always count on for a wide variety of occasions, from casual pitch-ins to formal buffets.

1	19.5- to 19.8-ounce package brownie mix
½	cup (1 stick) plus 3 tablespoons unsalted butter, melted, divided
3	large eggs
1	cup dark brown sugar
1	cup dark corn syrup
2	cups coarsely chopped pecans
1	cup miniature semisweet chocolate chips

Preheat oven to 350° (325° for dark-coated metal pan). Position a rack in the lower third of the oven. Spray the bottom only of a 13 x 9-inch baking pan with nonstick cooking spray (or foil-line pan; see page 11).

In a medium mixing bowl mix the brownie mix and ½ cup (1 stick) melted butter with a wooden spoon until just blended and all dry ingredients are moistened. Press mixture into prepared pan.

Bake 15 minutes. Remove from oven (leave oven on).

While crust bakes, in a medium mixing bowl whisk the eggs, brown sugar, corn syrup, and remaining 3 tablespoons melted butter until well blended. Stir in pecans and miniature chocolate chips; pour over hot crust.

Bake 35–40 minutes longer, until just set and topping is golden brown. Transfer to a wire rack and cool completely. Cut into bars. Makes 24 large or 36 small bars.

Walnut Fudge Bars

1   19.5- to 19.8-ounce package brownie mix
½   cup (1 stick) unsalted butter, melted
¼   cup water
2   large eggs
2   cups quick-cooking oats
2   cups chopped walnuts
2   cups semisweet chocolate chips
1   14-ounce can sweetened condensed milk

Preheat oven to 350° (325° for dark-coated metal pan). Position a rack in the lower third of the oven. Spray the bottom only of a 13 x 9-inch baking pan with nonstick cooking spray (or foil-line pan; see page 11).

In a large mixing bowl combine brownie mix, melted butter, water, and eggs with a wooden spoon until just blended and all dry ingredients are moistened; mix in oats and walnuts.

In a medium saucepan set over low heat melt the chocolate chips with the condensed milk, stirring until smooth.

Spread half of brownie batter in the prepared pan. Spread melted chocolate mixture over batter. Drop remaining brownie mixture by spoonfuls over chocolate layer (brownie mixture will not completely cover chocolate layer).

Bake 29–33 minutes or until brownie topping feels dry and edges begin to pull away from sides of pan. Transfer to wire rack and cool completely. Refrigerate at least 2 hours. Cut into bars. Makes 24 large or 36 small bars.

Having simple luxuries on hand for hungry friends and loved ones who just happen to pop in is a saving grace during the holidays or any time of year. Here is a homey but luxurious treat worth offering any time.

Chapter 3
Cookies and Bite-Sized Confections

Store the cookies in this chapter in airtight plastic containers or metal tins between layers of waxed paper or aluminum foil at room temperature for up to one week. Cookies may also be frozen, tightly wrapped in foil and placed in a ziplock plastic freezer bag. When ready to eat, thaw the cookies at room temperature before serving.

Double Fudge Chewies with Coconut & Pecans

These cookies are dense and fudgy thanks to the addition of cream cheese and sweetened condensed milk. The coconut and pecans add just the right amount of toothsome chewy-ness. For an even more choco-late-chocolate cookie, substitute 1 cup sifted, unsweetened cocoa powder for the flour.

¼	cup (½ stick) unsalted butter, softened
1	8-ounce package cream cheese, softened
1	14-ounce can sweetened condensed milk
1	large egg
1	cup all-purpose flour
1	19.5- to 19.8-ounce package brownie mix
1	cup coarsely chopped pecans
1⅓	cups shredded sweetened coconut
2	cups semisweet chocolate chips

Preheat oven to 375°. Spray cookie sheets with nonstick cooking spray.

In a large mixing bowl beat butter and cream cheese with electric mixer set on high until smooth. Add condensed milk and egg; beat until blended. Add flour and brownie mix; stir with wooden spoon until blended and all dry ingredients are moistened. Stir in pecans, coconut, and chocolate chips.

Drop dough by teaspoonfuls, 1 inch apart, onto prepared cookie sheets.

Bake 9–12 minutes or until set at edges and just barely set at center when lightly touched. Cool 1 minute on sheets. Transfer to wire racks with metal spatula and cool completely. Makes about 5 dozen cookies.

Big Brownie Cookies

1	19.5- to 19.8-ounce package brownie mix
⅓	cup vegetable oil or melted unsalted butter
2	large eggs
1½	cups semisweet chocolate chips or chunks
1	cup chopped nuts, any variety, sprinkled on top of cookies before baking (optional)

Preheat oven to 350°. Spray cookie sheets with nonstick cooking spray.

In a large mixing bowl combine brownie mix, oil, and eggs with wooden spoon until just blended and all dry ingredients are moistened; stir in chocolate chips.

Drop dough by heaping tablespoonfuls, 2 inches apart, onto prepared cookie sheets. Sprinkled with nuts, if desired.

Bake 11–14 minutes until cracked in appearance and just barely set at center when lightly touched. Cool 1 minute on sheets. Transfer to wire racks with metal spatula and cool completely. Makes about 2½ dozen big cookies.

So easy, so good, and so very chocolate—who can resist a cookie with those credentials? These cookies are great last-minute makers because an entire batch comes together in well under an hour and the results are so very impressive. If you wish to make smaller cookies, drop by heaping teaspoons (rather than tablespoons) and proceed as directed, baking for 9–13 minutes, until set. This will make about 3 dozen cookies. If you choose to add nuts, sprinkle them on top of each cookie rather than stirring them into the batter. The nuts will get toasted this way, deepening their flavor.

Chocolate Rice Crispy Cookies

This homespun cookie is a sweet combination of crispy and chewy highlighted with a double dose of chocolate.

1	19.5- to 19.8-ounce package brownie mix
1	cup (2 sticks) butter, softened
2	large eggs
2	tablespoons water
1	cup miniature semisweet chocolate chips
3	cups crisp rice cereal, divided

Preheat oven to 350°. Spray cookie sheets with nonstick cooking spray.

In a large mixing bowl mix the brownie mix, butter, eggs, and water with an electric mixer set on low for 2 minutes until well blended. Fold in chocolate chips and 1½ cups cereal. Refrigerate at least 1 hour or up to overnight.

Crush remaining 1½ cups cereal into coarse crumbs; place in shallow dish.

Shape dough into 1-inch balls. Roll in crushed cereal. Place balls about 1 inch apart on prepared cookie sheets.

Bake 11–13 minutes, until set at edges and just barely set at center when lightly touched. Cool 1 minute on sheets. Transfer to wire racks with metal spatula and cool completely. Makes about 4½ dozen cookies.

Brownies & Cream Sandwich Cookies

1	19.5- to 19.8-ounce package brownie mix
⅓	cup vegetable oil
2	large eggs
1	recipe Cream Cheese Frosting (see page 261)

Preheat oven to 350°. Spray cookie sheets with nonstick cooking spray.

In a large mixing bowl mix the brownie mix, oil, and eggs with wooden spoon until just blended and all dry ingredients are moistened.

Drop by teaspoonfuls, 2 inches apart, onto prepared cookie sheet.

Bake 7–8 minutes or until cookies are set at edges and just barely set at center when lightly touched. Cool 1 minute on sheets. Transfer to wire racks with metal spatula and cool completely.

Prepare Cream Cheese Frosting. Spread frosting on the bottoms of half of the cooled cookies. Top each frosted cookie with another cookie. Gently press together. Makes about 2½ dozen sandwich cookies.

These humble sandwich cookies have what it takes to bring on the smiles: rich brownie cookies, creamy filling, and a big comfort factor. For a chocolate sandwich cookie, substitute Chocolate Cream Cheese Frosting (see page 252) or Chocolate Fudge Frosting (see page 250) for the cream cheese frosting.

White Chocolate Cherry Cookies

This is one of my signature cookie concoctions. The cookies taste like a temptation you might find at a high-end specialty store or bakery but are quick and easy to make—perfect when you need to make or bring an impressive dessert in short order.

1	19.5- to 19.8-ounce package brownie mix
⅓	cup vegetable oil
2	large eggs
½	teaspoon almond extract
1	cup tart dried cherries or dried cranberries
1	cup white chocolate chips

Preheat oven to 350°. Spray cookie sheets with nonstick cooking spray.

In a medium mixing bowl mix the brownie mix, oil, eggs, almond extract, cherries, and white chocolate chips with a wooden spoon until well blended.

Drop dough by teaspoonfuls, 2 inches apart, onto prepared cookie sheets.

Bake 9–12 minutes, until set at edges and just barely set at center when lightly touched. Cool 1 minute on sheets. Transfer to wire racks with metal spatula and cool completely. Makes about 4½ dozen cookies.

Cream Cheese Chocolate Softies

1   19.5- to 19.8-ounce package brownie mix
¼   cup (½ stick) unsalted butter, melted
4   ounces (half of an 8-ounce package) cream cheese, softened
1   large egg

Preheat oven to 350°. In a medium mixing bowl beat brownie mix, melted butter, cream cheese, and egg with a wooden spoon until all dry ingredients are moistened and well blended (dough will be sticky).

Drop dough by teaspoonfuls, 2 inches apart, onto ungreased cookie sheets; smooth edge of each to form round cookie.

Bake 9–12 minutes or until set at edges and just barely set at center when lightly touched (do not overbake; cookies will become more firm as they cool). Transfer to wire rack and cool completely. Makes 4 dozen cookies.

You're only four ingredients away from a batch of heavenly, soft chocolate cookies. Cream cheese adds a distinctive tanginess to these cookies, a fine foil to the chocolate. You can up the chocolate ante by adding a cup of semisweet, milk, or white chocolate chips.

Mocha Buttercream–Filled Double Chocolate Sandwich Cookies

I tend to like things gussied up, sometimes to excess. Here's a case where it works, to perfection. Two essentials for the success of these cream-filled coffee confections are (1) make sure the filling is semi-set (if fully set, it will be too hard to spread) and (2) make sure the cookies are completely cooled before assembly to avoid melting the buttery filling.

2	cups semisweet chocolate chips, divided
½	cup heavy whipping cream
1½	tablespoons instant espresso or coffee powder, divided
6	tablespoons (¾ stick) unsalted butter, room temperature
¾	cup powdered sugar
1	teaspoon vanilla extract
1	19.5- to 19.8-ounce package brownie mix
⅓	cup vegetable oil
3	tablespoons water
2	large eggs
1	cup coarsely chopped pecans

In a medium, heavy-bottomed saucepan set over medium–low heat stir ½ cup of the chocolate chips, cream, and 1 tablespoon espresso powder until chocolate melts and coffee dissolves. Remove from heat and cool to room temperature, about 20 minutes. In a medium mixing bowl beat the butter, powdered sugar, and vanilla with an electric mixer until blended. Beat in chocolate mixture. Refrigerate until slightly firm but not hard, about 10 minutes.

Preheat oven to 350°. Spray cookie sheets with nonstick cooking spray. In a large mixing bowl mix the brownie mix, oil, water, eggs, and remaining ½ tablespoon espresso powder with a wooden spoon until just blended and all dry ingredients are moistened. Stir in pecans and remaining 1½ cups chocolate chips.

Drop by teaspoonfuls, 2 inches apart, onto prepared cookie sheets. Bake 7–8 minutes or until set at edges and just barely set at center when lightly touched. Cool 1 minute on sheets. Transfer cookies to wire racks with metal spatula and cool completely.

Spread filling on half the cookies. Top each frosted cookie with another cookie. Gently press together. Makes about $2\frac{1}{2}$ dozen sandwich cookies.

Chocolate-Kissed
Peanut Butter Thumbprints

Every baker needs a few recipes they can rely on as all-around pleasers, whether it's for a bake sale, potluck, picnic, or after-school treats for the kids. This cute cookie is one such recipe. Traditional milk chocolate "kisses" are always wonderful, but the white chocolate-milk chocolate striped "hugs" candies look especially pretty perched atop the dark chocolate dough.

1	19.5- to 19.8-ounce package brownie mix
1	14-ounce can sweetened condensed milk
1	cup creamy-style peanut butter
1	large egg
2	teaspoons vanilla extract
	About 72 chocolate "kiss" or "hugs" candies (from a 13-ounce bag), unwrapped

Preheat oven to 350°. In a large mixing bowl mix the brownie mix, condensed milk, peanut butter, egg, and vanilla with an electric mixer set on low spend for 1–2 minutes, until all dry ingredients are moistened and dough is well blended (dough will be very thick).

Shape dough into 1-inch balls and position 2 inches apart on ungreased cookie sheets.

Bake 8–10 minutes, until firm to the touch at the edges and slightly puffed in appearance. Remove sheets from the oven and immediately push a kiss candy, flat side down, into the center of each cookie. Cool 1 minute on sheets. Transfer cookies to wire racks with metal spatula and cool completely. Makes about 6 dozen cookies.

Jam-Filled Chocolate Thumbprints

1	19.5- to 19.8-ounce package brownie mix
1/3	cup unsweetened cocoa powder, sifted
1/4	cup (1/2 stick) unsalted butter, melted
2	teaspoons vanilla extract
2	large eggs
1/3	cup jam, preserves, marmalade, or jelly, stirred to loosen

In a medium mixing bowl mix the brownie mix, sifted cocoa powder, melted butter, vanilla, and eggs with a wooden spoon until all dry ingredients are moistened and dough is well blended. Cover bowl with plastic wrap and refrigerate dough at least 1 hour.

Preheat oven to 350°. Spray cookie sheets with nonstick cooking spray.

Shape dough into 1-inch balls and position 2 inches apart on prepared cookie sheets. Make a shallow indentation in each ball of dough with thumb or back of a 1/4-teaspoon measuring spoon. Fill each indentation with 1/4 teaspoon jam.

Bake 9–11 minutes, until firm to the touch at the edges. Cool 1 minute on sheets. Transfer to wire racks with metal spatula and cool completely. Makes about 4 1/2 dozen cookies.

Thumbprints are such friendly little cookies. They always stir up lots of warm-fuzzy memories for me—chatting with my mom, curling up with a good book, and counting the days until Christmas are but a few. I hope this easy chocolate version creates some favorite memories for you, too. You can use any jam or jelly you like. For a nutty thumbprint, roll each ball in finely chopped nuts (you'll need about a cup of nuts) before filling with jam. The nuts will toast as they bake, adding to the rich flavor of the cookies.

Chocolate Pantry Cookies

No eggs? No butter? No problem. Mayonnaise is the secret ingredient in these delicious cookies made from ingredients you are likely to have on hand. The mayonnaise is not as unusual as you might think—it's essentially eggs and oil. Be sure to use real mayonnaise as opposed to salad dressing for the best results.

1	19.5- to 19.8-ounce package brownie mix
2	cups semisweet chocolate chips
1	5.85-ounce package instant chocolate pudding mix
½	cup chopped pecans or walnuts (preferably lightly toasted)
1½	cups real mayonnaise

Preheat oven to 350°. Spray cookie sheets with nonstick cooking spray. In a large mixing bowl mix the brownie mix, chocolate chips, pudding mix, and nuts. Mix in the mayonnaise with a wooden spoon until just blended and all dry ingredients are moistened.

Shape dough into 1-inch balls. Place on prepared cookie sheets, spacing 2 inches apart. Bake 10–13 minutes until set at edges and just barely set at center when lightly touched. Cool 1 minute on sheets. Transfer to wire racks with metal spatula and cool completely. Makes about 4½ dozen cookies.

Chocolate Raisin Cookies

1	19.5- to 19.8-ounce package brownie mix
⅓	cup vegetable oil
2	large eggs
½	teaspoon ground cinnamon
1	cup raisins
1	cup miniature semisweet chocolate chips

Preheat oven to 350°. Spray cookie sheets with nonstick cooking spray.

In a medium mixing bowl mix the brownie mix, vegetable oil, eggs, and cinnamon with a wooden spoon until just blended and all dry ingredients are moistened; stir in raisins and chocolate chips.

Drop dough by teaspoonfuls, 2 inches apart, onto prepared cookie sheets.

Bake 9–11 minutes, until set at edges and just barely set at center when lightly touched. Cool 1 minute on sheets. Transfer to wire racks with metal spatula and cool completely. Makes about 4½ dozen cookies.

Forget the fuss—whip up a batch of these simple and oh-so-homey chocolate raisin cookies and get cozy. They're easy enough to justify a party for one and fancy enough to serve on a platter to share with guests.

Jumbo Triple-Chocolate Oatmeal Cookies

Here's a real treat for the lunch box or bag (for both kids and adults). A chocolate cookie dough and two kinds of chocolate chips turn plain oatmeal cookies into something new and exciting.

1	19.5- to 19.8-ounce package brownie mix
2	cups quick-cooking oats, uncooked
½	cup (1 stick) unsalted butter, melted
3	large eggs
1	cup white chocolate chips
1	cup semisweet chocolate chips

Preheat oven to 350°. Spray cookie sheets with nonstick cooking spray.

In a large mixing bowl combine brownie mix, oats, melted butter, eggs, white chocolate chips, and semisweet chocolate chips. Stir with a wooden spoon until well blended (dough will be very stiff).

Drop dough by level ¼-cupfuls, 2 inches apart, onto prepared cookie sheets; flatten slightly with the bottom of a glass.

Bake 13–17 minutes, until set at edges and just barely set at center when lightly touched. Cool 1 minute on sheets. Transfer to wire racks with metal spatula and cool completely. Makes 2 dozen big cookies.

Peppermint White Chocolate Crinkles

1	19.5- to 19.8-ounce package brownie mix
⅓	cup vegetable oil
2	large eggs
1	teaspoon peppermint extract
1½	cups white chocolate chips
12	red and white striped round peppermint hard candies, crushed

Preheat oven to 350°. Spray cookie sheets with nonstick cooking spray.

In a medium mixing bowl mix the brownie mix, oil, eggs, and peppermint extract with a wooden spoon until just blended and all dry ingredients are moistened; stir in white chocolate chips.

Drop dough by teaspoonfuls, 2 inches apart, onto prepared cookie sheets. Sprinkle tops with crushed candies.

Bake 9–12 minutes, until set at edges and just barely set at center when lightly touched. Cool 1 minute on sheets. Transfer to wire racks with metal spatula and cool completely. Makes about 4 dozen cookies.

A batch of these minty chocolate cookies makes a wonderful winter holiday gift, but chances are you'll want to keep them for yourself. Perhaps you'll succumb to the spirit of the season and share them with friends nonetheless. Or make two batches!

Kahlua White Chocolate Chunk Chewies

These incredible cook- ies, rich with white chocolate chunks and Kahlua, got a high approval rating first from my husband, then from everyone at work. While testing recipes, I made sure to send lots of "samples" to friends and co-workers, and they gave this particu- lar recipe an approval rating of 100 percent.

¼	cup Kahlua or other coffee liqueur
1	tablespoon instant coffee or espresso powder
1	19.5- to 19.8-ounce package brownie mix
¼	cup (½ stick) unsalted butter, melted
1	large egg
1	6-ounce box white chocolate baking bars, chopped into chunks
1	recipe Kahlua Coffee Icing (see page 260)

Preheat oven to 350°. Spray cookie sheets with nonstick cook- ing spray.

In a large mixing bowl mix the Kahlua and coffee powder. With a wooden spoon, mix in the brownie mix, melted but- ter, and egg until just blended and all dry ingredients are mois- tened; mix in the white chocolate chunks.

Drop dough by teaspoonfuls, 2 inches apart, onto prepared cookie sheets.

Bake 10–13 minutes, until set at edges and just barely set at center when lightly touched. Cool 1 minute on sheets. Transfer to wire racks with metal spatula and cool completely. Prepare Kahlua Coffee Icing. Drizzle icing over cooled cookies. Makes about 4 dozen cookies.

German Chocolate Thumbprint Cookies

1	cup packed light brown sugar
1	cup canned evaporated milk
½	cup (1 stick) plus ⅓ cup butter, softened, divided
3	large egg yolks, lightly beaten with a fork
1	teaspoon vanilla extract
1½	cups sweetened shredded coconut
1½	cups chopped pecans
1	19.5- to 19.8-ounce package brownie mix

In a medium, heavy-bottomed saucepan combine brown sugar, evaporated milk, ½ cup butter, and beaten egg yolks. Cook over medium heat for 10–13 minutes or until thickened and bubbly, whisking frequently. Stir in vanilla, coconut, and pecans. Remove from heat and cool to room temperature. Reserve 1¼ cups topping mixture. Set aside.

Preheat oven to 350°. Position a rack in the lower third of the oven. In a medium mixing bowl combine brownie mix, remaining ⅓ cup softened butter, and remaining topping mixture. Stir with a wooden spoon until all dry ingredients are thoroughly moistened.

Shape dough into 1-inch balls. Place 2 inches apart on ungreased cookie sheets. With thumb or back of a ¼ teaspoon measure, make an indentation in center of each ball and fill with mounded ½ teaspoonful of reserved topping.

Bake 10–13 minutes or until just barely set. Cool on sheets 2 minutes. Transfer cookies with spatula to wire racks and cool completely. Makes about 4½ dozen thumbprints.

These cookies top my list for holiday cookie plates, and although they take a bit more time to make (with the cooling and cooking times), the overall effort is well worth it. I've found, in particular, that people who claim they do not like coconut are easily converted with these thumbprints, each of which tastes like a miniature German chocolate cake.

Irish Cream–Frosted Milk Chocolate Cookies

Because I love frosting, it's not surprising that this yummy, liqueur-frosted chocolate cookie tops my list. Depending on your preference and what you have available, change out the liqueur in both the cookie and the frosting (although the Irish cream version is wickedly good). The best way to eat them is with complete abandon, with no thoughts of calories and not a twinge of guilt.

1	19.5- to 19.8-ounce package brownie mix
¼	cup (½ stick) unsalted butter, melted
¼	cup Irish cream liqueur
1	large egg
1½	cups milk chocolate chips
1	recipe Irish Cream Frosting (see page 260)

Preheat oven to 350°. Spray cookie sheets with nonstick cooking spray.

In a large mixing bowl mix the brownie mix, melted butter, liqueur, and egg with a wooden spoon until just blended and all dry ingredients are moistened; stir in the chocolate chips.

Drop dough by teaspoonfuls, 2 inches apart, onto prepared cookie sheets.

Bake 10–13 minutes, until cracked in appearance and just barely set at center when lightly touched. Cool 1 minute on sheets. Transfer to wire racks with metal spatula and cool completely. Prepare Irish Cream Frosting; frost cooled cookies. Makes about 4½ dozen cookies

Sean's Very Chocolate Cookies

1	19.5- to 19.8-ounce package brownie mix
1	5⅛-ounce package instant chocolate pudding mix
¼	cup dark rum
½	cup (1 stick) butter, melted
2	large egg
1½	cups semisweet chocolate chunks or chips

Preheat oven to 350°. Position racks in lower and upper thirds of oven. Spray cookie sheets with nonstick cooking spray.

In a large mixing bowl mix the brownie mix, cocoa powder, rum, melted butter, and eggs with a wooden spoon until just blended and all dry ingredients are moistened; mix in chocolate chunks.

Drop by teaspoonfuls, 2 inches apart, onto prepared cookie sheets.

Bake 10–13 minutes, until cracked in appearance and just barely set at center when lightly touched. Cool 1 minute on sheets. Transfer to wire racks with metal spatula and cool completely. Makes about 4½ dozen cookies.

When it comes to birthdays, my brother Sean is easy to satisfy. All he really wants is his favorite birthday cake, known by my family as "Very Chocolate Cake." It's a simple yet intensely chocolate pound cake that starts with a chocolate cake mix. These cookies follow the same basic formula as the cake but start with brownie mix. One bite and you'll understand why the name is so very fitting.

Apricot-Frosted Chocolate Cookies

The contrast of tart-sweet apricot—both in the cookie dough and in the frosting—and deep, dark chocolate makes for one very sophisticated cookie. Cardamom—a popular flavor in Scandinavian baking—adds just the right hint of spice to the blend. If you don't have it, ground coriander or nutmeg may be substituted.

1	19.5- to 19.8-ounce package brownie mix
⅓	cup butter, melted
2	large eggs
½	teaspoon ground cardamom
1	cup chopped dried apricots
1	cup miniature semisweet chocolate chips
1	recipe Apricot Frosting (see page 262)

Preheat oven to 350°. Spray cookie sheets with nonstick cooking spray.

In a large mixing bowl mix the brownie mix, melted butter, eggs, and cardamom with a wooden spoon until just blended and all dry ingredients are moistened; mix in chopped apricots and miniature chocolate chips.

Drop by teaspoonfuls, 2 inches apart, onto prepared cookie sheets.

Bake 10–13 minutes, until set at edges and just barely set at center when lightly touched. Cool 1 minute on sheets. Transfer to wire racks with metal spatula and cool completely.

Prepare the Apricot Frosting. Spread frosting over each cooled cookie. Makes about 4½ dozen cookies.

Toffee Apple Chocolate Cookies

1	19.5- to 19.8-ounce package brownie mix
½	cup (1 stick) unsalted butter, melted
¼	cup packed light brown sugar
2	large eggs
2	teaspoons vanilla extract
1	6-ounce package dried apples, chopped
1¼	cups English toffee baking bits

Preheat oven to 350°. Position racks in lower and upper thirds of oven. Spray cookie sheets with nonstick cooking spray.

In a large mixing bowl mix the brownie mix, melted butter, brown sugar, eggs, vanilla, dried apples, and toffee bits with a wooden spoon until all dry ingredients are moistened.

Drop by teaspoonfuls, 2 inches apart, onto prepared cookie sheets.

Bake 10–13 minutes, until just barely set at center when lightly touched. Cool 2 minutes on sheets. Transfer to wire racks with metal spatula and cool completely. Makes about 4½ dozen cookies.

I've made this same cookie with a sugar cookie dough for years, but I have to admit that it is even better made with chocolate dough. The dried apples together with the toffee bits give these cookies a crunchy-chewy consistency, making them great partners for tall glasses of milk on cool autumn afternoons. To send these cookies over the top, dip or drizzle them with melted white chocolate, place on waxed paper–lined cookie sheets, and refrigerate until chocolate is set. Outstanding!

Macadamia & Toasted Coconut Chocolate Cookies

This island-inspired cookie is just the thing for warm summer days, beach parties, outdoor barbecues, and lazy twilit picnics. Don't forget the lemonade and iced tea.

1⅔	cups sweetened shredded coconut
1	19.5- to 19.8-ounce package brownie mix
⅓	cup canned unsweetened coconut milk
¼	cup (½ stick) unsalted butter, melted
1	large egg
1	cup coarsely chopped roasted, lightly salted macadamia nuts

Preheat oven to 350°.

Spread coconut evenly over an ungreased cookie sheet. Place sheet on lower rack and toast coconut until golden brown and fragrant, about 7–8 minutes. Transfer to a large mixing bowl and cool completely.

Spray cookie sheets with nonstick cooking spray. To the bowl with the coconut add the brownie mix, coconut milk, melted butter, egg, and macadamia nuts. Mix with a wooden spoon until blended and all dry ingredients are moistened.

Drop by teaspoonfuls, 2 inches apart, onto prepared cookie sheets.

Bake 10–13 minutes until set at edges and just barely set at center when lightly touched. Cool 1 minute on sheets. Transfer to wire racks with metal spatula and cool completely. Makes about 4½ dozen cookies.

Cashew Butter Brickle Brownie Cookies

1	19.5- to 19.8-ounce package brownie mix
½	cup (1 stick) unsalted butter, melted
¼	cup packed light brown sugar
2	large eggs
2	teaspoons vanilla extract
1	cup lightly salted roasted cashews, coarsely chopped
1	cup English toffee baking bits

Preheat oven to 350°. Position racks in lower and upper thirds of oven. Spray cookie sheets with nonstick cooking spray.

In a large mixing bowl mix the brownie mix, melted butter, brown sugar, eggs, vanilla, cashews, and toffee bits with a wooden spoon until all dry ingredients are moistened.

Drop by teaspoonfuls, 2 inches apart, onto prepared cookie sheets.

Bake 10–13 minutes, until cracked in appearance and just barely set at center when lightly touched. Cool 1 minute on sheets. Transfer to wire racks with metal spatula and cool completely. Makes about 4½ dozen cookies.

Packed with buttery cashews and toffee baking bits, these newfangled chocolate cookies are a saving grace when I want to make an impressive cookie for a gift or gathering but don't have much time. Be prepared to share the recipe!

Peanut Butter–Chip Chocolate Cookies

My favorite way to make these peanut-buttery chocolate cookies is with peanut butter chips, but I also think they are pretty incredible made with semisweet or milk chocolate chips. If you can't decide, go half and half: ¾ cup chocolate chips and ¾ cup peanut butter chips. You can't go wrong!

1	19.5- to 19.8-ounce package brownie mix
1	cup creamy peanut butter (not old-fashioned or natural style)
½	cup (1 stick) unsalted butter, melted
¼	cup packed dark brown sugar
2	large eggs
2	teaspoons vanilla extract
1½	cups peanut butter–flavored baking chips

Preheat oven to 350°. Spray cookie sheets with nonstick cooking spray.

In a medium mixing bowl mix the brownie mix, peanut butter, melted butter, brown sugar, eggs, and vanilla with a wooden spoon until well blended. Stir in peanut butter baking chips.

Drop dough by teaspoonfuls, 2 inches apart, onto prepared cookie sheets.

Bake 10–13 minutes, until set at edges and just barely set at center when lightly touched. Cool 1 minute on sheets. Transfer to wire racks with metal spatula and cool completely. Makes about 5 dozen cookies.

Cinnamon-Chip Chocolate Cookies

1	19.5- to 19.8-ounce package brownie mix
⅓	cup vegetable oil
2	large eggs
¾	teaspoon ground cinnamon
1½	cups cinnamon baking chips

Preheat oven to 350°. Spray cookie sheets with nonstick cooking spray.

In a medium mixing bowl mix the brownie mix, oil, eggs, cinnamon, and cinnamon chips with a wooden spoon until blended and all dry ingredients are moistened.

Drop dough by teaspoonfuls, 2 inches apart, onto prepared cookie sheets.

Bake 9–12 minutes, until set at edges and just barely set at center when lightly touched. Cool 1 minute on sheets. Transfer to wire racks with metal spatula and cool completely. Makes about 4 dozen cookies.

Remember the first time you baked a batch of cookies? Chances are they were some sort of permutation of either chocolate or cinnamon. These double cinnamon chocolate cookies are bound to bring back warm fuzzy memories, both as they bake and as you eat them.

Pecan & White Chocolate Chunk Brownie Cookies

White chocolate, pecans, brown sugar, and dark chocolate dough—cookies don't get much better than this. Ready from start to finish in well under an hour, they're terrific with a cappuccino or glass of ice-cold milk.

1	19.5- to 19.8-ounce package brownie mix
½	cup (1 stick) unsalted butter, melted
¼	cup packed dark brown sugar
2	large eggs
1	6-ounce package white chocolate baking squares, coarsely chopped into chunks
1	cup coarsely chopped pecans

Preheat oven to 350°. Spray cookie sheets with nonstick cooking spray.

In a medium mixing bowl mix the brownie mix, melted butter, brown sugar, eggs, and white chocolate chunks with a wooden spoon until well blended.

Drop dough by teaspoonfuls, 2 inches apart, onto prepared cookie sheets. Sprinkle tops with a few pecans.

Bake 9–12 minutes, until set at edges and just barely set at center when lightly touched. Cool 1 minute on sheets. Transfer to wire racks with metal spatula and cool completely. Makes about 4½ dozen cookies.

Mocha Almond Fudge Cookies

1	19.5- to 19.8-ounce package brownie mix
⅓	cup vegetable oil
2	large eggs
1	tablespoon espresso or coffee powder
1	teaspoon almond extract
1	cup semisweet chocolate chips
1	cup sliced almonds
1	recipe Kahlua Coffee Icing (see page 260)

Yes, these fudgy cookies are very rich, but they're worth every bite. They're perfect for afternoon (or, if you cannot wait, morning) coffee breaks.

Preheat oven to 350°. Spray cookie sheets with nonstick cooking spray.

In a medium mixing bowl, mix the brownie mix, oil, eggs, espresso powder, almond extract, and chocolate chips with a wooden spoon until well blended.

Drop dough by teaspoonfuls, 2 inches apart, onto prepared cookie sheets. Sprinkle tops with a few sliced almonds; gently press almonds into dough.

Bake 9–12 minutes, until set at edges and just barely set at center when lightly touched. Cool 1 minute on sheets. Transfer to wire racks with metal spatula and cool completely.

Prepare the Kahlua Coffee Icing; drizzle over cooled cookies. Makes about 4 dozen cookies.

To-Die-For Chocolate Hazelnut Sandwich Cookies

1	19.5- to 19.8-ounce package brownie mix
1⅔	cup chocolate-hazelnut spread (e.g., Nutella®), divided
⅓	cup unsalted butter, melted
2	large eggs

I personally refer to these as "true believer" cookies because they have turned many foodie friends and acquaintances into brownie mix converts in just a few nibbles. They nearly flip when I tell them the recipe is made with only four ingredients. Sophisticated and intensely chocolate, they are as pretty as they are easy to make. The flavor of chocolate and hazelnut may not be familiar to many Americans, but it is a common, and much loved, European combination. But you only need to love chocolate to go nuts over these cookies. You can find chocolate hazelnut spread in most supermarkets these days, right next to the peanut butter or in the international foods section.

Preheat oven to 350°. Spray cookie sheets with nonstick cooking spray.

In a large mixing bowl mix the brownie mix, 1 cup chocolate-hazelnut spread, melted butter, and eggs with a wooden spoon until well blended (mixture will be very thick).

Roll dough into ¾-inch balls and place 2 inches apart on prepared cookie sheets. Flatten slightly with the bottom of a glass or the tines of a fork.

Bake 8–11 minutes until set at edges and just barely set at center when lightly touched and cookies have a cracked appearance (cookies will be flat and round). Cool 1 minute on sheets. Transfer to wire racks with metal spatula and cool completely.

Spread bottom side of one cookie with a teaspoon of remaining chocolate-hazelnut spread; sandwich with a second cookie. Repeat with remaining cookies. Makes about 3 dozen sandwich cookies.

Soft Banana Brownie Cookies

1   medium-sized, ripe banana
1   large egg
1   tablespoon vegetable oil
1   19.5- to 19.8-ounce package brownie mix
1   cup milk or white chocolate chips
1   cup chopped walnuts (optional)

Preheat oven to 350°. Spray cookie sheets with nonstick cooking spray.

In a medium mixing bowl mash the banana. Add the egg, oil, and brownie mix. Mix with a wooden spoon until just blended and all the dry ingredients are moistened. Stir in chocolate chips.

Drop by teaspoonfuls, 2 inches apart, onto prepared cookie sheets. Sprinkle with chopped walnuts, if desired.

Bake 10–13 minutes, until set at edges and just barely set at center when lightly touched (do not overbake). Cool 1 minute on sheets. Transfer to wire racks with metal spatula and cool completely. Makes about 4 dozen cookies.

Chocolate and banana are clearly made for each other in these soft, cake-like cookies. They're great to pack into lunchbags. Moreover, it's quite likely you have all the ingredients you need in your kitchen right now.

Buttery Brownie Cut-Outs

Making cookie cut-outs with my sister Rebecca and brother Sean is one of my favorite childhood Christmas memories. It was typically an all-day affair that began with my mother creaming what seemed like vats of butter and sugar (all by hand!) for multiple batches of her perfect butter cookie dough, followed by lots of giggling, icing, squirting, and sprinkling, all to the tune of Christmas carols in the background. These easy cut-outs are every bit as buttery as my mother's, but so very different in deep, dark chocolate form. Moreover, they come together in a flash. You'll have a ball decorating them, whether you choose a simple sprinkle of cocoa powder (easy & elegant— my favorite) or a smooth finish of icing.

1	19.5- to 19.8-ounce package brownie mix
¾	cup (1½ sticks) butter, softened
1	large egg
2	teaspoons vanilla extract
	Unsweetened cocoa powder powdered sugar for dusting (optional)
	Cookie Decorating Icing (see page 244; optional)

In a large mixing bowl mix the brownie mix, butter, egg, and vanilla with an electric mixer set on low for 1 minute (dough will be very thick). Scrape the dough off of the beaters and wrap the bowl in plastic wrap. Chill at least 4 hours or up to overnight.

Preheat oven to 350°. Position racks in upper and lower thirds of the oven. Sprinkle a work surface with a thin layer of flour. Set out rolling pin, cookie cutters, metal spatula, and two cookie sheets.

Remove the dough from the refrigerator and divide into fourths. Place one fourth of the dough on a floured surface (cover and return remaining dough to refrigerator). Flour the rolling pin and roll dough to ¼-inch thickness. Flour cookie cutters and cut out shapes. Transfer cut-outs to ungreased cookie sheets with spatula. Re-roll any scraps, then repeat with remaining dough, rolling one fourth at a time.

Place one cookie sheet on each oven rack. Bake 4 minutes. Rotate the sheets (place the sheet from the bottom rack on the top rack and the sheet from the top rack on the bottom rack) to ensure even baking. Bake 2–3 minutes longer for small shapes, 5–7 minutes for large shapes, or until center is puffed and sinks back.

Cool 1 minute on sheets. Transfer to wire racks with metal spatula and cool completely. If desired, sprinkle with cocoa powder or powdered sugar, or ice with icing. Makes about 5 dozen 2½-inch cookies.

Chocolate Oatmeal Cookies
(Any Way You Like Them)

1   19.5- to 19.8-ounce package brownie mix
½   cup vegetable oil or melted butter
2   large eggs
1¼   cups old-fashioned or quick-cooking oats
1 or 2 stir-in options (see below)
½   cup sugar

This recipe is fun to play around with—add your favorite ingredient from the list below or mix up an eclectic combination of stir-ins to suit your fancy. It's virtually impossible to miss with this very versatile cookie.

Preheat oven to 375°. Spray cookie sheets with nonstick cooking spray.

In a large mixing bowl mix the brownie mix, oil, and eggs until blended and all the dry ingredients are moistened. With a wooden spoon, stir in the oats and 1 or 2 of the stir-in options, if desired; stir until well blended.

Roll dough into 1½-inch balls; place on the prepared cookie sheets. Place sugar in a shallow dish. Dip bottom of a drinking glass in sugar; slightly flatten one of the cookies using the sugar-coated spoon. Repeat with remaining cookies.

Bake 9–12 minutes until set at edges and just barely set at center when lightly touched (do not overbake). Cool 1 minute on sheets. Transfer to wire racks with metal spatula and cool completely. Makes about 3 dozen cookies with no stir-ins, about 3½ dozen with 1 stir-in and about 4 dozen with 2 stir-ins.

Optional stir-ins (Stir in 1 or 2 of any of the following):
• 1 cup baking chips or chunks (e.g., semisweet chocolate chips or chunks, milk chocolate chips or chunks, white chocolate chips or chunks, butterscotch chips, peanut butter chips, cinnamon chips, or English toffee baking bits)
• 1 cup dried fruit bits (e.g., cranberries, raisins, coconut or chopped dried apricots)
• 1 cup chopped nuts (e.g., pecans, walnuts, macadamia nuts, or peanuts)

Big Brownie Buttercream "Pies"

It took me a long time to get these dreamy treats exactly as I wanted them—loaded with chocolate chips and rich with buttercream. If time is an issue, you can always substitute ready-to-spread frosting for the homemade filling, but if you have the time, the buttercream is well worth the effort.

1	19.5- to 19.8-ounce package brownie mix
⅓	cup vegetable oil
2	large eggs
2	cups miniature semisweet chocolate chips, divided

Filling:

1	cup (2 sticks) salted butter, softened
1	tablespoon vanilla extract
4	cups sifted powdered sugar

Preheat oven to 350°. Spray cookie sheets with nonstick cooking spray.

In a large mixing bowl combine brownie mix, oil, eggs, and half (1 cup) of the chocolate chips until well blended. Shape dough into 24 balls (about 1½ inches). Place 2 inches apart on prepared cookie sheets. Flatten slightly with bottom of a glass.

Bake 12–14 minutes, until set at edges and just barely set at center when lightly touched. Cool 1 minute on sheets. Transfer to wire racks with metal spatula and cool completely.

While cookies cool, prepare the filling. In a large mixing bowl beat the butter with electric mixer 2 minutes, scraping sides with rubber spatula. Add the vanilla and powdered sugar and beat 2–3 minutes longer; scrape down sides of the bowl and beat and additional 2 minutes, until light and fluffy. Stop the mixer, add the remaining mini chocolate chips and mix 30 seconds to combine.

Place half of the cookies, top side down, onto waxed paper. Spoon 3 tablespoons filling onto center of each cookie. Place remaining cookies top side up onto the filling to make a sandwich. Gently but firmly press down on the top cookie to spread the filling to the edges. Serve immediately or wrap in plastic wrap and store in tightly sealed plastic container. Makes 12 big pies.

Black & White Cookies

1	19.5- to 19.8-ounce package brownie mix
1/3	cup unsweetened cocoa powder, sifted
1/4	cup (1/2 stick) unsalted butter, melted
2	teaspoons vanilla extract
2	large eggs
1 1/2	cups white chocolate chips
3	tablespoons vegetable shortening, divided
1 1/2	cups semisweet chocolate chips

In a medium mixing bowl mix the brownie mix, sifted cocoa powder, melted butter, vanilla, and eggs with a wooden spoon until all dry ingredients are moistened and dough is well blended. Cover bowl with plastic wrap and refrigerate dough at least 1 hour.

Preheat oven to 350°. Spray cookie sheets with nonstick cooking spray.

Shape dough into 1-inch balls and position two inches apart on prepared cookie sheets. Flatten each ball to 1/4-inch thickness with the bottom of a glass.

Bake 8–10 minutes, until firm to the touch at the edges. Cool 1 minute on sheets. Transfer to wire racks with metal spatula and cool completely.

Line cooled cookie sheets with waxed paper. In a small, heavy-bottomed saucepan set over low heat melt the white chocolate chips with 1 1/2 tablespoons shortening, stirring until smooth. Dip one half of each cooled cookie in white chocolate; place on waxed paper. Refrigerate 30 minutes.

In a small heavy-bottomed saucepan set over low heat, melt the semisweet chocolate chips with remaining 1 1/2 tablespoons shortening, stirring until smooth. Dip second half of each cooled cookie in semisweet chocolate; place on waxed paper. Refrigerate 30 minutes to 1 hour to set the chocolate. Makes about 4 1/2 dozen cookies.

Whatever the occasion, an offering of elegant cookies at the end seems to make any meal—from a simple barbecue to a salad supper to a classic afternoon tea with friends—more special. This ebony and ivory offering fits the bill in high style.

Chocolate Rancho Roundup Cookies

Corral the kids or some friends for a night of old-fashioned movies and a roundup of these rancho cookies, some hot buttered popcorn, and big mugs of hot cocoa.

1	19.5- to 19.8-ounce package brownie mix
¾	cup old-fashioned or quick-cooking oats
⅔	cup vegetable oil
1	cup creamy peanut butter
2	large eggs
1	cup roasted lightly salted or honey roasted peanuts
1	cup semisweet chocolate chips

Preheat oven to 350°. Spray cookie sheets with nonstick cooking spray.

In a large mixing bowl combine brownie mix, oats, oil, peanut butter, and eggs until well blended; mix in peanuts and chocolate chips. Chill 1 hour.

Shape dough into 2-inch balls; place 2 inches apart on prepared cookie sheets. Flatten slightly with bottom of a glass.

Bake 11–14 minutes, until set at edges and just barely set at center when lightly touched. Cool 1 minute on sheets. Transfer to wire racks with metal spatula and cool completely. Makes about 2½ dozen large cookies.

Peppery Ginger Chocolate Cookies

1	19.5- to 19.8-ounce package brownie mix
2	teaspoons ground ginger
½	teaspoon ground black pepper
½	cup (1 stick) unsalted butter, melted
¼	cup packed dark brown sugar
2	large eggs
⅔	cup very finely chopped crystallized ginger
1	cup semisweet chocolate chips

Preheat oven to 350°. Spray cookie sheets with nonstick cooking spray.

In a large mixing bowl mix the brownie mix, ground ginger, black pepper, melted butter, brown sugar, and eggs with wooden spoon until just blended and all dry ingredients are moistened; mix in crystallized ginger and chocolate chips.

Drop by teaspoonfuls, 2 inches apart, onto prepared cookie sheets.

Bake 9–12 minutes, until cracked in appearance and just barely set at center when lightly touched. Cool 1 minute on sheets. Transfer to wire racks with metal spatula and cool completely. Makes about 4 dozen cookies.

These simple cookies celebrate one of my favorite flavors: ginger. Fragrant and speckled with bits of candied ginger and miniature chocolate chips, these cookies are the ticket for anyone who likes a bit of spice with their chocolate.

Nutty Chocolate Caramel Bull's-Eyes

Not sure which cookie to make for the kids? This is it. They will clamor for this yummy cookie, especially if you get them involved in unwrapping and pressing the choco-late-covered caramel "bull's-eyes" into the center of each treat. And for the record, grown-up "kids" love these cookies, too. Do be sure, however, to cool the cookies com-pletely before serving (the hot caramel may burn tender mouths).

1	19.5- to 19.8-ounce package brownie mix
$\frac{1}{3}$	cup unsweetened cocoa powder, sifted
$\frac{1}{4}$	cup ($\frac{1}{2}$ stick) unsalted butter, melted
2	teaspoons vanilla extract
2	large eggs
1	cup finely chopped nuts (e.g., pecans, peanuts, walnuts, almonds, or macadamia nuts)
54	chocolate-covered caramel candies (e.g., Rolos®), unwrapped

In a medium mixing bowl mix the brownie mix, sifted cocoa powder, melted butter, vanilla, and eggs with a wooden spoon until all dry ingredients are moistened and dough is well blended. Cover bowl with plastic wrap and refrigerate dough at least 1 hour.

Preheat oven to 350°. Spray cookie sheets with nonstick cooking spray.

Place chopped nuts into a shallow dish. Shape dough into 1-inch balls; roll each ball in nuts to coat evenly. Place balls 2 inches apart on prepared cookie sheets.

Bake 9–11 minutes, until firm to the touch at the edges. Remove from oven and immediately press one candy into center of each cookie. Return to oven 1 minute longer to melt candy slightly; remove from oven. Cool 1 minute on sheets. Transfer to wire racks with metal spatula and cool completely. Makes about $4\frac{1}{2}$ dozen cookies.

Chocolate Hermits

1	19.5- to 19.8-ounce package brownie mix
¼	cup packed light brown sugar
2	teaspoons pumpkin pie spice
½	cup (1 stick) unsalted butter, melted
2	large eggs
1	cup semisweet chocolate chips
½	cup raisins or currants
1	cup chopped walnuts or pecans

Hermits are spicy, spunky, cake-like cookies that date back to the early 1800s. Here their appeal is boosted with a double dose of chocolate.

Preheat oven to 350°. Spray cookie sheets with nonstick cooking spray.

In a large mixing bowl mix the brownie mix, brown sugar, pumpkin pie spice, melted butter, and eggs with a wooden spoon until just blended and all dry ingredients are moistened; mix in chocolate chips and raisins.

Drop by teaspoonfuls, 2 inches apart, onto prepared cookie sheets. Sprinkle tops with nuts.

Bake 9–12 minutes, until edges are firm and center is just barely set when lightly touched. Cool 1 minute on sheets. Transfer to wire racks with metal spatula and cool completely. Makes about 4½ dozen cookies.

Chocolate Fudge–Frosted Raspberry Softies

Here thick raspberry fudge frosting gilds almond-accented, cream-cheese chocolate cookies for an irresistible treat. During summer berry season, consider adding a fresh raspberry to the center of each frosted cookie.

1	19.5- to 19.8-ounce package brownie mix
¼	cup (½ stick) unsalted butter, melted
4	ounces (½ of an 8-ounce package) cream cheese, softened
1	large egg
½	teaspoon almond extract
1	recipe Chocolate-Raspberry Frosting (see page 257)

Preheat oven to 350°.

In a medium mixing bowl mix the brownie mix, melted butter, cream cheese, egg, and almond extract with a wooden spoon until all dry ingredients are moistened and well blended (dough will be sticky).

Drop dough by teaspoonfuls, 2 inches apart, onto ungreased cookie sheets; smooth edge of each to form round cookie.

Bake 10–14 minutes or until edges are set. Transfer to wire rack and cool completely.

Prepare Chocolate Raspberry Frosting. Frost cooled cookies. Makes 4 dozen big cookies.

Wicked Whiskey Chocolate Cookies

1   19.5- to 19.8-ounce package brownie mix
¼   cup whiskey
¼   cup (½ stick) unsalted butter, melted
1   large egg
1½   cups semisweet chocolate chunks or chips

1   recipe Chocolate Whiskey Frosting (see page 255)

Preheat oven to 350°. Position racks in lower and upper thirds of oven.

Spray cookie sheets with nonstick cooking spray. In a large mixing bowl mix the brownie mix, whiskey, melted butter, and egg with a wooden spoon until just blended and all dry ingredients are moistened; mix in chocolate chunks.

Drop dough by teaspoonfuls, 2 inches apart, onto prepared cookie sheets.

Bake 9–12 minutes, until cracked in appearance and just barely set at center when lightly touched. Cool 1 minute on sheets. Transfer to wire racks with metal spatula and cool completely.

Prepare Chocolate Whiskey Frosting. Generously frost cooled cookies. Makes about 4 dozen cookies.

It's pretty easy to take your favorite feel-good chocolate cookies from standard to sensational when you add more chocolate and a generous splash of whiskey.

Caramel Pecan Turtle Cookies

If you like the candies called Turtles—milk chocolate, pecan, and caramel clusters— you'll do a cartwheel when you taste these cookies.

1	19.5- to 19.8-ounce package brownie mix
1/3	cup unsweetened cocoa powder, sifted
1/4	cup (1/2 stick) unsalted butter, melted
2	teaspoons vanilla extract
2	large eggs
2	cups whole pecan halves
24	milk caramels, unwrapped
3	tablespoons milk

In a medium mixing bowl mix the brownie mix, sifted cocoa powder, melted butter, vanilla, and eggs with a wooden spoon until all dry ingredients are moistened and dough is well blended. Cover bowl with plastic wrap and refrigerate dough at least 1 hour.

Preheat oven to 350°. Spray cookie sheets with nonstick cooking spray.

Shape dough into 1-inch balls. Place balls 2 inches apart on prepared cookie sheets. Press one whole pecan half in center of each cookie.

Bake 9–11 minutes, until firm to the touch at the edges. Cool 1 minute on sheets. Transfer to wire racks with metal spatula and cool completely.

In a small saucepan set over low heat melt the caramels with the milk, stirring until melted and smooth; remove from heat and let cool. Drizzle caramel across cooled cookies using a spoon or fork. Makes about 4$\frac{1}{2}$ dozen cookies.

Trail Mix Cookies

1	19.5- to 19.8-ounce package brownie mix
½	cup vegetable oil
2	large eggs
⅔	cup quick-cooking oats
½	cup miniature chocolate chips
½	cup mixed dried fruit bits
½	cup roasted, lightly salted sunflower seeds

Preheat oven to 350°. Position racks in lower and upper thirds of oven. Spray cookie sheets with nonstick cooking spray.

In a large mixing bowl mix the brownie mix, oil, eggs, oats, chocolate chips, fruit bits, and sunflower seeds with a wooden spoon until all dry ingredients are moistened.

Drop by teaspoonfuls, 2 inches apart, onto prepared cookie sheets.

Bake 10–12 minutes until cracked in appearance and just barely set at center when lightly touched. Cool 1 minute on sheets. Transfer to wire racks with metal spatula and cool completely. Makes about 4½ dozen cookies.

A great portable cookie, these oat-, fruit-, and seed-filled treats will keep your energy going for a hike up the mountain or a stroll across town. Packages of assorted dried fruit bits can be found alongside raisins in your supermarket. If you cannot find them, raisins, dried cranberries, or chopped dried apricots may be substituted.

Cookies and Bite-Sized Confections

Chocolate Snickerdoodles

Sugar and spice and everything nice are what old-fashioned snickerdoodles are made of. Here the soft, cake-like cookies get a chocolate twist before being rolled in their traditional coating of cinnamon sugar.

1	19.5- to 19.8-ounce package brownie mix
¼	cup (½ stick) unsalted butter, melted
3	large eggs, lightly beaten
1	cup chopped walnuts, preferably lightly toasted
½	cup dried currants
⅔	cup sugar
1	tablespoon ground cinnamon
½	teaspoon ground nutmeg

Preheat oven to 350°. Position racks in lower and upper thirds of oven. Spray cookie sheets with nonstick cooking spray.

In a large mixing bowl mix the brownie mix, melted butter, and eggs with a wooden spoon until just blended and all dry ingredients are moistened; stir in chopped walnuts and currants. Chill dough at least 1 hour.

Combine the sugar, cinnamon, and nutmeg in a shallow dish or bowl. Form dough into 1-inch balls; roll in cinnamon sugar. Place 2 inches apart on prepared cookie sheets.

Bake 9–12 minutes, until set at edges and just barely set at center when lightly touched. Cool 1 minute on sheets. Transfer to wire racks with metal spatula and cool completely. Makes about 4 dozen cookies.

Peanut Butter–Frosted Double Chocolate Cookies

1	19.5- to 19.8-ounce package brownie mix
1/3	cup unsweetened cocoa powder, sifted
1/3	cup vegetable oil or melted butter
1	large egg
2	cups creamy peanut butter, divided
2	cups miniature semisweet chocolate chips, divided
1/4	cup powdered sugar

Preheat oven to 350°. Spray cookie sheets with nonstick cooking spray.

In a large mixing bowl mix the brownie mix, sifted cocoa powder, oil, egg, and 1 cup of the peanut butter with a wooden spoon until well blended (mixture will be very stiff). Mix in half (1 cup) of the chocolate chips. Cover bowl with plastic wrap and chill 1 hour.

Shape dough into 1-inch balls; place 2 inches apart on prepared cookie sheets. Flatten slightly with bottom of a glass.

Bake for 9–11 minutes, until set at edges and just barely set at center when lightly touched. Cool 1 minute on sheets. Transfer to wire racks with metal spatula and cool completely.

While cookies cool, make the icing by combining the remaining 1 cup peanut butter and the powdered sugar in a small mixing bowl. Mix by hand or with electric mixer until smooth. Spread cooled cookies with icing and sprinkle with remaining mini chocolate chips. Makes about 5 dozen cookies.

This is a cookie I know I can count on time and again, year in and year out. With the all-American combination of chocolate and peanut butter, the appeal is decidedly old-fashioned and down-home. It's just what you want from a cookie.

Chocolate Madeleines

Always a favorite in my book, these deeply ridged, delicate madeleines taste like tender little chocolate cakes and look like little shells. They are sure to garner attention on any cookie platter. A madeleine pan is a metal mold with scallop-shaped indentations (like a muffin tray), sold at cookware stores.

Vegetable shortening and all-purpose flour to coat pans

1	19.5- to 19.8-ounce package brownie mix
½	cup (1 stick) unsalted butter, melted
¼	cup water
4	large eggs, separated
2–3	tablespoons powdered sugar or unsweetened cocoa powder

Preheat oven to 350°. Grease molds of large madeleine pan (about 3 x 1¼-inch shell molds) with vegetable shortening. Sprinkle with flour to coat pan, shaking off excess.

In a large mixing bowl combine brownie mix, melted butter, water, and egg yolks until well blended; set aside.

In a medium mixing bowl beat egg whites with electric mixer set on high until soft peaks form. Stir ¼ of the beaten egg whites into the brownie batter to lighten it; fold remaining whites into batter.

Spoon 1 heaping tablespoon batter into center of each indentation in pan (do not overfill; batter will spread as it bakes). Bake until puffed and set at center, about 8–10 minutes. Cool in pan 5 minutes; gently remove madeleines to wire rack. Repeat process, greasing and flouring pan before each batch. Sift powdered sugar or cocoa powder over cooled cookies. Makes about 30 madeleines.

Chocolate-Orange Madeleines

Vegetable shortening and all-purpose flour
to coat pans

1	19.5- to 19.8-ounce package brownie mix
½	cup (1 stick) unsalted butter, melted
¼	cup fresh-squeezed orange juice
4	large eggs, separated
2	teaspoons grated orange zest
2–3	tablespoons unsweetened cocoa powder

Preheat oven to 350°. Grease molds of large madeleine pan (about 3 x 1¼-inch shell molds) with vegetable shortening. Sprinkle with flour to coat pan, shaking off excess.

In a large mixing bowl, combine brownie mix, melted butter, orange juice, egg yolks, and orange zest until well blended; set aside.

In a medium mixing bowl beat egg whites with electric mixer set on high until soft peaks form. Stir ¼ of the beaten egg whites into the brownie batter to lighten it; fold remaining whites into batter.

Spoon 1 heaping tablespoon batter into center of each indentation in pan (do not overfill; batter will spread as it bakes). Bake until puffed and set at center, about 8–10 minutes. Cool in pan 5 minutes; gently remove madeleines to wire rack. Repeat process, greasing and flouring pan before each batch. Sift cocoa powder over cooled cookies. Makes about 30 madeleines.

Ideal for coffee with a friend, these orange-accented chocolate madeleines are also elegant enough for a dinner party dessert. A dunk in dark, milk, or white chocolate makes a delicious and beautiful final flourish in place of the dusting of cocoa powder.

Brownie Biscotti

Prepare for the best chocolate biscotti you have ever tasted. These biscotti are exactly the way I prefer all biscotti: dense, crunchy and very dunk-able. For complete chocolate euphoria, dip, spread or drizzle each biscotti with melted semisweet, milk, or white choco-late. These make great gifts because they keep well and look fes-tive wrapped in tinted cellophane bags tied with a silk ribbon or raffia, or packed into petite holiday bags.

1	19.5- to 19.8-ounce package brownie mix
1	cup all-purpose flour
½	cup (1 stick) unsalted butter, melted and cooled
2	large eggs
1	cup very coarsely chopped nuts (e.g., walnuts, pecans, macadamia nuts), optional
1	recipe Chocolate Dip (see page 247), optional

Preheat oven to 350°. Position rack in center of oven. Line a cookie sheet with parchment paper.

In a large mixing bowl combine the brownie mix, flour, melted butter, eggs, and nuts, if desired. Blend with an electric mixer set on low until well blended, about 1–2 minutes, scrap-ing down sides of bowl (mixture will be stiff).

Transfer dough to prepared cookie sheet. With floured hands, shape dough into 2 rectangles, each 14 inches long by 3 inches wide, and ¾-inch thick, spacing about 4–5 inches apart on sheet. Mound the dough so it is slightly higher in the center than at the edges. Place cookie sheet in oven.

Bake 30–35 minutes, until firm to touch; remove from oven and cool on sheet for 10 minutes, (leave oven on).

With spatula, transfer logs to cutting board. Use a sharp kitchen knife to slice each rectangle into (approximately) ¾-inch slices on the diagonal. Return slices to sheet, cut sides down.

Return sheet to oven. Bake biscotti 10 minutes. Turn oven off and let biscotti remain in oven until crisp, about 30–40 minutes longer. Remove from oven and transfer biscotti to a rack. Cool completely. If desired, prepare Chocolate Dip and with a butter knife or small offset spatula spread over one side of each biscotti. Place on waxed paper–lined cookie sheet and refrigerate at least 1 hour to set chocolate. Store in an airtight container or plastic ziplock bag for up to 3 weeks. Makes about 32 biscotti.

Coffee Toffee Chocolate Biscotti

1	19.5- to 19.8-ounce package brownie mix
1	cup all-purpose flour
1	tablespoon instant coffee or espresso powder
½	cup (1 stick) unsalted butter, melted and cooled
2	large eggs
1	cup English toffee baking bits
1	recipe Chocolate Dip (see page 247; optional)

You'll want to keep a stash of these handy for yourself or for very, very good friends.

Preheat oven to 350°. Position rack in center of oven. Line a cookie sheet with parchment paper.

In a large mixing bowl combine the brownie mix, flour, coffee powder, melted butter, eggs, and toffee bits. Blend with an electric mixer set on low until well blended, about 1–2 minutes, scraping down sides of bowl (mixture will be stiff).

Transfer dough to prepared cookie sheet. With floured hands, shape dough into 2 rectangles, each 14 inches long by 3 inches wide, and ¾-inch thick, spacing about 4–5 inches apart on sheet. Mound the dough so it is slightly higher in the center than at the edges. Place cookie sheet in oven.

Bake 30–35 minutes, until firm to touch; remove from oven and cool on sheet for 10 minutes (leave oven on).

With spatula, transfer logs to cutting board. Use a sharp kitchen knife to slice each rectangle into (approximately) ¾-inch slices on the diagonal. Return slices to sheet, cut sides down.

Return sheet to oven. Bake biscotti 10 minutes. Turn oven off and let biscotti remain in oven until crisp, about 30–40 minutes longer. Remove from oven and transfer biscotti to a rack. Cool completely. If desired, prepare Chocolate Dip and with a butter knife or small offset spatula spread over one side of each biscotti. Place on waxed paper–lined cookie sheet and refrigerate at least 1 hour to set chocolate. Store in an airtight container or plastic ziplock bag for up to 3 weeks. Makes about 32 biscotti.

Gorgeous White Chocolate–Dipped Coconut Brownie Biscotti

If you decide to give these decked-out beauties as gifts, package them prettily, perhaps in decorative tins or in clear cellophane bags festooned with ribbons. For a bonus, include the recipe on your gift card.

1	7-ounce bag (about 2⅔ cups) shredded coconut, divided
1	19.5- to 19.8-ounce package brownie mix
1	cup all-purpose flour
½	cup (1 stick) unsalted butter, melted and cooled
2	large eggs
1	recipe White Chocolate Dip (see page 247)

Preheat oven to 350°. Position rack in center of oven. Line a cookie sheet with parchment paper.

Finely chop 1 cup of the coconut by hand or in food processor. In a large bowl combine the chopped coconut, brownie mix, flour, melted butter, and eggs. Blend with an electric mixer set on low until well blended, about 1–2 minutes, scraping down sides of bowl (mixture will be stiff).

Transfer dough to prepared cookie sheet. With floured hands, shape dough into two rectangles, each 14 inches long by 3 inches wide, and ¾-inch thick, spacing about 4–5 inches apart on sheet. Mound the dough so it is slightly higher in the center than at the edges. Place cookie sheet in oven.

Bake 30–35 minutes, until firm to touch; remove from oven and cool on sheet for 10 minutes (leave oven on).

With spatula, transfer logs to cutting board. Use a sharp kitchen knife to slice each rectangle into (approximately) ¾-inch slices on the diagonal. Return slices to sheet, cut sides down.

Return sheet to oven. Bake biscotti 10 minutes. Turn oven off and let biscotti remain in oven until crisp, about 30–40 minutes longer. Remove from oven and transfer biscotti to a rack. Cool completely.

Spread cookie sheet with waxed paper. Prepare White Chocolate Dip. With a butter knife or small offset spatula, spread one side of each biscotti with melted chocolate. Immediately sprinkle with some of the remaining coconut, shaking off excess. Place on waxed paper. Refrigerate at least 1 hour to set chocolate. Store in an airtight container or plastic ziplock bag for up to 3 weeks. Makes about 32 biscotti.

Cinnamon Stick Chocolate Biscotti

After a brisk winter day, these cinnamon-laced biscotti, paired with steaming mugs of marshmallow-topped cocoa, are just the ticket to warm up a crowd.

1	19.5- to 19.8-ounce package brownie mix
1	cup all-purpose flour
1½	teaspoons ground cinnamon
½	cup (1 stick) unsalted butter, melted and cooled
2	large eggs
1	recipe Chocolate Dip made with cinnamon chips (see page 247)

Preheat oven to 350°. Position rack in center of oven. Line a cookie sheet with parchment paper.

In a large mixing bowl place the brownie mix, flour, cinnamon, melted butter, and eggs. Blend with an electric mixer set on low until well blended, about 1-2 minutes, scraping down sides of bowl (mixture will be stiff).

Transfer dough to prepared cookie sheet. With floured hands, shape dough into two rectangles, each 14 inches long by 3 inches wide, ¾-inch thick, spacing about 4–5 inches apart on sheet. Mound the dough so it is slightly higher in the center than at the edges. Place cookie sheet in oven.

Bake 30–35 minutes, until firm to touch; remove from oven and cool on sheet for 10 minutes, (leave oven on).

With spatula, transfer logs to cutting board. Use a sharp kitchen knife to slice each rectangle into (approximately) ¾-inch slices on the diagonal. Return slices to sheet, cut sides down.

Return baking sheet to oven. Bake biscotti 10 minutes. Turn oven off and let biscotti remain in oven until crisp, about 30–40 minutes longer. Remove from oven and transfer biscotti to a rack. Cool completely.

If desired, prepare Cinnamon Chocolate Dip and with a butter knife or small offset spatula spread over one side of each biscotti. Place on waxed paper–lined cookie sheet and refrigerate at least 1 hour to set melted chips. Store in an airtight container or plastic ziplock bag for up to 3 weeks. Makes about 32 biscotti.

Christmas Cranberry-Pistachio Biscotti

1	19.5- to 19.8-ounce package brownie mix
1	cup all-purpose flour
½	cup (1 stick) unsalted butter, melted and cooled
2	large eggs
¾	cup coarsely chopped dried cranberries
1	cup shelled pistachios
2	teaspoons grated orange zest
1	recipe White Chocolate Dip (see page 247; optional)

Preheat oven to 350°. Position rack in center of oven. Line a cookie sheet with parchment paper.

In a large mixing bowl combine the brownie mix, flour, melted butter, eggs, cranberries, pistachios, and orange zest. Blend with an electric mixer set on low until well blended, about 1–2 minutes, scraping down sides of bowl (mixture will be stiff).

Transfer dough to prepared cookie sheet. With floured hands, shape dough into two rectangles, each 14 inches long by 3 inches wide, and ¾-inch thick, spacing about 4–5 inches apart on sheet. Mound the dough so it is slightly higher in the center than at the edges. Place cookie sheet in oven.

Bake 30–35 minutes, until firm to touch; remove from oven and cool 10 minutes (leave oven on).

With spatula, transfer logs to cutting board. Use a sharp kitchen knife to slice each rectangle into (approximately) ¾-inch slices on the diagonal. Return slices to sheet, cut sides down.

Return baking sheet to oven. Bake biscotti 10 minutes. Turn oven off and let biscotti remain in oven until crisp, about 30-40 minutes longer. Remove from oven and transfer biscotti to a rack. Cool completely. If desired, prepare White Chocolate Dip, and with a butter knife or small offset spatula spread over one side of each biscotti. Place on waxed paper–lined cookie sheet and refrigerate at least 1 hour to set chocolate. Store in an airtight container or plastic ziplock bag for up to 3 weeks. Makes about 32 biscotti.

Dotted with ruby-red cranberries and bright green pistachios, these bejeweled biscotti are a must-make when the temperature goes down and the holiday decorations go up.

Charlotte's Ginger-Jeweled Chocolate Biscotti

My mother is as crazy about ginger as I am, so this boldly spiced biscotti recipe is just for her. Two kinds of ginger give these cookies a lively hit of heat.

1	19.5- to 19.8-ounce package brownie mix
1	cup all-purpose flour
2½	teaspoons ground ginger
½	cup (1 stick) unsalted butter, melted and cooled
2	large eggs
⅔	cup finely chopped crystallized ginger

Preheat oven to 350°. Position rack in center of oven. Line a cookie sheet with parchment paper.

In a large bowl combine the brownie mix, flour, ground ginger, melted butter, eggs, and crystallized ginger. Blend with an electric mixer set on low until well blended, about 1–2 minutes, scraping down sides of bowl (mixture will be stiff).

Transfer dough to prepared cookie sheet. With floured hands, shape dough into two rectangles, each 14 inches long by 3 inches wide, and ¾-inch thick, spacing about 4–5 inches apart on sheet. Mound the dough so it is slightly higher in the center than at the edges. Place cookie sheet in oven.

Bake 30–35 minutes until firm to touch; remove from oven and cool on sheet for 10 minutes (leave oven on).

With spatula, transfer logs to cutting board. Use a sharp kitchen knife to slice each rectangle into ¾-inch slices on the diagonal. Return to sheet, cut sides down.

Return baking sheet to oven. Bake biscotti 10 minutes. Turn oven off and let biscotti remain in oven until crisp, about 30–40 minutes longer. Remove from oven and transfer biscotti to a rack. Cool completely. Store in an airtight container or plastic ziplock bag for up to 3 weeks. Makes about 32 biscotti.

Almond-Orange Chocolate Biscotti

1	19.5- to 19.8-ounce package brownie mix
1	cup all-purpose flour
½	cup (1 stick) unsalted butter, melted and cooled
2	large eggs
1	tablespoon grated orange zest
1	teaspoon almond extract
1	cup coarsely chopped whole almonds

Combining two classic biscotti flavors in a dark chocolate dough, these biscotti are great for tea and coffee breaks, not to mention gift-giving.

Preheat oven to 350°. Position rack in center of oven. Line a cookie sheet with parchment paper.

In a large mixing bowl combine the brownie mix, flour, melted butter, eggs, orange zest, almond extract, and almonds. Blend with an electric mixer set on low until well blended, about 1–2 minutes, scraping down sides of bowl (mixture will be stiff).

Transfer dough to prepared cookie sheet. With floured hands, shape dough into two rectangles, each 14 inches long by 3 inches wide, and ¾-inch thick, spacing about 4–5 inches apart on sheet. Mound the dough so it is slightly higher in the center than at the edges. Place cookie sheet in oven.

Bake 30–35 minutes, until firm to touch; remove from oven and cool on sheet for 10 minutes (leave oven on).

With spatula, transfer logs to cutting board. Use a sharp kitchen knife to slice each rectangle into ¾-inch slices on the diagonal. Return to sheet, cut sides down.

Return baking sheet to oven. Bake biscotti 10 minutes. Turn oven off and let biscotti remain in oven until crisp, about 30–40 minutes longer. Remove from oven and transfer biscotti to a rack. Cool completely. Store in an airtight container or plastic ziplock bag for up to 3 weeks. Makes about 32 biscotti.

Chocolate-Dipped Brownie "Truffles"

These double chocolate confections—part candy, part brownie—are melt-in-your-mouth good. Just one is eminently satisfactory. Beautiful plain, they are fun to personalize with sprinkles, nuts, or edible glitter.

1	19.5- to 19.8-ounce package brownie mix
½	cup vegetable oil
¼	cup water
2	large eggs
1	8-ounce box semisweet baking chocolate squares, coarsely chopped
1	14-ounce can sweetened condensed milk
1	teaspoon vanilla extract
1	tablespoon unsalted butter
	Decorations: chopped nuts, candy sprinkles, white chocolate or confectioner's (edible) glitter (optional)

Preheat oven to 350° (325° for dark-coated metal pan). Position a rack in the lower third of the oven. Spray the bottom only of a 13 x 9-inch baking pan with nonstick cooking spray (or foil-line pan; see page 11).

In a medium mixing bowl mix the brownie mix, oil, water, and eggs with a wooden spoon until just blended and all dry ingredients are moistened. Spread batter into prepared pan.

Bake 28–30 minutes, until just set at center (do not overbake). Transfer brownies to a wire rack and immediately cut into 48 pieces. Working quickly, roll each piece into a ball; place on wire racks and cool completely.

In heavy saucepan or double broiler over low heat melt chocolate with condensed milk, stirring until smooth. Turn heat to lowest possible setting; stir in vanilla and butter.

Place one brownie ball at a time on a fork; dip into chocolate and coat thoroughly. Place on rack for excess chocolate to drip off. If desired, sprinkle truffles with nuts, white chocolate, or decorator candies. Refrigerate at least 1 hour to set the chocolate. Store in refrigerator. Makes 48 truffles.

Chocolate Peppermint Petits Fours

1	19.5- to 19.8-ounce package brownie mix
½	cup plus 2 tablespoons vegetable oil, divided
¼	cup water
2	large eggs
1¾	cups crushed red and white peppermint hard candies or candy canes, divided
1	cup semisweet chocolate chips
1	16-ounce tub ready-to-spread chocolate frosting
¾	teaspoon peppermint extract

Preheat oven to 350°. Line a 13 x 9-inch pan with foil, extending foil over sides of pan (see page 11); spray bottom of foil with nonstick cooking spray.

In a large mixing bowl mix the brownie mix, ½ cup of the vegetable oil, water, and eggs with a wooden spoon until just blended and all dry ingredients are moistened; stir in 1 cup crushed candies. Spread batter into prepared pan.

Bake 28–30 minutes or until toothpick inserted 2 inches from side of pan comes out clean or almost clean (do not overbake). Transfer to a wire rack and cool completely. Cover in foil and freeze brownies 30 minutes.

Remove brownies from pan by lifting foil. Trim off crusty edges. Cut brownies into 1-inch squares. Return to freezer while preparing icing.

In a medium-sized, heavy-bottomed saucepan set over low heat melt chocolate chips and remaining 2 tablespoons vegetable oil. Cook and stir until melted and smooth. Stir in frosting and peppermint extract. Heat 1–2 minutes or until well blended and smooth, stirring constantly. Remove from heat.

To coat each brownie with icing, place brownie on a fork and hold over the saucepan; spoon icing over brownie, coating all sides except bottom. (If icing thickens, heat over low heat until of desired consistency.) Place petits fours on plate. Sprinkle with remaining ¾ cup crushed candies. Refrigerate at least 1 hour to set coating. Makes about 4 dozen petits fours.

I love a recipe that delivers an impressive result without much fuss. These petits fours, a simple but sophisticated nibble, fit the bill. The crushed candies are ideal decorations (easy, affordable, and pretty) if serving the petits fours as part of a winter holiday dessert buffet. For a spring gathering, consider substituting orange extract for the mint extract, then finish by using small tubes of decorator icing (available in the baking section of the supermarket) to pipe on some pastel ribbons.

Lemon–White Chocolate Petits Fours

These raspberry-

accented, lemon white

chocolate–coated

petits fours are the

perfect choice for

baby and bridal show-

ers. If you're feeling

particularly ambitious,

you can even fill each

petit four with seed-

less raspberry jam. The

easiest way to do this

is to split the 13 x 9-

inch brownie in half

1	19.5- to 19.8-ounce package brownie mix
½	cup plus 2 tablespoons vegetable oil, divided
¼	cup raspberry liqueur or cranberry-raspberry juice
2	large eggs
1	cup white chocolate chips
1	16-ounce tub ready-to-spread white cake frosting
1½	teaspoons lemon extract
	Decorator frosting, fresh raspberries, gold edible glitter

Preheat oven to 350°. Line 13 x 9-inch pan with foil, extending foil over sides of pan (see page 11); spray bottom of foil with nonstick cooking spray.

In a large mixing bowl mix brownie mix, ½ cup of the oil, liqueur, and eggs with a wooden spoon until just blended and all dry ingredients are moistened. Spread batter into prepared pan.

Bake 28–30 minutes or until toothpick inserted 2 inches from side of pan comes out clean or almost clean (do not over-bake). Transfer to a wire rack and cool completely. Cover in foil and freeze brownies 30 minutes.

Remove brownies from pan by lifting foil. Trim off crusty edges. Cut brownies into 1-inch squares. Return to freezer while preparing icing.

In a medium-sized, heavy-bottomed saucepan set over low heat melt white chocolate chips and remaining 2 tablespoons vegetable oil. Cook and stir until melted and smooth. Stir in frosting and lemon extract. Heat 1–2 minutes or until well blended and smooth, stirring constantly. Remove from heat.

To coat each brownie with icing, place brownie on fork over saucepan; spoon icing over brownie, coating all sides except bottom. (If icing thickens, heat over low heat until of desired consistency.) Place petits fours on plate. Decorate as desired with decorator frosting or top each petits four with a fresh raspberry and a sprinkle of edible gold glitter. Refrigerate at least 1 hour to set coating. Makes about 4 dozen petits fours.

with a serrated knife; spread with ⅔ cup jam and replace with second half. Freeze 30 minutes and then proceed as directed.

Brownie Macaroons

I love a good maca-
roon, especially one
with a slightly crisp
exterior and a chewy
interior. Rich and deli-
cious, this version
does it. The added
bonus of chocolate
takes these macaroons
in a delectable new
direction.

1	19.5- to 19.8-ounce package brownie mix
1	7-ounce package (2⅔ cups) sweetened shredded coconut
3	tablespoons vegetable oil
2	tablespoons water
2	large eggs
1	teaspoon almond extract

Preheat oven to 350°. Spray cookie sheets with nonstick cook-ing spray.

In a large mixing bowl combine brownie mix and coconut; mix well. Mix in the oil, water, eggs, and almond extract with a wooden spoon until all dry ingredients are moistened (dough will be stiff).

Shape dough into 1-inch balls. Place 2 inches apart on pre-pared cookie sheets; flatten slightly with bottom of a glass.

Bake 10–12 minutes or until edges are set (centers will be slightly soft.) Transfer cookies to wire rack with metal spatula and cool completely. Makes about 5 dozen cookies.

Chapter 4
Assorted
Brownie Desserts

Caramel–White Chocolate Brownie Pie

Finish eating a slice of this outrageously decadent dessert and you'll want to stretch out on the sofa with an audible sigh. Or maybe you'll want to get up for a second helping.

1	8-ounce package cream cheese, softened
1	12-ounce jar caramel ice cream topping, divided
3	large eggs
1	19.5- to 19.8-ounce package brownie mix
¼	cup vegetable oil
1	tablespoon water
1	10-inch unbaked frozen deep-dish pie crust (do not thaw)
1	cup white chocolate chips, divided
½	cup chopped pecans

Preheat oven to 350°. Position a rack in the lower third of the oven.

In a medium mixing bowl beat cream cheese, 2 tablespoons caramel topping, and 1 of the eggs with electric mixer set on medium until blended and smooth. Set aside.

In a medium mixing bowl mix the brownie mix, oil, water, and remaining 2 eggs with a wooden spoon until just blended and all dry ingredients are moistened. Stir in ½ cup of the white chocolate chips.

Spread ½ cup brownie mixture in bottom of crust. Spoon and carefully spread cream cheese mixture over brownie layer; drizzle with ½ cup of caramel topping. Top with remaining brownie mixture; spread evenly. Sprinkle with remaining white chocolate chips and pecans.

Bake 43–48 minutes or until center is puffed and crust is golden brown. If desired, place foil strips around crust edge during last 25 minutes of baking time to avoid overbrowning. Transfer to wire rack and cool. Drizzle remaining caramel over top of pie. Serve warm or completely cooled. Store in refrigerator. Makes 8 servings.

Brownie Soufflé Cake with One-Step Custard Sauce

All-purpose flour for dusting pan
1 **19.5- to 19.8-ounce package brownie mix**
½ **cup milk**
½ **cup (1 stick) butter, melted**
4 **large eggs, separated**
1–2 **tablespoons powdered sugar or unsweetened cocoa powder**
1 **cup premium vanilla or coffee ice cream, melted**

Preheat oven to 375°. Spray a 9- or 10-inch springform pan with nonstick cooking spray; dust with flour.

Meanwhile, in a large mixing bowl combine brownie mix, milk, melted butter, and egg yolks with a wooden spoon until blended and all dry ingredients are moistened; set aside.

In a medium mixing bowl beat egg whites with electric mixer set on high until soft peaks form. Gradually fold into brownie mixture. Pour batter into prepared pan.

Bake 33–38 minutes or until center is almost set. Cool 30 minutes (center will sink slightly). Carefully remove sides of pan. Sift top of cake with powdered sugar or unsweetened cocoa powder.

Just before serving, spoon some of the melted ice cream onto each plate. Cut cake into wedges and place one piece on each prepared plate. Makes 8 servings.

Imagine your favorite dark chocolate brownies puffed up into a light and airy cake—here it is. And yes, melted vanilla ice cream makes a dreamy accompanying custard sauce. Use the ice cream flavor of your choice. For some crowning touches, garnish the plates with fresh berries and mint sprigs.

Marbled Chocolate & Vanilla Brownie Cake

I'm very fond of this cake, which I would describe as quintessential comfort food. Simple to make but beautiful in presentation, it is a grand solution for those who cannot decide between chocolate brownies and vanilla cake.

1	19.5- to 19.8-ounce package brownie mix
3	large eggs
¼	cup water
½	cup vegetable oil
2	8-ounce packages cream cheese, softened
1	18.25-ounce package white cake mix
2	teaspoons vanilla extract
1	cup milk

Preheat oven to 350°. Position a rack in the lower third of the oven. Spray a 15 x 10 x 1-inch baking pan with cooking spray; set aside.

In a medium mixing bowl mix the brownie mix, eggs, water, and oil with a wooden spoon until blended and all dry ingredients are moistened. Spread half of the batter into prepared pan.

In a medium mixing bowl beat the cream cheese with an electric mixer set on high until smooth. Gradually beat in the cake mix, vanilla, and milk until well blended, stopping the mixer periodically to scrape down the sides of the bowl. Spoon the mixture atop brownie batter in pan. Spoon remaining brownie batter over cake batter. Draw a knife through the layers of batter to marbleize.

Bake 25–30 minutes or until toothpick inserted near center comes out clean. Transfer to a wire rack; cool completely. Cut into bars or squares. Makes 36 large or 48 small servings.

Chocolate-Chip Brownie Trifle

1	19.5- to 19.8-ounce package brownie mix
½	cup vegetable oil
¼	cup water
3	large eggs
2	cups miniature semisweet chocolate chips, divided
1	8-serving-size package chocolate instant pudding and pie filling mix
2⅔	cups cold milk
1	2-cup recipe Sweetened Whipped Cream (see page 269) or 2 cups frozen whipped topping, thawed

Looking for an alternative to birthday cake? This may be exactly what you're looking for. Here the traditional trifle gets several new twists that are definitely worthy of celebration: brownies in place of cake, layers of dark chocolate pudding, a scattering of chocolate chips, and a crown of whipped cream.

Preheat oven to 350° (325° for dark-coated metal pan). Position a rack in the lower third of the oven. Spray the bottom only of a 13 x 9-inch baking pan with nonstick cooking spray (or foil-line pan; see page 11).

In a medium mixing bowl mix the brownie mix, oil, water, and eggs with a wooden spoon until just blended and all dry ingredients are moistened; stir in ¾ cup chocolate chips. Spread batter into prepared pan.

Bake 28–30 minutes or until toothpick inserted 2 inches from side of pan comes out clean or almost clean (do not overbake). Transfer brownies to a wire rack and cool completely. Cut cooled brownies into 1-inch squares; set aside.

In a medium mixing bowl whisk the pudding mix with milk until pudding begins to thicken; set aside. Stir 1 cup of the remaining chocolate chips into the Sweetened Whipped Cream or whipped topping (reserving last ¼ cup for top).

Place half of the brownie squares in the bottom of a 3-quart glass bowl or trifle dish. Spread half of pudding over brownies in bowl followed by half of the whipped cream. Repeat with remaining brownies, pudding, and whipped cream. Sprinkle with reserved ¼ cup chocolate chips. Cover and refrigerate at least 2 hours before serving. Makes 10–12 servings.

Triple Chocolate Pudding Cake

Presenting the ultimate treat for the die-hard chocolate fan. It's part chocolate pudding, part chocolate cake, and 100 percent chocolate delirium.

1	19.5- to 19.8-ounce package brownie mix
½	teaspoon baking powder
½	cup milk
⅓	cup butter, melted
1	teaspoon vanilla extract
1½	cups water
1½	teaspoons instant espresso or coffee powder
1	cup ready-to-spread chocolate frosting (from a 16-ounce tub)
1	recipe Sweetened Whipped Cream (see page 269) or vanilla ice cream (optional)

Preheat oven to 350° (325° for dark-coated metal pan). Position a rack in the lower third of the oven. Spray the bottom only of an 8-inch square baking pan with nonstick cooking spray.

In a medium mixing bowl combine the brownie mix and baking powder; mix in milk, melted butter, and vanilla with a wooden spoon until just blended and all dry ingredients are moistened. Spread batter into prepared pan.

In a medium saucepan set over medium heat bring the water to a boil. Add the espresso powder and frosting; cook and stir over low heat until melted and smooth. Slowly pour over batter in pan. Do not stir.

Bake 40–45 minutes or until edges are bubbly and cake begins to pull away from sides of pan (the top of the cake may appear shiny in spots). Transfer to a wire rack and cool 30 minutes. Serve warm or cooled with Sweetened Whipped Cream or ice cream. Store in refrigerator. Makes 8 servings.

Chocolate-Chip Brownie Cones

1	19.5- to 19.8-ounce package brownie mix
½	cup vegetable oil
¼	cup water
3	large eggs
2	cups semisweet chocolate chips, divided
12	flat-bottom wafer ice cream cones
2	teaspoons vegetable shortening
	Assorted candy sprinkles (optional)

Preheat oven to 350°. Position a rack in the lower third of the oven.

In a medium mixing bowl mix the brownie mix, oil, water, and eggs with a wooden spoon until just blended and all dry ingredients are moistened; stir in 1 cup of the chocolate chips. Divide batter between the 12 cones. Stand the cones upright in a standard-size muffin pan (2¾ x 1¼-inch muffin cups).

Bake 25–30 minutes or until toothpick inserted in center comes out clean or almost clean (do not overbake). Transfer pan to a wire rack and cool completely.

In a small saucepan set over low heat melt the remaining 1 cup chocolate chips with the vegetable shortening, stirring until melted and smooth. Remove from heat. Dip tops of brownie cones into melted chocolate. Stand cones upright and sprinkle with assorted sprinkles. Place in refrigerator 30 minutes to set the chocolate. Makes 12 cones.

Chocoholics will undoubtedly delight in these whimsical brownies. If you're into balancing acts, plant a scoop of ice cream atop the brownie just before serving.

Boston Brownie Cream Pie

Growing up, my mother was an avid Co-op shopper and I was fortunate enough to accompany her there most Saturday mornings for her weekly shopping trip. The best part of the expedition was the final turn to the cash registers because we would pass through the Co-op's wonderful in-house bakery where, more often than not, Mom would pick up one of their scrumptious Boston cream pies for dessert. Golden cake, vanilla custard filling and a dark chocolate glaze smoothed over the top—I've never forgotten how good they were. Here I've created a simplified chocolate version, equally unforgettable, and one you'll want to make again and again.

1	19.5- to 19.8-ounce package brownie mix
3	large eggs
½	cup vegetable oil
1½	cups cold milk, divided
1	3.5-ounce package instant vanilla pudding and pie filling
¼	cup (½ stick) unsalted butter, melted
½	cup unsweetened cocoa powder
1	cup powdered sugar
1	teaspoon vanilla extract
¼	cup hot water

Preheat oven to 350°. Spray 2 9-inch round baking pans with nonstick cooking spray.

In a medium mixing bowl mix the brownie mix, eggs, oil, and ¼ cup of the milk with a wooden spoon until blended and all dry ingredients are moistened. Divide batter evenly between prepared pans, smoothing tops.

Bake for 21–24 minutes, until just set at edges of pans. Transfer to a wire rack and cool completely.

In a small mixing bowl whisk the pudding mix and remaining 1¼ cups cold milk until blended and just starting to thicken. Refrigerate at least 5 minutes to thicken.

Place one brownie layer on serving plate; spread with thickened pudding and top with second brownie layer. Place in refrigerator while preparing glaze.

In a small mixing bowl whisk the melted butter, cocoa powder, powdered sugar, vanilla, and hot water until smooth. Pour glaze over top of cake, smoothing over top and allowing glaze to drip over sides. Refrigerate at least 30 minutes before serving. Makes 10–12 servings.

Nutty Drumstick Ice Cream Bars

1	19.5- to 19.8-ounce package brownie mix
½	cup vegetable oil
¼	cup water
2	large eggs
2	cups lightly salted roasted peanuts, coarsely chopped, divided
1	quart vanilla ice cream, softened slightly
1	16-ounce jar chocolate fudge ice cream topping
1	4-ounce package sugar cones (12 cones), coarsely crushed

Preheat oven to 350° (325° for dark-coated metal pan). Position a rack in the lower third of the oven. Foil-line a 13 x 9-inch pan (see page 11). Lightly spray bottom only with non-stick cooking spray.

In a medium mixing bowl mix the brownie mix, oil, water, and eggs with a wooden spoon until just blended and all dry ingredients are moistened; stir in 1 cup of the chopped peanuts. Spread batter into prepared pan.

Bake 28–30 minutes or until toothpick inserted 2 inches from side of pan comes out clean or almost clean (do not over-bake). Transfer brownies to a wire rack and cool completely.

Spread the softened ice cream evenly over the cooled brownies. Loosely cover with foil and freeze 20 minutes. Meanwhile, warm the fudge sauce in a small saucepan set over low heat until smooth and spreadable, but not hot. Remove bars from freezer and spread evenly with fudge sauce. Sprinkle with the crushed cones and remaining cup of chopped peanuts; press gently into fudge sauce. Cover with foil and freeze at least 4 hours, until firm.

To serve, remove from freezer and let stand 5 minutes (for easier cutting). Remove using foil liner. Cut into squares. Makes 24 big bars.

As the name implies, these yummy ice cream treats have the flavor of the classic frozen cone. They're great for big gatherings because everyone, of every age, will love them. For easiest presentation at your gathering, cut into bars ahead of time, arrange on a platter, then cover and return to the freezer until serving time. And to soften the ice cream for the assembly, simply place it in the refrigerator 15–20 minutes, until spreadable but not melted.

Raspberry Dark Chocolate Ganache Tart

Raspberries and dark chocolate are my idea of simple elegance under any circumstance. Here the liqueur-spiked ganache does double duty, spread over the torte's top for drama and layered under the filling for a sweet surprise. Orange liqueur or brandy may be substituted for the raspberry liqueur, depending on what you have available.

1½	cups gingersnap crumbs
2	tablespoons packed dark brown sugar
10	tablespoons (1¼ sticks) unsalted butter, melted, divided
1	cup heavy whipping cream
5	tablespoons raspberry liqueur, divided
2	cups semisweet chocolate chips
1	19.5- to 19.8-ounce package brownie mix
3	large egg whites
2	cups (1 pint) fresh raspberries
1	2-cup recipe Sweetened Whipped Cream (see page 269) or vanilla ice cream (optional)

Spray bottom only of 10-inch springform pan with nonstick cooking spray. In a medium mixing bowl mix gingersnap crumbs, brown sugar, and 4 tablespoons melted butter with fork until crumbs are coated. Press in bottom of prepared pan; set aside.

In a medium saucepan heat whipping cream over medium-low heat until hot but not boiling. Stir in 2 tablespoons liqueur. Whisk in chocolate chips until melted and smooth; remove from heat. Set aside 1 cup chocolate mixture in a small bowl for topping. Carefully spread remaining chocolate mixture over crust. Freeze crust 20 minutes.

Meanwhile, preheat oven to 325°. In a large mixing bowl mix the brownie mix, remaining 6 tablespoons melted butter, and remaining 3 tablespoons liqueur with a wooden spoon until just blended and all dry ingredients are moistened. In small mixing bowl beat egg whites with electric mixer set on high 1–2 minutes or until soft peaks form. Add to brownie mixture, and beat with electric mixer set on low until just blended (batter will appear lumpy).

Remove crust from freezer. Spread batter over chocolate layer. Bake 45–50 minutes or until center is puffed and set and edges are firm (middle will be slightly soft; do not overbake) Transfer to wire rack and cool completely.

Run knife around edge of pan; remove side. In a small saucepan reheat reserved chocolate mixture over low heat until drizzling consistency. Spoon and spread over top of tart, letting it run down the sides. Garnish top with raspberries. Refrigerate at least 30 minutes to set the chocolate. Makes 8 servings.

Chocolate Fudge Banana Baby Cakes

Update your dessert menu with these dainty banana fudge cakes. Whether you're hosting a birthday party, bridal shower, or just having friends over for dinner, these sassy and surprisingly simple treats will surely delight everyone who is lucky enough to get one.

½   cup (1 stick) unsalted butter
1¼   cups semisweet chocolate chips
1   19.5- to 19.8-ounce package brownie mix
1   cup (about 2½ medium) mashed bananas
2   teaspoons vanilla extract
3   large eggs
1   12-ounce jar chocolate fudge ice cream topping
1   cup chopped pecans or macadamia nuts
        Sifted powdered sugar (optional)
        Vanilla ice cream (optional)

Preheat oven to 350°. Position a rack in the lower third of the oven. Spray 12 2¾ x 1¼-inch nonstick muffin cups with non-stick cooking spray.

In a small saucepan set over low heat melt the butter with the chocolate chips, whisking to blend (need not be perfectly blended). In a medium mixing bowl mix the chocolate-butter mixture, brownie mix, mashed bananas, vanilla, and eggs with a wooden spoon until just blended and all dry ingredients are moistened. Divide half of the batter evenly into sprayed muffin cups (cups will be slightly less than half full).

Spoon 1 teaspoon chocolate fudge topping into center of batter in each muffin cup. Top with remaining batter. Sprinkle pecans over batter; press in gently.

Bake 21–25 minutes or until edges are set (centers will still be slightly soft). Transfer to wire rack; cool 3 minutes in pan. Run knife around edge of each cake to loosen; remove from muffin cups.

Warm remaining chocolate fudge topping in small saucepan set over low heat. Place cakes on serving plates and drizzle with warm fudge. If desired, sprinkle with powdered sugar and serve with vanilla ice cream. Makes 12 little cakes.

Triple Chocolate Torte

1	cup heavy whipping cream
1	12-ounce package (2 cups) semisweet chocolate chips
1	19.5- to 19.8-ounce package brownie mix
6	tablespoons ($^3/_4$ stick) unsalted butter, melted
$^1/_4$	cup water
1	tablespoon instant espresso or coffee powder
3	large eggs
1	8-ounce package cream cheese, softened
1	recipe Sweetened Whipped Cream (see page 269; optional)

Preheat oven to 350°. Spray 10-inch springform pan with nonstick cooking spray.

In a medium saucepan set over low heat, heat whipping cream until very hot (do not boil). Remove from heat and stir in chocolate chips; stir until melted and smooth. Set aside.

In a medium mixing bowl mix the brownie mix, melted butter, water, espresso powder, and 2 eggs with a wooden spoon until just blended and all dry ingredients are moistened. Spread batter into prepared pan.

In a small mixing bowl beat cream cheese until light and fluffy. Add remaining egg; beat until smooth. Add ½ cup of the chocolate mixture; blend well. Spread evenly over brownie mixture in pan.

Bake until just set in center, about 38–42 minutes. Cool 10 minutes. Run knife around edge of pan to loosen; remove sides of pan. Transfer to wire rack; cool completely.

Place torte on serving platter. Spread remaining chocolate mixture over top of torte, letting mixture run down sides. Refrigerate at least 1 hour or until chilled. If desired, serve with Sweetened Whipped Cream or vanilla ice cream. Store in refrigerator. Makes 10–12 servings.

The search for the premium chocolate indulgence ends here. If you make no other recipe in this book, make this one to receive oodles of praise, adoration, and requests for the recipe. Gussy it up with chocolate shavings, whipped cream or a few fresh mint sprigs, if you like. But in truth, no adornment is needed.

Molten Mocha Lava Cakes

These cakes are slightly underbaked so that the chocolate center oozes when your spoon hits the center. Need I say more? Except perhaps ooh-la-la and don't forget the ice cream.

1	cup semisweet chocolate chips
½	cup (1 stick) unsalted butter
4	large eggs
3	large egg yolks
1	19.5- to 19.8-ounce package brownie mix
2	teaspoons instant espresso or coffee powder
3½	tablespoons coffee liqueur
1–2	tablespoons powdered sugar or unsweetened cocoa powder (optional)
	Vanilla or coffee ice cream (optional)

Preheat oven to 400°. Position a rack in the lower third of the oven. Spray 12 2¾ x 1¼-inch nonstick muffin cups with non-stick cooking spray.

In a medium saucepan set over low heat combine chocolate chips and butter. Cook and stir until melted and smooth. Remove from heat and cool 5 minutes.

Meanwhile, in a large mixing bowl beat the eggs and egg yolks with electric mixer set on high for 4–5 minutes or until foamy and doubled in size. Gradually add brownie mix and espresso powder to egg mixture, beating on medium until well blended. Fold in melted chocolate chip mixture and liqueur. Divide batter evenly into greased muffin cups (cups will be full).

Bake 11–14 minutes or until edges are set (centers will still be slightly soft). Cool 2 minutes in pans. Run knife around edge of each cake to loosen. Place warm cakes on serving plates and, if desired, sift with powdered sugar or cocoa powder. Serve warm, with ice cream, if desired. Makes 12 servings.

Black-Bottom Brownie Rum Fudge Pie

1   10-inch deep-dish frozen pie crust (thawed) or homemade 10-inch pie crust, unbaked

1¼   cups semisweet chocolate chips

1   19.5- to 19.8-ounce package brownie mix

½   cup (1 stick) unsalted butter, melted

¼   cup dark rum

2   large eggs

Vanilla or coffee ice cream (optional)

Preheat oven to 350°. Position a rack in the lower third of the oven. Sprinkle the chocolate chips evenly over bottom of unbaked pie crust; set aside.

In a medium mixing bowl mix the brownie mix, melted butter, rum, and eggs with a wooden spoon until all dry ingredients are moistened and blended. Carefully spoon large portions of the batter over the chocolate chips (try to keep the chocolate chips on the bottom of pie). Gently smooth the top with the back of a spoon.

Bake 43–48 minutes or until center is puffed and crust is golden brown. If desired, place foil strips around crust edge during last 25 minutes of baking time to avoid over-browning. Transfer to wire rack and cool completely. Cut cooled pie into slices and, if desired, serve with ice cream. Makes 8 servings.

Holy moly! That's what a good friend quipped when I served her a warm slice of this rum-rich pie. And who wouldn't say the same once they fork into this fudgy, deep-dished delight? The chocolate chips, sprinkled on the pie-crust bottom before adding the filling, melt during baking to create the pure chocolate "black bottom." If you want a non-alcoholic version while still keeping the rum flavor, substitute ¼ cup buttermilk plus 2 teaspoons rum-flavored extract for the dark rum. I'm not partial to an overly browned pie crust, so I suggest placing a few strips of aluminum foil over the pie crust edges during the last 25 minutes of baking.

"Hugs" & "Kisses" Brownie Bites

These appealing, junior-sized cocoa cakes know their place: at the top of your baking list. You can use traditional milk chocolate "kisses" or the newer white & milk chocolate striped "hugs"—or some of each. As you can probably imagine, other small chocolate candies also work very well here—the sky's the limit. But be forewarned: these are highly addictive!

1	19.5- to 19.8-ounce package brownie mix
½	teaspoon baking powder
½	cup (1 stick) unsalted butter, melted
¼	cup milk
3	large eggs
28	chocolate "kiss" or "hugs" candies, unwrapped
1	recipe Chocolate or White Chocolate Cream Cheese Frosting (see page 252; optional)

Preheat oven to 350°. Spray mini-muffin pans with nonstick cooking spray (or line with paper liners).

In a medium mixing bowl mix the brownie mix, baking powder, melted butter, milk, and eggs with a wooden spoon until just blended and all dry ingredients are moistened. Spread batter into prepared pan.

Drop 1 heaping tablespoon of batter into each muffin cup; top with candy. Press candy down into batter. Cover candy with additional teaspoon of brownie batter.

Bake 15–17 minutes or until set; cool in pans 5 minutes. Carefully loosen brownie muffins from pan. Transfer to wire racks and cool completely. If desired, frost with Chocolate or White Chocolate Cream Cheese Frosting. Makes about 28 brownie bites.

Snickery Sunken Treasure Cupcakes

1   19.5- to 19.8-ounce package brownie mix
½   cup vegetable oil
¼   cup water
3   large eggs
12   square chocolate covered caramel-peanut nougat nuggets (i.e., Snickers®), unwrapped

1   recipe Milk Chocolate Frosting (see page 251) or Cream Cheese Frosting (see page 261; optional)

Preheat oven to 350°. Position a rack in the lower third of the oven. Place paper baking cups in 12 2¾ x 1¼-inch nonstick muffin cups.

In a medium mixing bowl mix the brownie mix, oil, water, and eggs with a wooden spoon until just blended and all dry ingredients are moistened. Fill cups about three-fourths full (each about ¼ cup). Place a candy in each cup; gently press into batter.

Bake 25–28 minutes, until brownie portion springs back when touched. Cool 10 minutes; remove from pan. If desired, prepare Milk Chocolate or Cream Cheese Frosting; spread over cooled cakes. Serve warm or room temperature. Makes 12 servings.

Here's a dessert that epitomizes the difference between making dessert and making their day. To push these already irresistible treats right over the top, frost with chocolate or cream cheese frosting and sprinkle with more chopped Snickers bars.

Brownie-Bottomed Crème Brulée

Creamy custard coalesces with a rich brownie base in this luxurious, make-ahead dessert.

1	19.5- to 19.8-ounce package brownie mix
½	cup vegetable oil
¼	cup water
2	large eggs
3	cups heavy whipping cream
6	large egg yolks
6	tablespoons plus 8 teaspoons sugar, divided

Preheat oven to 350° (325° for dark-coated metal pan). Position a rack in the lower third of the oven. Spray the bottom only of an 8-inch square baking pan with nonstick cooking spray (or foil-line pan; see page 11).

In a medium mixing bowl mix the brownie mix, oil, water, and eggs with a wooden spoon until just blended and all dry ingredients are moistened. Spread batter into prepared pan.

Bake 40–44 minutes or until toothpick inserted 2 inches from side of pan comes out clean or almost clean (do not overbake). Transfer brownies to a wire rack and cool completely. Cut into 9 equal squares; trim crusty edges.

In a medium bowl whisk the whipping cream, egg yolks, and 6 tablespoons of the sugar until blended and smooth. Set aside.

Press 1 brownie square into each of 8 ¾-cup custard cups (there will be 1 extra brownie). Evenly divide custard into cups. Arrange cups in a large baking pan. Pour enough very hot water into pan to come halfway up sides of cups. Loosely cover pan with foil.

Bake 35 minutes, until custards are softly set at centers. Transfer cups to wire rack and cool completely. Refrigerate 3 hours or up to overnight, until well chilled.

Preheat broiler. Arrange chilled custard cups on a large baking sheet. Sprinkle top of each custard with 1 teaspoon sugar. Broil until sugar melts and turns golden, about 2 minutes (watch carefully to avoid burning). Refrigerate until cold, at least 2 hours. Makes 8 servings.

Chocolate Fudge Brownie Cheesecake

1	19.5- to 19.8-ounce package brownie mix
3	tablespoons butter, melted
2	8-ounce packages cream cheese, softened
1½	cups heavy whipping cream
1	12-ounce jar chocolate fudge ice cream topping

Preheat oven to 350°. Position a rack in the lower third of the oven.

In a medium mixing bowl mix 1½ cups of the brownie mix and the melted butter until blended. Press into bottom of an ungreased 9-inch springform pan. Set aside.

Meanwhile, beat cream cheese in a large mixing bowl with electric mixer set on medium for 2 minutes, scraping sides of bowl with rubber a spatula, until smooth. Add remaining brownie mix, whipping cream, and ⅓ cup fudge topping. Beat on medium speed, scraping bowl frequently, until smooth. Pour over crust in pan.

Bake 35–40 minutes, until set (do not overbake). Transfer to wire rack. Run knife around edge of cheesecake to loosen; cool completely. Warm chocolate fudge topping in a small saucepan set over low heat until warm. Drizzle over top of cheesecake. Refrigerate at least 4 hours or overnight. Cut into slices; serve. Cover and refrigerate any remaining cheesecake. Makes 10–12 servings.

No misprint here—five ingredients are all it takes to make this deeply chocolate, truffle-like cheesecake. No one will ever guess it began with a box of brownie mix, so why tell them—unless they ask for the recipe, which is highly likely. Please share it!

Petite Tuxedo Tarts

Perfect for your spring soiree, these dainty white chocolate–filled, strawberry-topped tarts are quick, easy, and—best of all— taste as great as they look.

1	19.5- to 19.8-ounce package brownie mix
½	cup vegetable oil
¼	cup water
3	large eggs
2	1-ounce white chocolate baking squares
2	tablespoons milk
1	8-ounce package cream cheese, softened
¼	cup powdered sugar
1	1-cup recipe Sweetened Whipped Cream (see page 269) or 1 cup frozen whipped topping, thawed
1	pint small strawberries, sliced, or 1 pint raspberries Fresh mint leaves (optional)

Preheat oven to 325°. Spray cups of mini-muffin pan with non-stick cooking spray or line with paper liners.

In a medium bowl mix the brownie mix, oil, water, and eggs with a wooden spoon until just blended and all dry ingredients are moistened. Fill prepared muffin cups two-thirds full.

Bake 12–14 minutes until edges are just set (do not overbake). Transfer to wire racks. Immediately press down tops of brownie with rounded 1-teaspoon measure or a cork to make indentations in each brownie, forming each into a tart shell. Cool in pan 15 minutes. Loosen edges; carefully remove from pan. Cool completely. Repeat with remaining batter.

In a small microwave-safe bowl microwave white chocolate and milk, uncovered, 1 minute on high, stirring until smooth. Cool slightly. In a medium bowl beat cream cheese and powdered sugar with electric mixer set on medium-high until blended and smooth. Gradually stir in white chocolate mixture until blended and smooth. Fold in Sweetened Whipped Cream.

Spoon or pipe white chocolate mixture into cooled brownie cups. Arrange strawberry slices on top. Garnish with mint leaves, if desired. Refrigerate 1–2 hours before serving. Makes 4 dozen tarts.

Brownie Swirl Vanilla Cheesecake

1½	cups graham cracker crumbs
4	tablespoons (½ stick) unsalted butter, melted
1	tablespoon sugar
4	8-ounce packages cream cheese, softened
1	cup sugar
2½	teaspoons vanilla extract
5	large eggs
1	19.5- to 19.8-ounce package brownie mix
⅓	cup water
3	tablespoons vegetable oil

Preheat oven to 350°. In a medium mixing bowl combine crumbs, melted butter, and sugar. Pat into bottom of ungreased 10-inch springform pan. Refrigerate.

In a large mixing bowl beat cream cheese with electric mixer set on medium until smooth. Mix in sugar and vanilla. Add 4 of the eggs, one at a time, continuing to beat on medium until well blended and smooth. Set aside.

In a medium mixing bowl mix brownie mix, water, oil, and remaining egg with a wooden spoon until just blended and all dry ingredients are moistened. Stir in 1 cup cheesecake batter until well blended.

Pour half of cream cheese batter into pan. Spoon half of brownie batter in dollops on top of cheesecake batter. Repeat layering. Swirl the batters with the tip of a knife to marbleize.

Bake 50–55 minutes, until just set in center. Transfer to wire rack. Run knife around edge of cheesecake to loosen; cool completely. Refrigerate at least 4 hours or overnight. Makes 10–12 servings.

This impressive dessert features two all-American favorites, brownies and cheese-cake, swirled together in one great concoction. It's essential that the cheesecake be chilled at least 4 hours, but is best made a full day ahead, so the flavors can marry overnight in the refrigerator.

Cherry Chocolate Baby Cakes

These tasty little cherry-filled cakes can be prepared and frozen, unfrosted, up to a month ahead of time, just right for entertaining or spur-of-the-moment chocolate cravings. The cakes thaw in about 30–45 minutes at room temperature (avoid using the microwave; it alters the consistency). Finish with the frosting and cherries.

1	19.5- to 19.8-ounce package brownie mix
½	cup vegetable oil
¼	cup water
2	large eggs
⅔	cup cherry preserves
2½	cups sifted powdered sugar
2½	tablespoons milk
¼	teaspoon almond extract
1	drop red food coloring (optional)
60	maraschino cherries with stems, drained and patted dry with paper towels

Preheat oven to 350°. Position a rack in the lower third of the oven. Line 60 miniature muffin cups with miniature paper liners; set aside.

In a medium mixing bowl mix the brownie mix, oil, water, and eggs with a wooden spoon until just blended and all dry ingredients are moistened. Spoon 1 scant teaspoon of batter into each muffin cup. Add ½ teaspoon of cherry preserves and top with 1 teaspoon additional batter.

Bake 10–12 minutes, until just set at center and toothpick inserted in center comes out clean. Cool in pans on wire rack 5 minutes. Remove from pans and transfer to a wire rack and cool completely.

Meanwhile, in a small mixing bowl combine sifted powdered sugar, milk, almond extract, and food coloring, if desired, and mix until smooth. Drizzle each baby cake with ½ teaspoon icing. Dip half of each cherry into remaining icing; place one on top of each cake. Makes 60 little cakes.

Baker's Note: If you do not have miniature muffin pans, a standard-size muffin tin (2½-inch cups) lined with paper liners may be used. Prepare batter as directed. Spoon 1 tablespoon batter into each

prepared cup. Add 1 teaspoon preserves and top with 1 tablespoon batter (you will use about ⅓ cup preserves total). Bake at 350° for 15 minutes, until toothpick inserted in centers comes out clean. Frost with icing and cherries (24 cherries). Makes 24 cakes.

Black-Bottom Raspberry Cheesecake

Of all the birthday cakes I've made for friends and colleagues over the years, this is the one most requested. Given the combination of fla- vors— brownie bot- tom, velvety vanilla cheesecake, and ruby red raspberries sand- wiched in between— it's not surprising. Forget about the calo- ries—this is (mental) health food.

1	19.5- to 19.8-ounce package brownie mix
⅓	cup oil
3	tablespoons water
5	large eggs
1	10-ounce package frozen raspberries, thawed, drained
1	cup seedless raspberry jam, divided
3	8-ounce packages cream cheese, at room temperature
¾	cup sugar
1	teaspoon vanilla extract
2	tablespoons powdered sugar
	Fresh raspberries and mint sprigs (optional)

Preheat oven to 350°. Spray bottom of 10-inch springform pan with nonstick cooking spray. In a medium mixing bowl mix the brownie mix, oil, water, and 2 eggs with a wooden spoon until just blended and all dry ingredients are moistened. Spread batter into prepared pan.

Bake 27–30 minutes (brownies will be partially set). Transfer to wire rack and cool 15 minutes (leave oven on).

In small mixing bowl combine raspberries and ½ cup of the raspberry jam until well blended. Set aside.

In a large mixing bowl beat cream cheese with electric mixer set on medium until blended and smooth. Beat in sugar and vanilla. Add remaining 3 eggs, one at a time, until well blended.

Spoon raspberry mixture evenly over top of brownie in pan. Slowly pour cheesecake batter on top.

Bake 50–55 minutes or until cheesecake is just barely set at the center when the pan is jiggled. Transfer to wire rack. Run knife around edge of cheesecake to loosen; cool completely. Refrigerate at least 4 hours or overnight.

To serve, heat the remaining $\frac{1}{2}$ cup raspberry jam in small saucepan over low heat until just melted. Let cool 10 minutes. Sift top of cheesecake with powdered sugar. Drizzle top of cake with melted raspberry jam in a zigzag pattern. Refrigerate until ready to serve. If desired, garnish with fresh raspberries and mint sprigs. Makes 10–12 servings.

White Chocolate Eggnog Cheesecake

Move over fruitcake—this eggnog-spiced, rum-spiked cheesecake is a guaranteed holiday pleaser at all of my Christmas parties, even among people who claim they do not care for eggnog. But don't limit your making of it to the holiday season. The delicate balance of flavors is welcome all autumn and winter long.

1	19.5- to 19.8-ounce package brownie mix
⅓	cup vegetable oil
3	tablespoons water
5	large eggs
3	8-ounce packages cream cheese, at room temperature
¾	cup sugar
¼	cup dark rum or brandy
2	tablespoons cornstarch
¾	teaspoon ground nutmeg
⅛	teaspoon ground cinnamon
⅓	cup heavy whipping cream
1	cup white chocolate chips
	Additional ground nutmeg for sprinkling atop the cheesecake (optional)

Preheat oven to 350°. Spray bottom of 10-inch springform pan with nonstick cooking spray. In a medium mixing bowl mix the brownie mix, oil, water, and 2 eggs with a wooden spoon until just blended and all dry ingredients are moistened. Spread batter into prepared pan.

Bake 27–30 minutes (brownies will be partially set). Transfer to wire rack and cool 15 minutes (leave oven on).

In a large mixing bowl beat cream cheese with electric mixer set on medium until blended and smooth. Beat in sugar, rum, cornstarch, nutmeg, and cinnamon. Add remaining 3 eggs, one at a time, until well blended. Pour cheesecake batter on top of cooled brownie base.

Bake 50–55 minutes or until cheesecake is just barely set at the center when the pan is jiggled. Transfer to wire rack.

Meanwhile, in a small saucepan set over low heat, heat the whipping cream until hot but not boiling. Remove from heat and add the white chocolate chips, whisking until smooth. Cool 15 minutes then pour over cheesecake. Sprinkle with additional nutmeg, if desired. Cool completely. Run knife around of cheesecake to loosen. Refrigerate at least 4 hours or overnight. Makes 10–12 servings.

Cranberry Chocolate Upside Down Cake

Ready to shake things up at the Thanksgiving dessert table this year? Bejeweled with cranberries and laced with cinnamon and orange, this gorgeous chocolate cake is dazzling in both appearance and taste. Just be sure to make clean up easy by placing the cake pan on a cookie sheet—upside down cakes have a tendency to spill over a bit. Foil-lining the cookie sheet means that cleanup is as simple as scrunching the foil into a ball

14	tablespoons (1¾ sticks) unsalted butter, divided
⅔	cup packed light brown sugar
½	teaspoon ground cinnamon
2	cups (about ½ pound) fresh or frozen (thawed) cranberries, rinsed and picked over
4	large egg whites, room temperature
1	19.5- to 19.8-ounce package brownie mix
1	tablespoon grated orange zest
¼	cup fresh-squeezed orange juice
3	large egg yolks, room temperature

Preheat oven to 350°. Line a cookie sheet with foil. Melt 6 tablespoons (¾ stick) of the butter in a saucepan over medium-low heat; pour into a small bowl and set aside. Melt remaining 8 tablespoons (1 stick) butter in same saucepan over medium heat. Stir in the brown sugar and cinnamon and cook until the sugar begins to dissolve. Pour the mixture into a 9-inch square cake pan or a 9- to 10-inch ovenproof skillet and tilt to coat well. Add the cranberries in an even layer; set aside.

In a medium mixing bowl beat the egg whites with electric mixer set on high until soft peaks form; set aside.

In a large mixing bowl mix reserved 6 tablespoons melted butter, brownie mix, orange zest, orange juice, and egg yolks with electric mixer set on medium until the dry ingredients are moistened. With mixer set on medium speed, beat half of the whipped egg whites into brownie mixture until just barely combined. With a rubber spatula, fold in remaining egg whites (do not worry if some white streaks still appear). Carefully pour batter over cranberries, spreading to edges of pan.

Place pan on prepared cookie sheet (to catch any overflow

splatters). Bake 47–50 minutes, until a toothpick inserted at the cake's center comes out with just a few moist crumbs attached. Transfer to wire rack and run a knife around the edge. Cool 30 minutes. Invert the cake onto a serving platter. Makes 8 servings.

and tossing into the garbage can. That's my kind of cleaning!

Bananas Foster Chocolate Upside Down Cake

Just when you think chocolate dessert can't get any better, along comes a treat like this to blow your mind. I'm a big fan of upside down cakes in general, and although I will always have a soft spot in my heart for my mom's traditional pineapple recipe, this bananas foster–inspired chocolate version does, pardon the cliché, take the cake. It's best eaten on the same day you make it (the bananas get a bit gooey by days two and three) so either invite

14	tablespoons (1¾ sticks) butter, divided
⅔	cup packed light brown sugar
⅓	cup coarsely chopped pecans
4	large ripe bananas, peeled, cut diagonally into ¼-inch-thick slices
4	large egg whites, room temperature
1	19.5- to 19.8-ounce package brownie mix
¼	cup brandy or dark rum
3	large egg yolks, room temperature, lightly beaten

Preheat oven to 350°. Line a cookie sheet with foil. Melt 6 tablespoons (¾ stick) of the butter in a saucepan over medium-low heat; set aside for the cake. Melt remaining 8 tablespoons (1 stick) butter in same saucepan over medium heat. Stir in the brown sugar and cook until the sugar begins to dissolve. Pour the mixture into a 9-inch square cake pan or a 9- to 10-inch ovenproof skillet and tilt to coat well. Sprinkle pecans evenly over. Place banana slices in concentric circles on nuts, overlapping slightly and covering bottom; set aside.

In a medium mixing bowl beat the egg whites with an electric mixer set on high until soft peaks form; set aside.

In a large mixing bowl mix reserved 6 tablespoons melted butter, brownie mix, brandy, and egg yolks with electric mixer set on medium until the dry ingredients are moistened. With mixer set on medium speed, beat half of the whipped egg whites into brownie mixture until just barely combined. With a rubber spatula, fold in remaining egg whites (do not worry if some white streaks still appear). Carefully pour batter over bananas; spread to edges of pan.

Place pan on prepared cookie sheet (to catch any overflow splatters). Bake 47–50 minutes, until a toothpick inserted at the cake's center comes out with just a few moist crumbs attached. Transfer to wire rack and run a knife around the edge. Cool 30 minutes. Invert the cake onto a serving platter. Makes 8 servings.

a crowd or deliver the excess to your neighbors (they'll let you borrow the lawn mower any time afterward).

Raspberry Cream Cheese Brownie Pie

This fabulous finale is simple but stylish. It will remind you of homey desserts past— think fruit pies, cheesecake, and brownies—but is updated for today.

1	8-ounce package cream cheese, softened
3	tablespoons sugar
3	large eggs
1	19.5- to 19.8-ounce package brownie mix
¼	cup vegetable oil
1	tablespoon water
1	teaspoon almond extract
1	10-inch unbaked frozen deep-dish pie crust (do not thaw)
½	cup raspberry preserves
½	cup semisweet chocolate chips
½	cup sliced almonds

Preheat oven to 350°. Position a rack in the lower third of the oven.

In a medium mixing bowl beat cream cheese, sugar, and 1 of the eggs with electric mixer set on medium until blended and smooth. Set aside.

In a medium mixing bowl mix the brownie mix, oil, water, almond extract, and remaining 2 eggs with a wooden spoon until just blended and all dry ingredients are moistened.

Spread half of brownie mixture in bottom of pie crust. Drop ½ cup preserves in spoonfuls over brownie. Spoon and carefully spread cream cheese mixture over preserves. Top with dollops of remaining brownie mixture; spread evenly. Sprinkle with chocolate chips and almonds.

Bake for 43–48 minutes or until center is puffed and crust is golden brown. If desired, place foil strips around crust edge during last 25 minutes of baking time to avoid overbrowning. Transfer to a wire rack and cool. Serve warm or completely cooled. Store in refrigerator. Makes 8 servings.

Mocha Cream Shortcakes

1	19.5- to 19.8-ounce package brownie mix
½	cup vegetable oil or ½ cup (1 stick) unsalted butter, melted
¼	cup water or buttermilk
2	large eggs
1	tablespoon instant espresso or coffee powder
1½	teaspoons vanilla extract
1	cup cold milk
1	package (4-serving size) vanilla instant pudding & pie filling
1	2-cup recipe Sweetened Whipped Cream (see page 269) or frozen whipped topping (thawed)
1	12-ounce jar chocolate fudge ice cream topping, warmed

Preheat oven to 350° (325° for dark-coated metal pan). Position a rack in the lower third of the oven. Spray the bottom only of an 8-inch square baking pan with nonstick cooking spray (or foil-line pan; see page 11).

In a medium mixing bowl mix the brownie mix, oil, water, and eggs with a wooden spoon until just blended and all dry ingredients are moistened. Spread batter into prepared pan.

Bake 40–44 minutes or until toothpick inserted 2 inches from side of pan comes out clean or almost clean (do not overbake). Transfer brownies to a wire rack and cool completely. Cut cooled brownie into 9 squares.

In a large mixing bowl dissolve the espresso powder in the vanilla. Add the milk and pudding mix. Whisk until well blended and pudding is slightly thickened. Refrigerate 5 minutes to thicken further. Gently fold in Sweetened Whipped Cream or whipped topping. Refrigerate at least 15 minutes.

Split each brownie horizontally in half. Place bottom halves of brownies, cut side up, on each of 9 dessert plates; top with pudding mixture, then the brownie tops. Drizzle with warm chocolate fudge topping. Serve immediately. Makes 9 servings.

Here's a dessert with a refined, sophisticated flavor profile that is lovely for entertaining and so simple to put together. The brownie "shortcakes" as well as the filling can be made ahead of time so that a quick final assembly is all that's needed. In the summer, consider adding a few fresh raspberries atop the filling or scattered around the plate. A light sifting of unsweetened cocoa powder or powdered sugar over the shortcake and plate will make this look like a swanky restaurant offering.

Brownie Ice Cream Sandwiches

No need to save these for summertime—they are perennial treats, especially if you vary the ice cream by season. The filling possibilities don't end with ice cream, either. For a to-die-for variation, sandwich raspberry or mango sorbet between the cookies—heavenly!

1	19.5- to 19.8-ounce package brownie mix
⅓	cup oil
2	large eggs
1	pint ice cream, any flavor
1¼	cups chopped nuts, shredded coconut, miniature chocolate chips, miniature baking M&Ms, or candy sprinkles (optional)

Preheat oven to 350°. Spray cookie sheets with nonstick cooking spray.

In a medium mixing bowl mix the brownie mix, oil, and eggs with a wooden spoon until just blended and all dry ingredients are moistened.

Drop dough by teaspoonfuls, 2 inches apart, onto prepared cookie sheets. Bake 9–10 minutes, until just barely set at center (do not overbake). Cool 2 minutes on baking sheet. Transfer to a wire rack and cool completely. Repeat with remaining dough.

Remove the ice cream from the freezer and let stand 15 minutes to soften. Scoop a heaping tablespoon of ice cream onto the bottom side of one cookie, then sandwich with a second cookie, pressing down gently so that the ice cream comes to the very edge of the cookie. If desired, roll the edge in one of the optional decorations. Wrap tightly in plastic wrap. Repeat with remaining cookies and ice cream.

Freeze sandwiches at least 30 minutes before serving. Makes about 2 dozen ice cream sandwiches.

Summer Berry Brownie Tart

1	19.5- to 19.8-ounce package brownie mix
½	cup vegetable oil
2	large eggs
1	8-ounce tub soft-spread strawberry cream cheese, room temperature
3	cups assorted fresh berries (e.g., raspberries, blueberries, and sliced strawberries)
¼	cup red currant jelly
	Fresh mint leaves for garnish (optional)

Preheat oven to 350°. Line 14-inch pizza pan with foil. Spray foil with nonstick cooking spray.

In a medium mixing bowl mix the brownie mix, oil, and eggs with a wooden spoon until just blended and all dry ingredients are moistened. Spread over foil-lined pan to within 1½ inches of the pan edge.

Bake 25–28 minutes until just set at center (do not overbake). Transfer to wire rack and cool completely.

Spread cream cheese over cooled brownie base. Arrange berries in decorative pattern over top.

In a small saucepan set over low heat melt the red currant jelly. Brush melted jelly over berries. Refrigerate tart at least 1 hour before serving. Garnish with mint leaves, if desired. Makes 10–12 servings.

This party-size dessert, with its bright berry topping, is a summer celebration. I use a 14-inch pizza pan so that the brownie base keeps its round shape when baking. However, you can also use a cookie sheet, shaping the brownie into a rectangular or oval shape. Other fruits may be substituted for the berries (e.g., bananas, mangos, nectarine slices, or canned apricot halves) depending on what's in season or what you have on hand. Use apple jelly in place of the red currant jelly if you choose to use lighter colored fruits.

Mandarin Orange Brownie Tart

Here's a spectacular dessert that looks like it takes considerable time and effort to prepare. Just the opposite is true. The brownie bottom is a snap to make and the layers of topping are quick to assemble.

1	19.5- to 19.8-ounce package brownie mix
½	cup vegetable oil
2	large eggs
1	8-ounce tub soft-spread honey nut cream cheese, room temperature
3	11-ounce cans mandarin orange segments, well drained and patted dry
½	cup white or semisweet chocolate chips
2	teaspoons vegetable shortening
½	cup sliced almonds, lightly toasted

Preheat oven to 350°. Line 14-inch pizza pan with foil. Spray foil with nonstick cooking spray.

In a medium mixing bowl mix the brownie mix, oil, and eggs with a wooden spoon until just blended and all dry ingredients are moistened. Spread over foil-lined pan to within 1½ inches of the pan edge.

Bake 25–28 minutes, until just set at center (do not overbake). Transfer to wire rack and cool completely.

Spread cream cheese over cooled brownie base. Arrange drained mandarin slices in concentric circles over top.

In small saucepan set over low heat melt the chocolate chips with the shortening, stirring until melted and smooth. Drizzle over tart in decorative pattern. Sprinkle with almonds. Refrigerate tart at least 1 hour before serving to set the chocolate. Makes 10–12 servings.

Chocolate Mint Brownie Pie

1	19.5- to 19.8-ounce package brownie mix
6	tablespoons butter (¾ stick), melted
¼	cup water
1	large egg
¾	teaspoon peppermint extract
1½	cups semisweet chocolate chips, divided
1	10-inch unbaked frozen deep-dish pie crust (do not thaw)
¾	cup white chocolate chips
	Fresh mint leaves (optional)

Preheat oven to 350°. Position a rack in the lower third of the oven.

In a medium mixing bowl mix the brownie mix, melted butter, water, egg, and peppermint extract until well blended. Stir in ¾ cup of the semisweet chocolate chips. Spoon and spread batter into crust.

Bake 43–48 minutes, until just set at center (do not over-bake). If desired, place foil strips around crust edge during last 25 minutes of baking time to avoid over-browning.

Remove pie from oven and immediately sprinkle with semisweet and white chocolate chips. Return to oven for 1–2 minutes to melt chips. Transfer to wire rack. With tip of knife, spread melted chips, creating a marble pattern. Cool completely. Refrigerate 1 hour to set the chocolate. If desired, garnish with mint leaves. Makes 8 servings.

Chocolate and mint, like all great pairings, bring out the best in each other. For delicious proof, whip up this easy-to-assemble pie. Ice cream is almost essential as an accompaniment. Vanilla is grand, but mint chip is even better.

Chocolate Brownie Tiramisu

Change can definitely be good, especially when it's for the sake of chocolate. I decided to take that notion and run with it in this very chocolate version of tiramisu. I confess to hiding leftovers in the back of the refrigerator to have them all to myself!

1	19.5- to 19.8-ounce package brownie mix
½	cup vegetable oil
½	cup water, divided
3	large eggs
¼	cup sugar
1	tablespoon instant espresso or coffee powder
5	tablespoons rum, brandy, or coffee-flavored liqueur
1	8-ounce package cream cheese, softened
1	cup heavy whipping cream
¼	cup sifted unsweetened cocoa powder
2	tablespoons powdered sugar
2	teaspoons vanilla extract
1	tablespoon unsweetened cocoa powder and/or chocolate curls (optional)

Preheat oven to 350°. Position a rack in the lower third of the oven. Spray two 8-inch square cake pans with nonstick cooking spray.

In a medium mixing bowl mix the brownie mix, oil, ¼ cup of the water, and eggs until well blended. Divide batter evenly between prepared pans, smoothing tops. Bake 20–24 minutes or until toothpick inserted in center comes out clean. Cool 10 minutes in pans. Remove from pans and place on wire racks. Cool completely. Cut each brownie into 16 1 x 4-inch "fingers."

Meanwhile, in small saucepan combine sugar, instant espresso powder, and remaining ¼ cup water. Bring to a boil over medium heat. Boil 1 minute. Remove from heat; stir in 4 tablespoons of the rum. Cool 30 minutes or until completely cooled.

In small mixing bowl beat the cream cheese, whipping

cream, cocoa powder, powdered sugar, vanilla, and remaining tablespoon rum with electric mixer set on low until blended. Beat at medium about 1 minute longer until thickened and smooth.

Arrange half of the brownie fingers in an 11 x 5-inch glass dish. Generously brush with half of the prepared syrup. Spread with half of the cheese mixture. Repeat the layering, topping with remaining cream cheese mixture. Place cocoa in fine strainer; sprinkle cake with cocoa and chocolate curls, if desired. Refrigerate, loosely covered with foil, at least 1 hour or up to overnight. Store in refrigerator. Cut into squares to serve. Makes 8 servings.

Grasshopper Brownie-Mallow Torte

Subtly flavored with mint, this is a dessert for celebrations. If you don't have crème de menthe, substitute $\frac{1}{4}$ cup milk, $\frac{1}{2}$ teaspoon peppermint extract and 2–3 drops green food coloring.

1	19.5- to 19.8-ounce package brownie mix
$\frac{1}{2}$	cup vegetable oil
$\frac{1}{4}$	cup water
2	large eggs
6	tablespoons green crème de menthe, divided
1	7-ounce jar marshmallow creme
1	2-cup recipe Sweetened Whipped Cream (see page 269) or 2 cups frozen whipped topping, thawed
	Fresh mint leaves (optional)

Preheat oven to 350° (325° for dark-coated metal pan). Position a rack in the lower third of the oven. Spray bottom only of a 9-inch springform pan with nonstick cooking spray.

In a medium mixing bowl mix the brownie mix, oil, water, and eggs with a wooden spoon until just blended and all dry ingredients are moistened. Spread batter into prepared pan.

Bake 38–42 minutes, until just set at center (do not overbake). Transfer brownies to a wire rack and cool completely (do not remove springform ring). Brush with 2 tablespoons crème de menthe.

In a large mixing bowl gradually beat remaining 4 tablespoons crème de menthe into marshmallow creme with wire whisk or electric mixer on low until well blended. Fold in Sweetened Whipped Cream or whipped topping. Pour mixture over cooled brownie. Refrigerate at least 4 hours or up to overnight. Run knife around edge of pan and remove springform ring. Garnish with mint leaves, if desired. Makes 8–10 servings.

Cherry Chocolate Crisp

1	19.5- to 19.8-ounce package brownie mix
1⅓	cups quick-cooking oats
¾	cup chopped pecans
½	cup (1 stick) unsalted butter, melted
2	21-ounce cans cherry pie filling
1	quart vanilla ice cream

Preheat oven to 350°.

In a large mixing bowl mix the brownie mix, oats, and pecans. Add the melted butter and stir with a wooden spoon until all dry ingredients are moistened (mixture will be relatively dry).

Spoon pie filling evenly into an ungreased 8-inch square glass baking dish. Sprinkle brownie mixture over pie filling.

Bake 30–35 minutes or until edges are bubbly. Transfer to wire rack and cool.

Serve the crisp scooped into bowls, warm or room temperature, and topped with vanilla ice cream. Makes 8 servings.

I can testify that this easy dessert is a no-fail crowd pleaser. Other fruit pie fillings may be substituted—for example, apricot is a good choice—but I think the contrast of the tart cherry filling with the chocolate topping is the best.

Brownie Baked Alaska

The steps for this impressive dessert are longer than most other recipes herein, but if you take your time, it's hard to go wrong. Moreover, you, and everyone else, will be dazzled by the finished product. For best results, be sure to use a rich, premium ice cream. It's more than an issue of taste: premium ice cream tends to be far more dense and hence freezes more firmly than other ice creams. To soften the ice cream uniformly, place the container (lid removed) in the microwave and

1½	pints chocolate ice cream, slightly softened
1	pint vanilla ice cream, slightly softened
1	21-ounce can cherry pie filling
1	19.5- to 19.8-ounce package brownie mix
3	large eggs
½	cup vegetable oil
¼	cup water
4	large egg whites
¼	teaspoon salt
⅛	teaspoon cream of tartar
⅔	cup sugar

Line a chilled 1½-quart mixing bowl with several layers of plastic wrap. With the back of a large spoon, spread chocolate ice cream to line bowl, being sure ice cream comes to the top of the bowl. Freeze 30 minutes. In a medium mixing bowl stir vanilla ice cream with cherry pie filling. Remove bowl with chocolate ice cream from freezer; spoon vanilla ice cream mixture in center; cover and freeze until firm, about 5 hours or overnight (Can be done up to 2 weeks ahead of time).

Preheat oven to 350°. Spray the bottom only of a 9-inch springform pan with nonstick cooking spray.

In a medium mixing bowl mix the brownie mix, eggs, oil, and water until well blended. Spread in prepared pan. Bake 38–42 minutes, until set. Transfer to wire rack and cool completely. Remove brownie round from pan and place on foil-lined cookie sheet. Invert prepared frozen ice cream on top; peel off plastic wrap. Wrap brownie ice cream cake with foil and freeze. (Can be done up to 3 days ahead of time.)

About 20 minutes before serving, preheat oven to 500°. In a medium mixing bowl beat egg whites, salt, and cream of tartar with electric mixer on high until soft peaks form. Gradually beat in sugar until completely dissolved (whites should stand in stiff, glossy peaks).

Unwrap ice cream cake; place on cookie sheet. Spread meringue over ice cream cake, sealing to edge, down to cookie sheet. Bake 4–5 minutes, until meringue is lightly browned. Remove from oven, cut into slices and serve immediately. Makes 16 servings.

heat for ten-second intervals on medium power.

Chocolate-Chip Cinnamon Rolls with Cream Cheese Frosting

Next time you want to show off at a brunch, unveil these indulgent treats. They take a bit more time to make, but I'm confident you will agree that the results make it all worth it.

3	.25-ounce packages active dry yeast
2½	cups lukewarm water (105°–115°)
1	19.5- to 19.8-ounce package brownie mix
4½	cups all-purpose flour
1	cup (2 sticks) unsalted butter, softened, divided
1¼	cups miniature chocolate chips
½	cup dark brown sugar
2	teaspoons ground cinnamon
¼	cup sugar
1	recipe Cream Cheese Frosting (see page 261; prepare the amount suitable for 13 x 9-inch pan of brownies)

In a small bowl dissolve the yeast in the lukewarm water. Let stand until foamy, about 10 minutes.

In a large bowl combine the yeast mixture with the brownie mix and 3 cups of the flour; stir with a wooden spoon to combine. Add the remaining flour, ½ cup at a time, stirring well after each addition. When the dough has pulled together, turn it out onto a lightly floured surface and knead until smooth and elastic, about 8 minutes.

Lightly oil a large bowl. Place the dough in the bowl and turn to coat with oil. Cover with a damp cloth and let rise in a warm place until doubled in volume, about 30 minutes.

Deflate the dough and turn it out onto a lightly floured surface. Roll the dough into a 10 x 16-inch rectangle. Spread ½ cup (1 stick) of the softened butter over the rectangle; sprinkle on miniature chocolate chips, brown sugar, and cinnamon.

Starting from one of the long sides, roll up the rectangle, jelly-roll style, and cut into 16 1-inch wide rolls.

Preheat oven to 375°. Generously spray two 9-inch round cake pans with nonstick cooking spray. Melt the remaining ½ cup butter in a small pan set over low heat. Place the rolls snugly into the prepared pans (8 per pan). Generously brush with the melted butter and sprinkle with sugar. Loosely cover the rolls with a damp cloth and let rise until doubled in volume, about 30 minutes.

Bake 20–24 minutes, until rolls are golden or lightly brown and sound hollow when lightly tapped. Transfer pans to wire racks and cool 10 minutes.

Prepare Cream Cheese Frosting; spread over warm rolls. Serve rolls warm or cooled. Makes 16 large rolls.

Very Raspberry Chocolate Trifle

This elegant trifle is the quintessential make-ahead dessert. The rich creamy filling will be a surefire hit for anyone who likes pudding—and that's just about everybody. If you like, add a final flourish of chocolate shavings (use a vegetable peeler on a 1-ounce square of semisweet baking chocolate), fresh mint leaves, or edible flowers to "wow" your guests.

1	19.5- to 19.8-ounce package brownie mix
½	cup vegetable oil
¼	cup water
3	large eggs
1	8-serving-size package vanilla instant pudding and pie filling mix
2⅔	cups cold milk
½	teaspoon almond extract
⅔	cup seedless raspberry preserves, divided
2	cups (1 pint) fresh raspberries, divided
1	2-cup recipe Sweetened Whipped Cream (see page 269) or 2 cups frozen whipped topping, thawed
	Chocolate shavings (optional)

Preheat oven to 350° (325° for dark-coated metal pan). Position a rack in the lower third of the oven. Spray the bottom only of a 13 x 9-inch baking pan with nonstick cooking spray (or foil-line pan; see page 11).

In a medium mixing bowl mix the brownie mix, oil, water, and eggs with a wooden spoon until just blended and all dry ingredients are moistened. Spread batter into prepared pan.

Bake 28–30 minutes or until toothpick inserted 2 inches from side of pan comes out clean or almost clean (do not overbake). Transfer brownies to a wire rack and cool completely. Cut cooled brownies into 1-inch squares; set aside.

In a medium mixing bowl mix pudding mix with milk and almond extract until pudding begins to thicken.

Place half of the brownie squares in the bottom of a 3-quart glass bowl or trifle dish. Spread half of pudding over brownies in bowl; dollop with ⅓ cup raspberry preserves and sprinkle with 1 cup raspberries. Spread with half of the

Sweetened Whipped Cream. Repeat with remaining brownies, pudding, raspberries, and whipped cream. Sprinkle with chocolate shavings, if desired. Cover and refrigerate at least 2 hours before serving. Makes 10–12 servings.

Peanut Butter–Chocolate Decadence Trifle

Here is another simple but impressive do-ahead dessert for people who love the combination of peanut butter and chocolate (who doesn't?). You can assemble the trifle in one large dish, or layer the brownies and filling parfait-style in individual dessert dishes or wine glasses.

1	19.5- to 19.8-ounce package brownie mix
½	cup vegetable oil
¼	cup water
2	large eggs
24	regular-sized (about 2 inches in diameter) peanut butter cups, divided
1	8-serving-size package vanilla instant pudding mix
2⅔	cups cold milk
½	cup creamy peanut butter
1	2-cup recipe Sweetened Whipped Cream (see page 269), or 2 cups frozen whipped topping, thawed

Preheat oven to 350° (325° for dark-coated metal pan). Position a rack in the lower third of the oven. Spray the bottom only of a 13 x 9-inch baking pan with nonstick cooking spray (or foil-line pan; see page 11).

In a medium mixing bowl mix the brownie mix, oil, water, and eggs with a wooden spoon until just blended and all dry ingredients are moistened. Spread batter into prepared pan.

Bake 28–30 minutes or until toothpick inserted 2 inches from side of pan comes out clean or almost clean (do not overbake). Transfer brownies to a wire rack and cool completely. Cut cooled brownies into 1-inch squares; set aside.

Coarsely chop 20 of the peanut butter cups, saving 4 for garnish.

In a large mixing bowl combine pudding mix and milk.

Beat at low with electric mixer for 2 minutes or until thickened. Add peanut butter; beat until smooth. Gently fold in half of the Sweetened Whipped Cream.

Place half of brownies in bottom of 3-quart glass bowl or trifle dish. Top with half of the pudding, half of the chopped candy. Repeat layers. Top with remaining whipped cream. Coarsely chop remaining candy and sprinkle on top of trifle. Cover and refrigerate at least 2 hours before serving. Makes 10–12 servings.

Black Forest Brownie Trifle

Easy to make, dressed to impress, and yet as comforting as an old friend, this oh-so-delicious combination of fruit, brownies, pudding, and whipped cream sets a new benchmark for American-style desserts.

1	19.5- to 19.8-ounce package brownie mix
½	cup vegetable oil
¼	cup water
2	large eggs
1	8-serving-size package chocolate instant pudding and pie filling mix
2⅔	cups milk
1	21-ounce can cherry pie filling
1	2-cup recipe Sweetened Whipped Cream (see page 269) or 2 cups frozen whipped topping, thawed
½	cup sliced almonds, lightly toasted

Preheat oven to 350° (325° for dark-coated metal pan). Position a rack in the lower third of the oven. Spray the bottom only of a 13 x 9-inch baking pan with nonstick cooking spray (or foil-line pan; see page 11).

In a medium mixing bowl mix the brownie mix, oil, water, and eggs with a wooden spoon until just blended and all dry ingredients are moistened. Spread batter into prepared pan.

Bake 28–30 minutes or until toothpick inserted 2 inches from side of pan comes out clean or almost clean (do not overbake). Transfer brownies to a wire rack and cool completely. Cut cooled brownies into 1-inch squares; set aside.

In a small mixing bowl whisk the pudding mix with the milk until pudding begins to thicken. Refrigerate 5 minutes.

Place half of the brownie squares in the bottom of a 3-quart glass bowl or trifle dish. Spread half of pudding over brownies in bowl; dollop with half of pie filling. Spread with half of the Sweetened Whipped Cream. Repeat layering with remaining brownies, pudding, pie filling, and whipped cream. Sprinkle with toasted almonds. Cover and refrigerate at least 2 hours before serving. Makes 10–12 servings.

Berry White Chocolate Cream Torte

1	19.5- to 19.8-ounce package brownie mix
½	cup vegetable oil
¼	cup water
2	large eggs
1	10-ounce package frozen raspberries in syrup, thawed
1	tablespoon sugar
1	tablespoon cornstarch
1	cup fresh raspberries
1	8-ounce package cream cheese, softened
2	tablespoons orange liqueur or orange juice
1	cup white chocolate chips, melted according to package directions
1	2-cup recipe Sweetened Whipped Cream (see page 269)
1	1-ounce square semisweet chocolate, grated or shaved into curls
	Fresh mint sprigs (optional)

When the occasion calls for splendor at the table, this is the dessert.

Preheat oven to 350°. Position a rack in the lower third of the oven. Spray the bottom only of a 9-inch springform pan with nonstick cooking spray.

In a medium mixing bowl combine brownie mix, oil, water, and eggs with a wooden spoon until well blended. Spread batter into the prepared pan. Bake 40–44 minutes or until toothpick inserted 2 inches from side of pan comes out clean or almost clean (do not overbake). Transfer to a wire rack.

In blender container or food processor bowl fitted with metal blade process thawed raspberries with syrup until smooth. Place strainer over small bowl; strain berry mixture, pressing with back of spoon through strainer to remove seeds. Discard seeds. *(continued on next page)*

In small saucepan combine sugar and cornstarch. Gradually whisk in raspberry puree. Bring to a boil over medium heat. Cook until mixture is slightly thickened and clear; cool 5 minutes. Spread over brownie layer to within ½ inch of edges. Arrange fresh raspberries evenly over raspberry mixture; refrigerate.

In medium bowl beat cream cheese and liqueur with electric mixer until blended and smooth. Beat in melted white chocolate until blended and smooth. Fold in Sweetened Whipped Cream. Cover and refrigerate 1 hour.

Stir cream cheese mixture until smooth; carefully spread over raspberry layer. Sprinkle with grated chocolate. Refrigerate at least 1 hour or until firm. Garnish with mint leaves, if desired. Store in refrigerator. Makes 16 servings.

Chapter 5
Frostings, Glazes, and Whipped Cream

Cookie Decorating Icing

Use this simple icing on the Brownie Cut-outs for a pretty white contrast against the dark chocolate dough or tint with food coloring paste for a rainbow of icing colors. The egg whites act as a stabilizer in this icing, allowing it to harden for decorating the cookies. Because the whites are not cooked, I prefer to use powdered egg whites (e.g., Just Whites). They are available in the baking section of most supermarkets.

1	16-ounce box powdered sugar
4	teaspoons powdered egg whites (not reconstituted)
⅓	cup water
1	tablespoon fresh-squeezed lemon juice
1	teaspoon vanilla
	Food coloring paste (optional)

In a large bowl combine all ingredients except food coloring and beat with an electric mixer set on medium until just blended, about 1 minute. Increase speed to high and beat icing, scraping down side of bowl occasionally, until it holds stiff peaks, about 3 minutes in standing mixer or 4–5 minutes with a handheld mixer.

Beat in food coloring if added color is desired. If you plan to spread (rather than pipe) icing on cookies, stir in more water, a few drops at a time, to thin to desired consistency. Makes about 3 cups.

No-Prep Frostings for Brownies and Brownie Cookies

+ Peanut Butter

+ Peanut Butter & Jelly

+ Soft-Spread Sweetened Cream Cheese

+ Chocolate hazelnut spread (e.g., Nutella)

+ Jam, preserves, or marmalade

+ Jarred lemon curd

+ Ready-to-spread canned cake frosting

+ Marshmallow creme/fluff

A plain batch of brownies can be dressed up quickly and deliciously with any one of these no-prep frosting options. Use approximately ¾ cup to 1 cup for an 8-inch square batch of brownies, and approximately 1½ to 2 cups to frost a 13 x 9-inch batch of brownies or 4–5 dozen cookies. You can add some final flourishes, too, by sprinkling on shredded coconut, chopped nuts, chocolate chips, toffee bits, or candy nonpareils from the baking aisle in the supermarket.

One-Step Chocolate-Chip/ Baking Chip "Frosting"

This is one of my favorite ways to dress up a plain pan of brownies. For an even fancier finish, first do this one-step frosting, then do a contrasting chocolate drizzle (for example, white chocolate drizzle over semisweet chocolate chip frosting) in the recipe that follows; drizzle over melted chip frosting in a decorative design. Gorgeous!

Prepare and bake 8-inch square pan Classic Brownies (see page 16). Remove from oven and sprinkle evenly with 1 cup chocolate chips (e.g., semisweet, milk, or white) or baking chips (e.g., butterscotch, peanut butter, cinnamon). Cover baking pan with cookie sheet for 3 minutes. Remove pan and spread melted chips with knife or small offset spatula to cover the brownies.

For thicker frosting on 8 x 8-inch batch: Increase chips to 1$\frac{1}{2}$ cups.
For 13 x 9-inch batch of brownies: Increase chips to 2 cups.

Chocolate Drizzle or Dip

1   cup semisweet, milk, or white chocolate, or cinnamon baking chips

1   tablespoon vegetable shortening

Melt chips and shortening in a small heavy saucepan over low heat, stirring often to avoid scorching. Makes about 1 cup melted chocolate, enough to drizzle over one 13 x 9-inch pan of brownies or 4–5 dozen cookies, or spread onto one batch of biscotti.

To use as a Chocolate Dip:
Dip a cookie or biscotti into the melted chocolate. Remove the excess chocolate by pulling the cookie across the edge of the pan.

To use as a Chocolate Drizzle:
Place cookies on a wire rack over waxed paper. Dip a fork or knife into melted chocolate and let the first clumpy drip land back in the pan. Then drizzle the chocolate over the edge of the pan onto the cookies. Let the cookies stand until the chocolate is set or refrigerate until chocolate is set.

Adding vegetable shortening to the chocolate chips makes the melted chocolate smooth, spreadable, and easy to work with. Be sure to keep the pan on very low heat and stir frequently to avoid scorching the chocolate.

Cinnamon Glaze

Depending on the degree to which you like cinnamon, you can increase or decrease the amount of cinnamon here. Alternatively, use the recipe as a template for other spicy glazes, substituting the ground spice of your choice, or a combination, for the ground cinnamon.

1½   cups powdered sugar, sifted
¾   teaspoon ground cinnamon
1½   tablespoons unsalted butter, melted
2–3   teaspoons milk

In a small bowl whisk the powdered sugar, cinnamon, and melted butter until blended and smooth. Add just enough milk, a teaspoon at a time, to make glaze a thin spreading consistency, whisking until smooth. Makes about ½ cup glaze, enough to glaze an 8-inch square pan of brownies.

Baker's note: For a 13 x 9-inch pan of brownies or 4–5 dozen cookies, double the ingredients listed above and proceed as directed.

Chocolate Velvet Frosting

2	tablespoons butter
½	cup semisweet chocolate chips
¼	cup sour cream
1¼	cups sifted powdered sugar

This frosting is everything that its name implies: rich, smooth, luxurious, and, of course, very chocolate.

In a medium saucepan set over low heat combine butter and chocolate chips; cook and stir until melted and smooth. Remove from heat and cool 5 minutes; whisk in sour cream. Gradually add powdered sugar, whisking until blended, shiny, and smooth. Makes about 1 cup frosting, enough to frost an 8-inch square pan of brownies.

 Baker's note: For a 13 x 9-inch pan of brownies or 4–5 dozen cookies, double the ingredients listed above and proceed as directed.

Chocolate Fudge Frosting

Anyone who tastes this rich, buttery, and very fudgy frosting will feel very lucky. It's a classic for spreading on plain or fancy brownies, just like what you would find on a premium coffeehouse brownie.

2	1-ounce squares unsweetened chocolate, coarsely chopped
3	tablespoons unsalted butter, cut into pieces
1½	cups powdered sugar, sifted, divided
1–2	tablespoons milk
½	teaspoon vanilla extract
Pinch	salt

In a double boiler melt the chopped chocolate with the butter; cook and stir until melted and smooth. Remove from heat and cool 10 minutes.

In a medium bowl mix the melted chocolate, ½ cup powdered sugar, 1 tablespoon milk, vanilla, and pinch of salt with an electric mixer set on medium until blended. Add the remaining powdered sugar, ½ cup at a time, beating on medium until blended and smooth. Add a few more drops milk, if necessary, to make the frosting spreading consistency. Makes about 1 cup frosting, enough to frost an 8-inch square pan of brownies.

 Baker's note: For a 13 x 9-inch pan of brownies or 4–5 dozen cookies, double the ingredients listed above and proceed as directed.

Milk Chocolate Frosting

2	2-ounce squares unsweetened baking chocolate, coarsely chopped
½	cup (1 stick) unsalted butter, softened
¾	cup powdered sugar, sifted
½	cup heavy whipping cream

Fill a large skillet with 1 inch of water. Bring to a low simmer over medium-low heat. Place the chopped chocolate in a large metal bowl; place the metal bowl in the skillet of water; stir chocolate until melted and smooth. Remove bowl from heat and cool 15 minutes.

Add the butter to bowl of melted chocolate. Beat with electric mixer set on medium until blended. Add the powdered sugar alternately with the cream, beating on medium until light and creamy. Add more sugar if too soft and more cream if too thick. Refrigerate 15 minutes. Makes about 1⅔ cups, enough to frost a 13 x 9-inch pan of brownies, a dozen cupcakes, or 4–5 dozen cookies.

 Baker's Note: For an 8-inch square pan of brownies, halve the ingredients listed above and proceed as directed.

This is my very favorite chocolate frosting. It's light and buttery with a smooth milk chocolate finish that makes a superb crowning touch to a host of dark chocolate brownie, cupcake, and cookie options.

Chocolate (Semisweet or White) Cream Cheese Frosting

Here's a dependable recipe I know I can turn to again and again to gussy up just about anything and everything sweet. Always divine on brownies, this tangy chocolate frosting is also delectable on brownie cookies and cupcakes.

3   1-ounce squares semisweet or white chocolate, chopped
2   tablespoons heavy whipping cream
4   ounces (half of an 8-ounce package) cream cheese, softened
1   cup powdered sugar, sifted

In a double boiler melt the chopped chocolate with the heavy cream, stirring until melted and smooth. Remove from heat.

In a medium mixing bowl the beat the cream cheese and powdered sugar with electric mixer set on medium until smooth. Slowly add the chocolate mixture, beating until incorporated and smooth. Cover and refrigerate at least 30 minutes (frosting will thicken up as the chocolate cools). Makes about 1 cup frosting, enough to frost an 8-inch square pan of brownies.

Baker's note: For a 13 x 9-inch pan of brownies or 4–5 dozen cookies, double the ingredients listed above and proceed as directed.

Chocolate Marshmallow Frosting

2¼	cups powdered sugar, sifted
⅔	cup unsweetened cocoa powder
6	large marshmallows
¼	cup (½ stick) unsalted butter, cut into small pieces
5–6	teaspoons milk
1	teaspoon vanilla extract

This silky chocolate concoction is a chocolate lover's sweet dreams come true.

In a large bowl combine the powdered sugar and cocoa powder. Set aside.

In a medium saucepan set over low heat combine the marshmallows and butter, stirring constantly until melted and smooth, about 3–4 minutes. Remove the pan from the heat. Pour the marshmallow mixture over the sugar-cocoa mixture. Add the milk and vanilla and stir until the frosting is smooth and satiny. Let stand 15–20 minutes to cool and thicken. Makes about 1½ cups, enough to frost a 13 x 9-inch pan of brownies or 4–5 dozen cookies.

 Baker's Note: For an 8-inch square pan of brownies, halve the ingredients listed above and proceed as directed.

Fluffiest Chocolate Buttercream

Curiously enough, this very fluffy, very buttery, very easy, and very delicious light chocolate frosting comes courtesy of a good friend who is a very avid exerciser and health food junkie and is also a dedicated chocolate aficionado. It is also heavenly on angel food cake.

2	1-ounce squares bittersweet or semisweet chocolate, coarsely chopped
½	of a 7-ounce jar marshmallow creme
¾	cup (1½ sticks) unsalted butter, softened and cut into chunks

In a double boiler set over simmering water melt the chocolate, stirring until melted and smooth. Remove from heat and let cool, about 15–20 minutes.

In a medium bowl beat the marshmallow creme with an electric mixer on high until smooth. Gradually add the chunks of butter, mixing until incorporated, smooth and fluffy. Scrape bowl well and add the melted, cooled chocolate. Mix on high until incorporated and smooth. Use immediately. Makes about 2 cups, enough to generously frost a 13 x 9-inch pan of brownies or 4–5 dozen cookies.

 Baker's Note: For an 8-inch square pan of brownies, halve the ingredients listed above and proceed as directed.

Chocolate Whiskey Frosting

6   **tablespoons (¾ stick) unsalted butter**

¼   **cup whiskey or bourbon**

¼   **cup light corn syrup**

4   **1-ounce squares unsweetened baking chocolate, coarsely chopped**

2   **teaspoons vanilla extract**

2   **cups powdered sugar, sifted**

In a medium saucepan set over medium-high heat combine the butter, whiskey, and corn syrup; bring to a boil. Remove from heat. Stir in the chocolate, whisking until melted. With wire whisk beat in vanilla and gradually add the powdered sugar until frosting is of spreading consistency. Cool. Refrigerate at least 30 minutes before using. Makes about 1½ cups, enough to frost a 13 x 9-inch pan of brownies or 4–5 dozen cookies.

Baker's Note: For an 8-inch square pan of brownies, halve the ingredients listed above and proceed as directed.

Your guess is correct: this frosting is sublime. Southern Comfort and framboise (raspberry liqueur) are equally exquisite substitutions for the whiskey.

Chocolate Rum Glaze

The crowning touch for Jim & Anna's Dark Rum Brownies (see page 45), this spiked glaze is also excellent drizzled over cookies. The glaze may look thin while it is still warm, but it thickens as it cools.

½	cup packed light brown sugar
3	tablespoons butter (not unsalted)
2	tablespoons dark rum
1	tablespoon milk
½	cup semisweet chocolate chips

In a small saucepan set over medium-low heat combine the brown sugar, butter, rum and milk . Cook, stirring constantly, until the mixture comes to a boil. Boil, stirring constantly, 1 minute longer. Remove the pan from the heat and stir in the chocolate chips. Stir the mixture until the chips are completely melted and the mixture is smooth. Cool 5 minutes. Pour the glaze over warm or cooled brownies. Makes about ¾ cup glaze, enough to glaze an 8-inch square pan of brownies.

Baker's note: For a 13 x 9-inch pan of brownies or 4–5 dozen cookies, double the ingredients listed above and proceed as directed.

Chocolate-Raspberry Frosting

1	cup semisweet chocolate chips
⅔	cup sour cream
¼	cup seedless raspberry preserves, whisked to loosen
2	tablespoons light corn syrup
1	teaspoon vanilla extract
1½	tablespoons unsalted butter, softened

Silky chocolate-raspberry frosting? It's even better than you can imagine.

In a double boiler set over simmering water stir chocolate until melted and smooth. Pour chocolate into a large bowl. Cool to room temperature. Beat in the sour cream, preserves, corn syrup, and vanilla with an electric mixer set on medium, beating until mixture is fluffy, smooth, and light in color, about 3 minutes. Beat in the butter. Makes about 2 cups, enough to generously frost a 13 x 9-inch pan of brownies or 4–5 dozen cookies.

Baker's note: For an 8-inch square pan of brownies, halve the ingredients listed above and proceed as directed.

Shiny Chocolate Glaze

Adding a bit of shimmery glamour to a basic batch of brownies is as easy as making and spreading this glaze.

1	cup semisweet chocolate chips
2	tablespoons unsalted butter
2	tablespoons corn syrup
1–3	teaspoons hot water

In a small saucepan set over low heat melt the chocolate chips, butter, and corn syrup, stirring occasionally, until melted and smooth. Stir in hot water, a few drops at a time, until mixture is thin enough to drizzle. Makes about 1¼ cups, enough to glaze a 13 x 9-inch pan of brownies.

Baker's Note: For an 8-inch square pan of brownies, halve the ingredients listed above and proceed as directed.

Caramel Penuche Frosting

¼   cup (½ stick) butter
½   cup packed dark brown sugar
2   tablespoons milk
1   cup powdered sugar, sifted
½   teaspoon vanilla extract

In a medium saucepan set over medium heat melt the butter with the brown sugar. Continue to cook and stir until the mixture comes to a boil. Add the milk; bring the mixture back to a boil. Remove the pan from the heat and stir in the sifted powdered sugar and vanilla. Spread over brownies or cookies while still warm. Makes about 1¼ cups frosting, enough to frost an 8-inch square pan of brownies.

 Baker's Note: For a 13 x 9-inch pan of brownies or 4–5 dozen cookies, double the ingredients listed above and proceed as directed.

This delicious frosting is incredible on brownies, cookies, and just about everything else. Be sure to spread while it's still warm. If left to cool completely, it sets up to a fudge consistency which, while still scrumptious, makes it almost impossible to spread.

Kahlua Coffee Icing

This doubly coffee icing can also be used with great success on the brownie biscotti in chapter three. Simply spread over one side of the biscotti with a butter knife or small offset spatula, then set on wire rack to harden.

3½	tablespoons Kahlua or other coffee liqueur
2	teaspoons instant espresso or coffee powder
1	teaspoon vanilla extract
Pinch	salt
3	cups powdered sugar, sifted

In a medium bowl combine the liqueur, espresso powder, vanilla, and pinch of salt until dissolved. Whisk in powdered sugar until blended and smooth. Makes about 1⅓ cups icing, enough to ice a 13 x 9-inch pan of brownies or 4–5 dozen cookies.

Irish Cream Frosting

This frosting is so good, it's very difficult to keep from eating it straight off of the spoon. Once you try it on brownies or chocolate cookies, though, you'll find it's worth the initial restraint.

¼	cup (½ stick) unsalted butter, softened
1	3-ounce package cream cheese, softened
2	tablespoons Irish cream liqueur
2	cups powdered sugar, sifted

In a medium mixing bowl beat the butter, cream cheese, and liqueur on medium until blended, smooth, and fluffy. Gradually add the powdered sugar, beating on medium until light and creamy. Add a little more powdered sugar if necessary to stiffen frosting. Makes about 1½ cups frosting, enough to frost a 13 x 9-inch pan of brownies or 4–5 dozen cookies.

 Baker's note: For an 8-inch square pan of brownies, halve the ingredients listed above and proceed as directed.

Cream Cheese Frosting

6	ounces cream cheese, softened
1/4	cup (1/2 stick) unsalted butter, softened
1	teaspoon vanilla extract
2 1/4	cups powdered sugar, sifted

In a medium bowl beat the cream cheese, butter, and vanilla extract with an electric mixer on medium until blended and smooth. Gradually add the powdered sugar, beating until incorporated and smooth. Makes about 1¾ cups frosting, enough to generously frost a 13 x 9-inch pan of brownies or 4–5 dozen cookies.

This very versatile frosting is classic on carrot cake, but I think you will soon agree that it is unbeatable on brownies.

Sour Cream Frosting

3/4	cup powdered sugar
1	8-ounce package cream cheese, room temperature
1/2	cup sour cream
1	teaspoon fresh-squeezed lemon juice

In a medium bowl beat the powdered sugar, cream cheese, sour cream, and lemon juice with an electric mixer on high until well blended and smooth. Makes about 1¾ cups frosting, enough to frost a 13 x 9-inch pan of brownies or 4–5 dozen cookies.

Baker's note: For an 8-inch square pan of brownies, halve the ingredients listed above and proceed as directed.

If you like flavor contrasts, you will adore this tangy, creamy frosting lavished over a pan of dark chocolate brownies or a batch of chocolate cookies. Be sure to store the frosted brownies or cookies in the refrigerator.

Apricot Frosting

Use this recipe as a template for other fruit frostings, substituting an equal amount of cherry, strawberry, peach, seedless raspberry, or pineapple preserves, for example, in place of the apricot preserves.

3	cups sifted powdered sugar
3	tablespoons butter, softened
⅔	cup apricot preserves

In a medium mixing bowl beat the powdered sugar, butter, and apricot preserves with an electric mixer on medium until smooth. Makes about 1½ cups frosting, enough to frost a 13 x 9-inch pan of brownies or 4–5 dozen cookies.

 Baker's note: For an 8-inch square pan of brownies, halve the ingredients listed above and proceed as directed.

Browned Butter Icing

3   tablespoons unsalted butter
1½   cups powdered sugar, sifted
1   teaspoon vanilla extract
2–4 teaspoons milk

In a medium saucepan set over medium heat melt the butter until light brown in color. (Watch butter carefully—it can burn quickly.) Remove from heat.

Stir powdered sugar, vanilla, and 1 tablespoon milk into browned butter. Stir in just enough more milk to make frosting smooth and spreadable. Stir in more milk if mixture is too thick or more powdered sugar if mixture is too thin. Makes about ¾ cup icing, enough to ice an 8-inch square pan of brownies.

Be sure to use real butter, not margarine, for this recipe. Margarine will not brown and get the nutty flavor that butter will.

Baker's note: For a 13 x 9-inch pan of brownies or 4–5 dozen cookies, double the ingredients listed above and proceed as directed.

Vanilla Butter Glaze

Vanilla and butter have a transformative effect on chocolate. In particular, this quickly assembled glaze makes already good brownies extraordinarily moist, irresistible masterpieces. For an even richer butter flavor, consider browning the melted butter (see page 6) before whipping up the glaze.

1½   cups powdered sugar, sifted
1½   tablespoons unsalted butter, melted
1   teaspoon vanilla extract
1–2   teaspoons milk

In a small bowl whisk the powdered sugar, melted butter, and vanilla until blended and smooth. Add just enough milk, a teaspoon at a time, to make glaze a thin spreading consistency, whisking until smooth. Makes about ½ cup glaze, enough to glaze an 8-inch square pan of brownies.

Baker's note: For a 13 x 9-inch pan of brownies or 4–5 dozen cookies, double the ingredients listed above and proceed as directed.

Whiskey Glaze

Three ingredients equals simple perfection here.

1¼   cups powdered sugar, sifted
1   tablespoon unsalted butter, melted
1   tablespoon whiskey or bourbon

In a small bowl combine the powdered sugar, melted butter, and whiskey. Whisk until smooth. Makes about ½ cup of glaze, enough to glaze an 8-inch square pan of brownies.

Mint Frosting

3　　cups powdered sugar, sifted

⅓　　cup butter, softened

¾　　teaspoon peppermint extract

2　　tablespoons milk

2　　drops green food coloring (optional)

This is a classic recipe for holiday brownies and cookies.

In a medium bowl beat the powdered sugar, butter, and peppermint extract with an electric mixer set on low until blended and smooth. Beat in milk, 1 tablespoon at a time, until smooth and spreadable. Beat in food coloring, if desired. Makes about 1½ cups frosting, enough to frost a 13 x 9-inch pan of brownies or 4 dozen cookies.

Baker's note: For an 8-inch square pan of brownies, halve the ingredients listed above and proceed as directed.

Orange Cream Cheese Frosting

I developed this recipe for my friend Elizabeth, who is of the mindset that all brownies should be frosted. She has a particular penchant for the combination of orange and chocolate, so this doubly orange frosting makes her very happy, especially when it is smoothed over a batch of Orange Cream–Frosted Brownies (see page 48).

1	8-ounce package cream cheese, softened
3	cups powdered sugar
2	tablespoons frozen orange juice concentrate, thawed
1	teaspoon grated orange zest
1–2	drops yellow food coloring
1–2	drops red food coloring

In a small bowl mix the cream cheese, powdered sugar, orange juice concentrate, orange zest, yellow food coloring, and red food coloring until smooth and spreadable. Makes about 1⅔ cups, enough to frost a 13 x 9-inch pan of brownies or 4–5 dozen cookies.

Baker's Note: For an 8-inch square pan of brownies, halve the ingredients listed above and proceed as directed.

Mocha Buttercream Frosting

1	tablespoon coffee powder or instant espresso
4	teaspoons hot water
2	cups powdered sugar
2	tablespoons unsweetened cocoa
½	cup (1 stick) butter, softened

In large bowl dissolve coffee powder in the hot water. Add powdered sugar, cocoa, and softened butter; beat with electric mixer on medium until smooth. Makes about 1 cup frosting, enough to frost an 8-inch square pan of brownies.

Butter plus cocoa plus espresso equals one of the very best frostings for gilding a pan of homemade brownies. It's easy to prepare, too.

Maple Frosting

1½	cups sifted powdered sugar
1	3-ounce package cream cheese, softened
1	tablespoon unsalted butter, softened
2	teaspoons maple flavored extract

In a medium bowl beat powdered sugar, cream cheese, softened butter, and maple flavoring until smooth. Makes about 1 cup frosting, enough to frost an 8-inch square pan of brownies.

Maple and chocolate may sound like an unusual combination, but the proof is in the tasting here. You will wonder why you haven't matched the two before now!

Baker's Note: For a 13 x 9-inch pan of brownies or 4–5 dozen cookies, double the ingredients listed above and proceed as directed.

Peanut Butter Frosting

Peanut butter and brownies are made for each other, and this quick-to-make frosting makes it easy to foster the relationship. And it's very likely you have all of the ingredients on hand.

6	tablespoons creamy style peanut butter (not natural or old-fashioned style)
¼	cup (½ stick) unsalted butter, softened
2	cups powdered sugar, sifted
3–4	tablespoons milk

In a medium mixing bowl beat the peanut butter and butter with an electric mixer set on medium until blended. Gradually add the powdered sugar alternately with the milk, beating on low until blended and smooth. Increase speed to medium and beat 1 minute longer until light and creamy. Makes about 1¾ cups, enough to generously frost a 13 x 9-inch pan of brownies or 4–5 dozen cookies.

Baker's Note: For an 8-inch square pan of brownies, halve the ingredients listed above and proceed as directed.

Sweetened Whipped Cream

For 1 cup:

½	cup heavy whipping cream
1	tablespoon granulated sugar
½	teaspoon vanilla extract

For 1½ cups:

¾	cup heavy whipping cream
2	tablespoons granulated sugar
1	teaspoon vanilla extract

For 2 cups:

1	cup heavy whipping cream
3	tablespoons granulated sugar
1½	teaspoons vanilla extract

For 3 cups:

1½	cups heavy whipping cream
¼	cup granulated sugar
2	teaspoons vanilla extract

Beat whipping cream, sugar, and vanilla extract in chilled mixing bowl with electric mixer on high until soft peaks form. Use immediately.

Frozen whipped topping may be fine in a pinch, but the real thing—sweetened whipped cream—is worth the splurge.

Glossary

Beat: To combine ingredients vigorously with a spoon, fork, wire whisk, hand beater, or electric mixer until the ingredients are smooth and uniform.

Blend: To combine ingredients with a spoon, wire whisk or rubber scraper until very smooth and uniform. A blender or food processor may also be used, depending on the job.

Boil: To heat a liquid until bubbles rise continuously and break on the surface and steam is given off. For a rolling boil, the bubbles form rapidly and will not stop forming even when the liquid is stirred.

Chop: To cut food into small pieces using a chef's knife, food processor, or blender.

Drain: To pour off extra liquid from a food, often with the use of a colander or strainer set over the sink. To reserve the drained liquid, place a bowl under the colander.

Drizzle: To slowly pour a liquid mixture, such as melted butter, chocolate, or glaze, in a very thin stream over a food.

Fold: To combine ingredients lightly while preventing loss of air by using two motions: Using a rubber spatula, first cut down vertically through the mixture. Next, slide the spatula across the bottom of the bowl and up the side, turning the mixture over. Repeat these motions after rotating the bowl one-fourth turn with each series of strokes.

Garnish: An edible decoration added to food or the act of adding such a decoration.

Grease: To rub the inside surface of a pan with solid shortening, using a pastry brush, wax paper, or paper towels, to prevent food from sticking during baking. Nonstick cooking spray may also be used; do not use butter or margarine (especially in a baked recipe), either may burn and/or sticking may occur.

Grease and Flour: To rub the inside surface of a pan with solid shortening before dusting it with flour, to prevent food from sticking during baking. After flouring the pan, turn it upside down, tapping the bottom to remove excess flour.

Mix: To combine ingredients in any way that distributes them evenly, integrating the ingredients. This can be accomplished using a hand utensil or an electric mixer.

Pipe: A decorating technique that involves forcing frosting, icing, or chocolate from a pastry bag or parchment cone to form specific designs on a cookie.

Preheat: To turn the oven controls to the desired temperature, allowing the oven to heat thoroughly before adding food. Preheating takes about 10–15 minutes.

Set: To allow a food to become firm.

Soften: To allow cold food, such as butter, margarine, or cream cheese, to stand at room temperature until no longer hard. Generally this will take 30–60 minutes.

Stir: To combine ingredients with a circular or "figure 8" motion until they are of a uniform consistency.

Whip: To beat ingredients with a wire whisk, hand rotary beater, or electric mixer to add air and increase volume until ingredients are light and fluffy, such as with whipping cream or egg whites.

Zest: The perfume-y outermost layer of citrus fruit that contains the fruit's essential oils. Zest can be removed with a zester, a small hand-held tool that separates the zest from the bitter white pith underneath, or with a grater, vegetable peeler, or sharp knife.

Index

almonds
    Almond Brickle Brownie Bars, 105
    Almond Fudge Brownies, 68
    Almond Joyful Coconut Brownies, 36
    Almond-Orange Chocolate Biscotti, 185
    Almond Toffee-Topped Brownies, 22
    Cardamom, Almond & Orange Bars, 102
    Chocolate Linzer Bars, 124
    Mocha Almond Fudge Cookies, 159
Amaretto Café Cream Brownies, 34
apples
    Caramel Apple Chocolate Crumble Bars, 98
    Toffee Apple Chocolate Cookies, 153
apricots
    Apricot Coconut Bars, 92
    Apricot-Frosted Chocolate Cookies, 152
    Apricot Frosting, 262
    Apricot Macaroon Brownies, 66
    Very Apricot Chocolate Streusel Bars, 101

Backpacker Bars, 106
bananas
    Bananas Foster Chocolate Upside Down
      Cake, 220
    Chocolate Fudge Banana Baby Cakes, 202
    Funky, Chunky Chocolate Banana Chip Bars,
      94
    Monkey Business Banana Brownies, 28

    Soft Banana Brownie Cookies, 161
Berry White Chocolate Cream Torte, 241
Berry-Berry Chocolate Streusel Bars, 95
Best "Boosted" Brownies, 24
Big-Batch Brownies, 19
Big Brownie Buttercream "Pies," 164
Big Brownie Cookies, 135
Black & Tan Layered Brownies, 23
Black & White Cookies, 165
Black-Bottom Brownie Rum Fudge Pie, 205
Black-Bottom Raspberry Cheesecake, 214
Black Forest Brownie Trifle, 240
Black Forest Brownies, 72
blueberries
    Berry-Berry Chocolate Streusel Bars, 95
Boston Brownie Cream Pie, 198
Brandy-Laced "Fruitcake" Brownies, 44
Brown Sugar & Toffee Cheesecake Bars, 114
Browned Butter Cashew Brownies, 55
Browned Butter Icing, 263
Brownie Baked Alaska, 232
Brownie Biscotti, 178
Brownie-Bottomed Crème Brulée, 208
Brownie Ice Cream Sandwiches, 224
Brownie Macaroons, 190
brownie mix, various brands of, 5
Brownie Soufflé Cake with One-Step Custard
    Sauce, 193

Brownie Swirl Vanilla Cheesecake, 211
Brownies & Cream Sandwich Cookies, 137
Buttery Brownie Cut-Outs, 162

Candy Bar Bars, 97
Cappuccino Brownies, 82
caramel
    Caramel Apple Chocolate Crumble Bars, 98
    Caramel-Butterscotch-Loaded Brownies, 53
    "Caramel Delightful" Bars, 118
    Caramelicious Turtle Brownies, 21
    Caramel Mallow Brownie Bars, 121
    Caramel Pecan Turtle Cookies, 172
    Caramel Penuche Frosting, 259
    Caramel–White Chocolate Brownie Pie, 192
    Chocolate Carmelitas, 112
    Chocolate-Chip Cinnamon Rolls with Cream
      Cheese Frosting, 234
    Dulce de Leche Cream Bars, 116
    Nutty Chocolate Caramel Bull's-Eyes, 168
Cardamom, Almond & Orange Bars, 102
cashews
    Browned Butter Cashew Brownies, 55
    Cashew Butter Brickle Brownie Cookies, 155
    Cashew Crunch Brownie Bars, 88
Charlotte's Ginger-Jeweled Chocolate Biscotti,
    184
cheesecake
    Black-Bottom Raspberry Cheesecake, 214
    Brown Sugar & Toffee Cheesecake Bars, 115
    Brownie Swirl Vanilla Cheesecake, 211
    Chocolate, Chocolate, Chocolate-Chip
      Cheesecake Bars, 108
    Cheesecake-Filled Chocolate Streusel Bars,
      89
    Chocolate Fudge Brownie Cheesecake, 209
    Mint-Chip Cheesecake Brownie Bars, 103
    New York Cheesecake Brownie Bars, 87

Peanut Butter Cheesecake Swirl Brownies,
    84
Pumpkin Swirl Cheesecake Bars, 110
Toasted Coconut Cheesecake Bars, 86
Turtle Cheesecake Brownies, 39
Ultimate Fresh Raspberry Cheesecake Bars,
    90
White Chocolate Eggnog Cheesecake, 216
cherries
    Black Forest Brownies, 72
    Black Forest Brownie Trifle, 240
    Brownie Baked Alaska, 232
    Cherry Chocolate Baby Cakes, 212
    Cherry Chocolate Crisp, 231
    Chocolate Covered Cherry Brownies, 71
    One Bowl Triple-Chocolate Cherry Bars,
      127
    White Chocolate Cherry Cookies, 138
chocolate, about, 6
Chocolate Brownie Tiramisu, 228
Chocolate Carmelitas, 112
Chocolate-Chip Brownie Cones, 197
Chocolate-Chip Brownie Trifle, 195
Chocolate-Chip Cinnamon Rolls with Cream
    Cheese Frosting, 234
Chocolate-Chip Cookie Bull's-Eye Brownies,
    43
Chocolate-Chip Pecan Pie Bars, 130
Chocolate, Chocolate, Chocolate-Chip
    Cheesecake Bars, 108
Chocolate Covered Cherry Brownies, 71
Chocolate Cream Cheese Chocolate-Chip
    Brownies, 18
Chocolate Date Bars, 113
Chocolate-Dipped Brownie "Truffles," 186
Chocolate Drizzle or Dip, 247
Chocolate Fudge Banana Baby Cakes, 202
Chocolate Fudge Brownie Cheesecake, 209

Chocolate Fudge–Frosted Raspberry Softies, 170

Chocolate Fudge Frosting, 250

Chocolate-Glazed Mint-Frosted Brownies, 47

Chocolate Hermits, 169

Chocolate-Kissed Peanut Butter Thumbprints, 142

Chocolate Linzer Bars, 124

Chocolate Madeleines, 176

Chocolate Marshmallow Frosting, 253

Chocolate Mint Brownie Pie, 227

Chocolate Oatmeal Cookies, 163

Chocolate-Orange Madeleines, 177

Chocolate Pantry Cookies, 144

Chocolate Peppermint Petits Fours, 187

Chocolate Raisin Cookies, 145

Chocolate Raisin Pecan Bars, 93

Chocolate Rancho Roundup Cookies, 166

Chocolate-Raspberry Frosting, 257

Chocolate Rice Crispy Cookies, 136

Chocolate Rum Glaze, 256

Chocolate (Semisweet or White) Cream Cheese Frosting, 252

Chocolate Snickerdoodles, 174

Chocolate Velvet Frosting, 249

Chocolate Whiskey Frosting, 255

Christmas Cranberry-Pistachio Biscotti, 183

cinnamon
    Cinnamon-Chip Chocolate Cookies, 157
    Cinnamon-Chip Cranberry Walnut Bars, 99
    Cinnamon Glaze, 248
    Cinnamon Stick Chocolate Biscotti, 182
    Julie's Cinnamon Buttermilk Brownies, 31

Classic Brownies, 16

Classic Brownie Variations, 17

coconut
    Almond Joyful Coconut Brownies, 36
    Apricot Coconut Bars, 92

Apricot Macaroon Brownies, 66

Brownie Macaroons, 190

Coconut, Rum, & White Chocolate Macadamia Bars, 104

Double Fudge Chewies with Coconut & Pecans, 134

Five-Layer Chocolate Marshmallow Brownie Bars, 120

German Chocolate Thumbprint Cookies, 149

Macadamia & Toasted Coconut Chocolate Cookies, 154

Milk Chocolate Macaroon Bars, 115

Toasted Coconut Cheesecake Bars, 86

Toasted Coconut White Chocolate Fudge Brownies, 62

coffee
    Amaretto Café Cream Brownies, 34
    Cappuccino Brownies, 82
    Chocolate Brownie Tiramisu, 228
    Coffee Toffee Chocolate Biscotti, 179
    Coffee Toffee Cream Bars, 117
    Mocha Almond Fudge Cookies, 159
    Mocha Buttercream Brownies, 56
    Mocha Buttercream–Filled Double Chocolate Sandwich Cookies, 140
    Mocha Buttercream Frosting, 267
    Mocha Cream Shortcakes, 223
    Molten Mocha Lava Cakes, 204
    Kahlua Coffee Icing, 260
    Kahlua White Chocolate Chunk Chewies, 148
    Triple-Shot Espresso Layered Brownies, 26

Cookie Decorating Icing, 244

Cookies 'n' Cream Brownies, 29

Craggy-Topped Toffee Fudge Brownies, 69

cranberries
    Backpacker Bars, 106
    Cinnamon-Chip Cranberry Walnut Bars, 99

Christmas Cranberry-Pistachio Biscotti, 183
Cranberry Brownies with Cranberry
  Ganache Topping, 67
Cranberry Chocolate Upside Down Cake,
  218
Sour Cream Cranberry Bars, 126
cream cheese, *see also* cheesecake
  Chocolate Cream Cheese Chocolate-Chip
    Brownies, 18
  Cream Cheese Chocolate Softies, 139
  Cream Cheese Frosting, 261
  Cream Cheese Swirled Brownies, 42
  Chocolate (Semisweet or White) Cream
    Cheese Frosting, 252
  Orange Cream Cheese Frosting, 266
  Raspberry Cream Cheese Brownies, 33

Dad's Double Peanut Butter Frosted Brownies,
  52
Dark Chocolate Gingerbread Brownies, 74
Double Fudge Chewies with Coconut &
  Pecans, 134
Dulce de Leche Cream Bars, 116

Easy Mississippi Mud Brownies, 30
equipment, baking, 10
Extra-Easy Chocolate-Frosted Rocky Road
  Bars, 125

Five-Layer Chocolate Marshmallow Brownie
  Bars, 120
Fluffiest Chocolate Buttercream, 254
Fudge-Frosted Walnut Brownies, 58
Funky, Chunky Chocolate Banana Chip Bars, 94

German Chocolate Thumbprint Cookies, 149
Gianduia Brownies (Italian Chocolate Hazelnut
  Brownies), 80

ginger
  Charlotte's Ginger-Jeweled Chocolate
    Biscotti, 184
  Dark Chocolate Gingerbread Brownies, 74
  Peppery Ginger Chocolate Cookies, 167
glossary, 271
Gooey Baby Ruthy Brownies, 70
Gorgeous White Chocolate–Dipped Coconut
  Brownie Biscotti, 180
Grasshopper Brownie-Mallow Torte, 230

hazelnut
  Gianduia Brownies, 80
  To-Die-For Chocolate Hazelnut Sandwich
    Cookies, 160
"Hugs" & "Kisses" Brownie Bites, 206

ice cream
  Brownie Baked Alaska, 232
  Brownie Ice Cream Sandwiches, 224
  Nutty Drumstick Ice Cream Bars, 199
ingredients
  measuring, 8
  selecting, 5
Irish Cream Frosting, 260
Irish Cream–Frosted Milk Chocolate Cookies,
  150

Jam-Filled Chocolate Thumbprints, 143
Jim & Anna's Dark Rum Brownies, 45
Julie's Cinnamon Buttermilk Brownies, 31
Jumbo Triple-Chocolate Oatmeal Cookies, 146

Kahlua Coffee Icing, 260
Kahlua White Chocolate Chunk Chewies, 148

Lemon–White Chocolate Petits Fours, 188

macadamias
  Macadamia & Toasted Coconut Chocolate
    Cookies, 154
  Macadamia & White Chocolate Chunk
    Brownies, 59
malt
  Milk Chocolate Malt Brownies, 37
Mandarin Orange Brownie Tart, 226
maple
  Maple-Frosted Brownies, 65
  Maple Frosting, 267
  Maple Pecan Bars, 107
Marbled Chocolate & Vanilla Brownie Cake,
  194
marshmallow
  Apricot Macaroon Brownies, 66
  Caramel Mallow Brownie Bars, 121
  Chocolate Marshmallow Frosting, 253
  Easy Mississippi Mud Brownies, 30
  Extra-Easy Chocolate-Frosted Rocky Road
    Bars, 125
  Five-Layer Chocolate Marshmallow Brownie
    Bars, 120
  Funky, Chunky Chocolate Banana Chip Bars,
    94
  Grasshopper Brownie-Mallow Torte, 230
  Rocky Road Brownies, 51
  S'mores Brownies, 60
  Tri-Level Peanut Butter Marshmallow Crispy
    Bars, 122
Milk Chocolate Buttermilk Brownies, 64
Milk Chocolate Frosting, 251
Milk Chocolate Macaroon Bars, 115
Milk Chocolate Malt Brownies, 37
mint
  Chocolate-Glazed Mint-Frosted Brownies, 47
  Chocolate Mint Brownie Pie, 227
  Chocolate Peppermint Petits Fours, 187

Grasshopper Brownie-Mallow Torte, 230
Mint-Chip Cheesecake Brownie Bars, 103
Mint Frosting, 265
Mint Julep Ganache Brownies, 32
Peppermint Patty–Frosted Brownies, 49
Peppermint White Chocolate Crinkles, 147
Mocha Almond Fudge Cookies, 159
Mocha Buttercream Brownies, 56
Mocha Buttercream–Filled Double Chocolate
  Sandwich Cookies, 140
Mocha Buttercream Frosting, 267
Mocha Cream Shortcakes, 223
Molten Mocha Lava Cakes, 204
Monkey Business Banana Brownies, 28

New York Cheesecake Brownie Bars, 87
No-Prep Frostings for Brownies and Brownie
  Cookies, 245
Nutty Chocolate Caramel Bull's-Eyes, 168
Nutty Drumstick Ice Cream Bars, 199

Oatmeal Cookie–Bottomed Brownies, 46
Oh-So-Orange Brownies, 78
One Bowl Triple-Chocolate Cherry Bars, 127
One-Step Chocolate-Chip/Baking Chip
  "Frosting," 246
orange
  Almond-Orange Chocolate Biscotti, 185
  Cardamom, Almond & Orange Bars, 102
  Chocolate-Orange Madeleines, 177
  Mandarin Orange Brownie Tart, 226
  Oh-So-Orange Brownies, 78
  Orange Cream Cheese Frosting, 266
  Orange Cream–Frosted Brownies, 48

peanut butter
  Chocolate-Kissed Peanut Butter
    Thumbprints, 142

Chocolate Rancho Roundup Cookies, 166
Dad's Double Peanut Butter Frosted
 Brownies, 52
Peanut Butter Cheesecake Swirl Brownies,
 84
Peanut Butter–Chip Chocolate Cookies,
 156
Peanut Butter–Chocolate Decadence Trifle,
 238
Peanut Butter Cup Brownies, 50
Peanut Butter–Frosted Double Chocolate
 Cookies, 175
Peanut Butter Frosting, 268
Peanut-Butterscotch Fudge-Filled Bars, 96
Tri-Level Peanut Butter Marshmallow Crispy
 Bars, 122
peanuts
 Rocky Road Brownies, 51
pecans
 Black & Tan Layered Brownies, 23
 "Caramel Delightful" Bars, 118
 Caramel Pecan Turtle Cookies, 172
 Chocolate-Chip Pecan Pie Bars, 130
 Chocolate Raisin Pecan Bars, 93
 Double Fudge Chewies with Coconut &
  Pecans, 134
 Maple Pecan Bars, 107
 Pecan & White Chocolate Chunk Brownie
  Cookies, 158
 Pecan Pie Brownies, 40
Peppermint Patty–Frosted Brownies, 49
Peppermint White Chocolate Crinkles, 147
Peppery Ginger Chocolate Cookies, 167
Petite Tuxedo Tarts, 210
Pineapple–White Chocolate Aloha Bars, 119
pistachios
 Christmas Cranberry-Pistachio Biscotti,
  183

Pretty-in-Pink Strawberry Streusel Bars, 128
Pumpkin Swirl Cheesecake Bars, 109

raisins
 Chocolate Hermits, 169
 Chocolate Raisin Cookies, 145
 Chocolate Raisin Pecan Bars, 93
 Rum Raisin Brownies, 54
raspberries
 Berry White Chocolate Cream Torte, 241
 Black-Bottom Raspberry Cheesecake, 214
 Chocolate Fudge–Frosted Raspberry
  Softies, 170
 Chocolate Linzer Bars, 124
 Chocolate-Raspberry Frosting, 257
 Raspberry Brownies, 61
 Raspberry Cream Cheese Brownie Pie, 222
 Raspberry Cream Cheese Brownies, 33
 Raspberry Dark Chocolate Ganache Tart,
  200
 Ultimate Fresh Raspberry Cheesecake Bars,
  90
 Very Raspberry Chocolate Trifle, 236
Rocky Road Brownies, 51
rum
 Black-Bottom Brownie Rum Fudge Pie, 205
 Chocolate Rum Glaze, 256
 Coconut, Rum, & White Chocolate
  Macadamia Bars, 104
 Jim & Anna's Dark Rum Brownies, 45
 Rum Raisin Brownies, 54

Sean's Very Chocolate Cookies, 151
Shiny Chocolate Glaze, 258
S'mores Brownies, 60
Snickery Sunken Treasure Cupcakes, 207
Snickery Supreme Brownies, 77
Soft Banana Brownie Cookies, 161

sour cream
  Sour Cream Brownies with Broiled Brown
    Sugar Topping, 79
  Sour Cream Brownies with Chocolate Velvet
    Frosting, 25
  Sour Cream Cranberry Bars, 126
  Sour Cream Frosting, 261
Spicy Aztec Brownies, 38
storing baked goods, 10
strawberries
  Pretty-in-Pink Strawberry Streusel Bars, 128
  Strawberries & Cream Brownies, 75
Summer Berry Brownie Tart, 225
Sweetened Whipped Cream, 269
Swirled Tuxedo-Top Brownies, 76

Tennessee Jam Cake Brownies, 57
Toasted Coconut Cheesecake Bars, 86
Toasted Coconut White Chocolate Fudge
  Brownies, 62
To-Die-For Chocolate Hazelnut Sandwich
  Cookies, 160
Toffee Apple Chocolate Cookies, 153
Trail Mix Cookies, 173
Tri-Level Peanut Butter Marshmallow Crispy
  Bars, 122
Triple Chocolate Pudding Cake, 196
Triple Chocolate Torte, 203
Triple-Shot Espresso Layered Brownies, 26
Truffle-Topped Brownies, 73
Turtle Cheesecake Brownies, 39

Ultimate Fresh Raspberry Cheesecake Bars, 90

Vanilla and Butter-Rich Glazed Buttermilk
  Brownies, 20
Vanilla Butter Glaze, 264
Very Apricot Chocolate Streusel Bars, 101

Very Raspberry Chocolate Trifle, 236

walnuts
  Cinnamon-Chip Cranberry Walnut Bars, 99
  Fudge-Frosted Walnut Brownies, 58
  Maple-Frosted Brownies, 65
  Swirled Tuxedo-Top Brownies, 76
  Walnut Fudge Bars, 131
whiskey
  Chocolate Whiskey Frosting, 255
  Mint Julep Ganache Brownies, 32
  Wicked Whiskey Chocolate Cookies, 171
  Whiskey Glaze, 264
  Whiskey-Glazed Double Chocolate
    Brownies, 41
white chocolate
  Berry White Chocolate Cream Torte, 241
  Caramel–White Chocolate Brownie Pie, 192
  Coconut, Rum, & White Chocolate
    Macadamia Bars, 104
  Gorgeous White Chocolate–Dipped
    Coconut Brownie Biscotti, 180
  Kahlua White Chocolate Chunk Chewies, 148
  Lemon–White Chocolate Petits Fours, 188
  Macadamia & White Chocolate Chunk
    Brownies, 59
  Pecan & White Chocolate Chunk Brownie
    Cookies, 158
  Peppermint White Chocolate Crinkles, 147
  Pineapple–White Chocolate Aloha Bars, 119
  Toasted Coconut White Chocolate Fudge
    Brownies, 62
  White Chocolate Brown Sugar Meringue
    Bars, 129
  White Chocolate Cherry Cookies, 138
  White Chocolate Eggnog Cheesecake, 216
  White Chocolate Fudge Fantasy Bars, 100
Wicked Whiskey Chocolate Cookies, 171